M⬤VING CRITICA╷ ␣ᚦORWARD

Taking the pulse of current efforts to do—and, in some cases, undo—critical literacy, this volume explores and critiques its implementation in learning contexts around the globe. An impressive set of international authors offer examples of productive critical literacy practices in and out of schools, address the tensions and gaps between these practices and educational policies, and attempt to forecast the future for critical literacy as a movement in the changing global educational policy landscape. This collection is unique in presenting the recent work of luminaries such as Allan Luke and Hilary Janks alongside relative newcomers who use innovative approaches and arguments to reinvigorate and redefine critical practice.

Moving Critical Literacies Forward:

- Gathers in one place current research in critical literacy organized around three themes: Theoretical Frameworks and Arguments for Critical Literacy; Critiquing Critical Literacy in Practice; Revisions of Critical Literacy
- Covers research that is international in scope
- Features a balanced mix of contributors—both leading theorists and emerging scholars

It is time for this cutting-edge inquiry into the state of critical literacy—not only because it is a complex and ever-evolving field, but perhaps more importantly, because it offers a reaction to, and powerful reworking of, standardization and high-stakes accountability measures in educational contexts around the globe.

Jessica Zacher Pandya is Associate Professor, California State University Long Beach, USA.

JuliAnna Ávila is Assistant Professor, University of North Carolina Charlotte, USA.

MOVING CRITICAL LITERACIES FORWARD

A New Look at Praxis Across Contexts

Edited by
Jessica Zacher Pandya
JuliAnna Ávila

Routledge
Taylor & Francis Group

NEW YORK AND LONDON

First published 2014
by Routledge
711 Third Avenue, New York, NY 10017

Simultaneously published in the UK
by Routledge
2 Park Square, Milton Park, Abingdon, Oxon OX14 4RN

Routledge is an imprint of the Taylor & Francis Group, an informa business

Library of Congress Cataloging in Publication Data
Moving critical literacies forward : a new look at praxis across contexts /
[edited] by Jessica Pandya, Julianna Ávila.
    pages cm
    Includes bibliographical references and index.
    1. Literacy—Social aspects. 2. Language arts—Social aspects. 3. Critical pedagogy.
    I. Ávila, JuliAnna. II. Pandya, Jessica Zacher.
    LC149.M545 2013
    370.11'5—dc23

                            2013022055

ISBN: 978-0-415-81813-1 (hbk)
ISBN: 978-0-415-81814-8 (pbk)
ISBN: 978-0-203-52186-1 (ebk)

Typeset in Bembo
by Swales & Willis Ltd, Exeter, Devon

This book is for Sande, Margie, Sylvia, Stephanie, Doris, Mayra, Leslie, Maggie, Samantha, Cindy, Janet, and Estela, for all that each of you do—and might do in the future—to move critical literacy forward.

—Jessica

This book is for my parents, who were my first teachers of both literacy and social justice.

—JuliAnna

CONTENTS

FOREWORD

Jerome C. Harste

The function of a foreword is to give perspective. To that end, I first want to make you aware of the semantic territory that this book encompasses. Further, and because this volume is literally "An International Who's Who in Critical Literacy," it seems appropriate to use an instructional strategy called "Postcards of the Mind" that Andy Manning (2013) uses in the Mount Saint Vincent's University's Master's Degree in Critical Literacy. "Postcards of the Mind" asks readers after reading an article, one week later, to write a postcard outlining what sticks with them. Students are asked to note a key idea, why that idea matters, how it affects their thinking, and how it is going to affect their practice. Said differently, I'm using "Postcards of the Mind" as a vehicle to introduce this book to readers; why the ideas presented here matter, for whom, and in what ways.

The Territory Covered

Allan Luke once said (2009) that he wanted the average citizen to see critical literacy not as subversive, but as a basic human right:

> When we wanted to sell critical literacy to Australians as a new competency, we certainly didn't tell them we were on about teaching them that the state was an evil corporate empire and we wanted to crack it . . . In today's environment if you don't have critical literacy you are a sucker, you are going to wind up in debt, you are going to end up on the streets, you are going to sign up with the first bank that offers you a crummy mortgage, you are going to wind up with a big Visa card debt, you are going to buy everything that is pushed your way (video opening).

Alan Luke's statement still holds. The goal of critical literacy is to make students agents of text rather than victims of text. Nonetheless, as this volume accentuates, the definitions of both "text" and "agency" have broadened and expanded. What follows are some of the key ideas that I jotted down on my personal "postcards" after I read through the volume:

Allan Luke defines critical literacy as the use of technologies of print and other media of communication to analyze, critique, and transform the norms, rule systems, and practice governing institutions and everyday life. What is new is his concern that critical literacy has become too "coldly technical" (my words, not his)—focused too much on text and discourse analysis rather than on moral and ethical issues. In addition to close readings, Luke argues that critical educators need to address whose readings or whose version of the world counts, and on what grounds. Luke's point is that critical literacy needs to be committed to the search for truth and facts, and anchored in the reality of the everyday.

Hilary Janks argues that, while new web 2.0 technology has made the world more democratized, powerful discourses continue "to speak to us and to speak through us." She argues for a renewed interest in supporting students in understanding and studying the social effects of text and image. Her emphasis is on the redesign of educational experience. I particularly liked her critique of Kress.

Patrick Finn maintains his interest in social class and how schools in different neighbors offer a very different curriculum. By contrasting the curriculum of an elite boarding school with that of working-class schools of today and the American Socialist Party schools of the 1920s, Finn highlights what aspects of school improvement we would do well to remember in reforming working-class education in America. Among his insights is the importance of having students understand the contributions that the working class has made to social progress, the focus on incorporating students into a larger like-minded community, and helping students see the value of education in terms other than socioeconomic mobility.

Beryl Exley, Annette Woods, and Karen Dooley argue that to be literate today requires students to understand, analyze, and transform worlds with written, oral, and multimedia texts. What is missing, they argue—and needed in order to make critical literacy essential—is a focus on student and community voice as it interfaces with place and space.

Amy Seely Flint and Tasha Tropp Laman argue that, with the emphasis on student achievement, teachers of writing often find themselves tied to a prescribed curriculum. By working in low socioeconomic communities they demonstrate how teachers might use poetry to highlight critical literacy by addressing the social injustices that students in these settings face.

Barbara Comber and Helen Nixon argue that very little critical literacy work in schools has explicitly addressed the politics of place and space in terms of access, design, and ownership. Working with primary teachers in a neighborhood experiencing urban renewal, Comber and Nixon demonstrate how students were invited to critique government planning documents as well as have a voice in the creation of a space that reflects "belonging" and corrects some of the social injustices that form the reality of their daily life.

Elisabeth Johnson and Lalitha Vasudevan argue that, rather than introduce what we see as important critical literacy topics, we would do better to focus on the ongoing daily literacy practices of our students that need interrogation; namely, the telling of classroom jokes to each other, the YouTube videos students share among themselves, the mock-machismo banter that goes on between students. Their argument is that the most effective critical literacy curriculum emerges when students are "caught with their hands in the cookie jar" (my take) or, to paraphrase as the authors themselves say it, from the ongoing lives of students as they enact a new way of being in the world.

Enid Rosario-Ramos and Laura Ruth Johnson emphasize the need for social action as part of a critical literacy curriculum. They implicitly argue that critical literacy often doesn't go far enough. They see civil engagement and social action as critical end components. In their chapter they demonstrate how the involvement of community organizations in an ethnically Puerto Rican community supported students in developing counter-narratives that critically examined the society in which they lived as well as allowed them to enact important changes in that community.

Michael Moore, Don Zancanella, and JuliAnna Ávila warn readers not to be taken in by the Common Core State Standards (CCSS) and what looks like their endorsement of critical literacy. While focusing on "close reading" and "text complexity," the standards, they argue, fail to really address the fundamentals of what it means to be critical literacy. Their chapter traces the history of the CCSS and its attempt underhandedly to divert attention away from critical literacy.

Shinya Takekawa addresses the interface between Japanese education and critical literacy, arguing that issues of implementation change as the notion of critical literacy is taken up globally. Using Japan as a case in point, Takekawa argues that a fundamental "unlearning" needs to take place before the politics and possibilities of critical literacy can see fruition in his country.

Jessica Zacher Pandya critiques California's attempt to standardize and mandate the teaching of critical literacy. Despite rhetoric like "critical literacy skills" and "inquiry-based learning," the step-by-step implementation of commercial programs negates the very processes students must engage in to take on a critical stance. Her overall message to teachers is to beware of Greeks bearing gifts, in this case commercial programs using all the right buzz words.

Vivian Vasquez continues to argue that critical literacy is a perspective that needs to begin from day one of the first day of school; that critical literacy is not something one reserves for older students, but needs to begin with the very youngest of learners. She recounts the ongoing, everyday literacy events that occurred in her classroom and life—events which continued to provide her opportunity and fodder to support her own ongoing understanding of critical literacy and well as that of her prekindergarten and advanced degree college students.

Cynthia Lewis concludes the volume by looking across all the chapters. She identifies three new directions that run through the volume. The first she calls "embodiment/spatiality," a trend away from seeing critical literacy as discourse analysis per se to a broadening of the definition to include the body as located in particular spaces and places. The second she labels "technologies/globalization," a trend that acknowledges the visual and global culture in which we live as well as the new skills that critical citizens will need to be able to "read" the linguistic, visual, and aural signs and symbols that inundate their lives, both public and private. The third trend she sees running through the volume is a growing concern about the relationship between "standardization," which she defines as the homogenizing effects of standards, testing, and accountability, and the sustainability of critical literacy globally. Throughout her discussion she shares insights as well as alluding to her current work on emotion and embodiment as it relates to what the authors of this volume are saying.

Why This Book Matters

With some awareness of the semantic territory that this book covers, why this book matters becomes obvious. First, *Moving Critical Literacies Forward* matters because it represents some of the key players in critical literacy and what it is that is currently on their minds. Together, the group of authors assembled here represent the forefront of where we are globally in our thinking about what it means to take on a critical stance as well as what issues we still have to contend with and solve.

Second, this volume is international in scope. Too often international scholars argue that their work is not recognized until some U.S. educator takes up the ideas and presents them as their own. *Moving Critical Literacies Forward* represents, from the standpoint of authorship, how advanced critical literacy is in countries outside of the United States. The United States is truly a Johnny-come-lately when it comes to the adoption of a critical literacy curriculum. This volume is proof that there is much to learn by listening to those who have forged new ground and gone before.

Third, the volume expands the territory of what critical literacy encompasses, as well as elaborates on the many dimensions of critical literacy that need to be taken into account. Not only are truth, morality, ethics and other heady topics addressed, but so are aesthetics, affect, and importance of "belonging." The medium may not be the entire message, but the imagery, emotional impact, and aesthetics of how something is said appears to be a natural extension to those wishing to implement a critical multimodal language art curricula.

Fourth, *Moving Critical Literacies Forward* is at once theoretical and practical. Theoretically, it expands what the field has previously thought of as critical literacy. Practically, it maps how such theoretical insights might be incorporated into everyday classroom practice. Overall, what you have in this volume is a much-needed balance between theoretical practice and practical theory.

Taken as a whole, but in a metaphorical sense, what readers are given in *Moving Critical Literacies Forward* is "lumber." Lumber to strengthen and expand our definition of critical literacy as well as lumber to rebuild our critical literacy curriculum as we sail full speed ahead come Monday morning.

Who Should Read This Book?

Anyone who feels the need to make the case that critical literacy ought to be front and center in the literacy curriculum. Far from passé, critical literacy takes on heightened importance as educators in a variety of capacities re-examine their world from a critical perspective. Then, who is this book for? Teachers who wish to deepen their understanding of what it means to take a critical literacy stance. Classroom teachers who want practical ideas as to how critical literacy might be enacted in classrooms with students of all ages. Teacher educators who wish to prepare critically literate preservice and inservice educators who in turn might support the students they teach in taking on critical literacy as a life perspective. Researchers who wish to write grants that explore the frontiers of critical literacy.

One last time, "Who is this book for?" Anyone who wants to write a postcard saying, "Wish you were here." The nice thing is that *Moving Critical Literacies Forward* gives readers not only this invitation but the plane ticket!

References

Luke, A. (2009). *The new literacies* (webcast for educators). Toronto, ON: Curriculum Services Canada.

Manning, A. (2013). Postcards of the mind (pp. 193, 197, 215). In C. Leland, M. Lewison, & J. Harste (Eds.) *Teaching children's literature: It's critical*. New York: Routledge.

ACKNOWLEDGMENTS

Thanks first of all to Allan Luke, for suggesting that we turn the *Theory Into Practice* issue in which we first pulled together some of these ideas into a book. Next, thanks to Naomi Silverman at Routledge for seeing the merits of our proposal(s) and gently shepherding us through the process. We also have appreciated the work of Naomi Silverman and Christina Chronister at Routledge and Julie Swales of Swales & Willis in getting this book to the presses. The book was strengthened by the insightful reviews of Alan Rogers, University of East Anglia, and Noah Asher Golden, Graduate Center, City University of New York. We're also thankful to Terry Locke and the journal *English Teaching: Practice & Critique* for permission to reprint Hilary Janks' article here (as Chapter 3). Jessica would also like to thank Mihir Pandya for support and encouragement.

1

INTRODUCTION

Making the Road by Talking: Moving Critical Literacies Forward

Jessica Zacher Pandya and JuliAnna Ávila

In this introduction, we solidify in writing some of the conversations about key issues in critical literacy that we have been having over the past 10 years. We began this process in homage to Miles Horton and Paulo Freire's conversations in *We Make the Road by Walking* (1990), aiming to discuss and reflect on critical literacy's place in the world today. Like them, we have purposefully used dialogue as a framework through which to articulate the need to, as our title suggests, move critical literacies forward. We have brought the authors in this book together to show what critical literacy as a set of practices and stances can help us accomplish in classrooms and in our worlds. We—the participants in this edited volume—argue that critical literacies offer powerful ways of engaging with the opportunities and inequalities accelerated by globalization. New student populations and new technologies are combining to change what it means to be literate and to teach literacy.

These changing contexts are fraught for present and future teachers, whose hesitancy about undertaking critical literacy practices[1] are reflective of larger societal tensions about turbulent economies and unstable job markets. Jobs are scarce, job retention is increasingly tied to assessments, and test preparation and curricular fidelity are often key job components. Critical literacies—whether seen as a way to cosmopolitanize youth (Hull & Stornaiuolo, 2010; Smith & Hull, 2012), a method through which to combat injustice (Janks, 2010; this volume), or a bricolage of these and other definitions—offer alternatives. They offer alternative ways to read and respond to some of the effects of globalization that are so visible in classrooms. To be useful in these ways, they need to be continuously retheorized and continually revisioned in practice. We think critical literacy has a fundamental role to play in the recruitment and retention of teachers who are able to not only withstand but also thrive in such exciting and challenging circumstances.

In the conversation we begin below, we use our own experiences to make some links between critical literacies in teacher education and in classroom and out-of-school contexts with children and youth. We begin with the issue of literacy vs. literacies, since its complexities illuminate crucial aspects of our subsequent critical literacy discussion. For instance, the multiple definitions of critical literacy and the looseness implied by the plural "literacies" provoke a certain degree of caution from those who want straightforward definitions and teachable skill sets. We then discuss the connections between critical literacy and multicultural education and education for social justice. We see them as interlinked movements, and think that critical literacy practices can, and do, move social justice itself forward. We also touch on some of the ways the global accountability movement has impacted critical literacies efforts in classrooms from preschool to college, as well as in teacher education. Critical literacies practices can offset the emotional, and cognitive, pressures of high-stakes assessment; they can also work as a set of methods through which teachers and students can make themselves heard in policy arenas. We have appreciated the chance to learn about and reflect on these topics as we make our own critical literacy journeys, and look forward to further conversation.

Our Conversation

JuliAnna: I find the trend of using "literacy" and "literacies" in seemingly interchangeable ways intriguing because it reflects, I would argue, some key frictions in literacy studies. Even as we have, in research and practice, shifted to a recognition that literacy is no longer a singular, agreed-upon entity, easily taught in linear and measurable ways (e.g., New London Group, 1996), habit and tradition seem to return us to the default: critical literacy. Does it even matter if it is singular or plural (except to an English teacher with idiosyncratic concerns)? I believe it does because, although perhaps benign in one sense, this choice represents the ways we're caught between one context, where mainstream education still treats literacy as singular in many ways (e.g., assessments) and the contexts we are working hard to create and share (e.g., plural contexts, where some elements might well transfer while others may not, leading again to unruliness I'll return to later). Critical literacies are hard to contain, in rows or boxes and even definitionally.

Another reason that we all move between "literacy" and "literacies" is that we want to reserve the right to move between the two forms as we see fit. This right is perhaps a *claim* made by those who traffic in language, with its affordances as well as its limitations. We know what both the reductive singular as well as the more expansive plural have meant and continue to mean as contested terms in the political struggle that can be literacy, or should I say literacies, education. I hope that we can teach our students that, at times in our lives, literacy is singular and must be coped with as a singular and monolothic entity to succeed in mainstream education, while at other times, there is more freedom and latitude, and hopefully self-definition, of what literacies encompass; and, ultimately, that our literacy identities can be expansive enough to deal with both forms.

Jessica: That may be one of the larger goals of critical literacy practitioners—to ensure that their own, and others', literacy identities are expansive. I think an expansive literacy identity is probably one of the most valuable assets in a globalizing world. Can we talk about our own literacy identities, to explain how we came to bring these authors together in this particular collection about critical literacy? My sense of self has long been tied up in being a good reader and writer, and my schooling experiences apprenticed me to a mix of what Patrick Finn (2009) would call middle-class and elite literacy practices. It wasn't until college, when I began tutoring children at a public school in Chicago's south side who did not share my privilege, or my positive associations with school literacies, that I got an inkling of what it might be like to be uncomfortable with the literacy practices that structure our lives. I spent my senior year volunteering in a local first-grade classroom, an experience that marked the beginning of my identity as a teacher in general, and as a teacher of urban children in particular.

I knew there were inequalities in the school system in which I worked, but I had not yet heard the term social justice, much less critical literacy; and I had even less sense of the idea that my students and I might attempt to make changes in our worlds. I suspect that this is where a lot of new teachers—from more and less privileged backgrounds—find themselves: knowing the world is unfair, but thinking that the only kind of positive change they can make is at the personal level, helping one student at a time. What about your own early experiences— did they lead you to a similar place?

JuliAnna: I felt that way starting out, although I've always wondered about the extent to which my experiences are typical. Since childhood I have always felt like I was in the borderlands; I grew up in southeast Los Angeles county in a mostly Latino neighborhood; as a girl who looked more White than Latina, although I am both, I was an outsider as long as I can recall. I ended up at an elite university but only for my last 2 years and after moving around, changing schools, and living a life that did not bode well for empowering anyone, least of all myself. I felt caught between cultures and social classes, and was not sure I deserved a university education since so many of my peers had not been able to attempt one, due primarily, I think, to not being raised to expect a post-secondary education or a social or economic station better than their parents'. I did not want my parents' life—or at least one of my parents: my father was a middle and secondary school teacher for 45 years, and I began college with the proclamation that I would *not* be an educator. Despite that, I had started volunteering as a teenager and became involved in a variety of social justice organizations. It would not be until I started teaching that I would connect education with social justice. As a college senior, I came to believe that those of us who achieve in literacy and English Education should be working with those who struggle with it and are outsiders in that particular sphere. Like you, I threw myself into the task of working with students who viewed literacy as an enemy and source of failure.

Jessica: So in both of our cases, I'd say the recognition of the centrality of literacy to individuals came first, and then that recognition expanded to the levels of social justice and community action. When I enrolled in the elementary teaching credential program at the New College of California, in San Francisco, I was immersed in the educational lingo for inequality, picking up terms like "social justice" and "multiculturalism." I was also introduced to Freire, learning explicitly how literacy was implicated in social justice issues: how children intuitively construct understandings of their worlds, and how those understandings can be profitably used in the service of literacy acquisition. We hosted monthly Spanish–English family literacy nights, learned songs in Spanish, and practiced whole-language teaching methods (especially literacy experience approaches—those were my favorite activities). I began to learn Spanish at New College out of self-defense, since, at the time (and now) it seemed to me that everyone I came into contact with in California spoke Spanish, and I had better do so, too.

I got my first teaching job the next year at a school I'll call Gonzales (a pseudonym). It was a very diverse school—a mix of Latino, African-American, White, and Asian families and teachers. I was encouraged by my colleagues to address social justice issues with my students, but looking back, I'd describe our efforts as what Sleeter and Grant (2008) would call a "multicultural education" approach rather than a critical literacy approach. We did not move from study to questioning, much less to taking action to change existing power relations. My own inability to go further into critical pedagogical approaches—either further along the multicultural education spectrum towards social change, or towards critical literacy—shows me how I did connect education with social justice, but in rather specific, and not very expansive, ways. I think this is where a lot of teachers find themselves—wanting to bring inequalities to their students' attention, or to talk about inequalities their students bring up, but not having a sense of what to do next![2] Critical literacies approaches offer a bridge for those people—from awareness to action, via literacy activities that are (mostly) valued at school.[3]

JuliAnna: I know what you mean about operating at a certain level of awareness and assumption. I had been a "good" student and did well on standardized tests so when I started teaching high school and was working with students who tested several years behind their grade levels, I did not know enough to question either the validity of the assessments that pinned the label of "struggling" to these students or the structure of schooling that tracks students in unjust and unsupported ways, or to challenge the "mentor" teacher who told me that I should promptly abandon my plans to read the grade-level texts that the district recommended; instead, she strongly suggested that I equip myself with "skill" workbooks and then commandeer the copy machine so that I could have enough copies for all of the students. I did buy some of those remedial workbooks but also proceeded to read grade-level "real" texts with students (e.g., *The Catcher in the Rye* [Salinger, 1951]; I bet Holden Caulfield would have a thing to say about the scenario I just described). I also asked the principal to assign me another mentor.

Despite my lack of awareness of critical literacy, and an inclination to be obedient that I credit to my Catholic childhood, I still believed it was a student's right to read the same texts that their "regular" peers were reading.

Jessica: You know, even with the institutional label of "struggling" placed on your students, you probably had more flexibility in that context than high school teachers of so-called "struggling" students do now. I had a similar flexibility, since I had only 20 students, lots of curricular resources, and, most importantly, the assessment pressures of No Child Left Behind (2001) were only distant clouds on the horizon. In fact, the only testing regime my students and I faced was administering the Brigance kindergarten readiness test in the few weeks allotted to me to get it done. Since then, I've made arguments about the injustice of overloading children with high-stakes testing regimes and highly structured curricula (Zacher Pandya, 2011), but at the time, I was unaware of these coming trends. I was, as many teachers are, busy enough just working with my students and happy to leave the larger world to its own devices. What about you? Did your awareness of social justice issues expand as you taught high school?

JuliAnna: I think my awareness of social justice found a different context since I had been aware of issues before due to volunteering with a range of organizations while in high school, as I mentioned before. The school that I taught at was diverse with Latino, African-American, and White students in, I would guess, roughly equal numbers (with a caveat about the tenuous nature of memory) and in a lower middle-class and working-class neighborhood. It was a scene I knew well, having attended this particular high school myself, a fact my students found amusing. I think they wondered if I had gotten out, why I had not *stayed* out. It was because I had done so well in English classes that I wanted to return to work with students who did not do well in English, still years away from understanding the complex and intricate landscape of "not doing well" in school. Although I had been enrolled in an Educating At-Risk Youth M.A. program immediately after earning a B.A., I felt that learning about education in the abstract was less useful to me at that time than making the abstract real by teaching full time. I continued to take graduate education classes at night, and despite the fact that I was learning, I did not yet have critical literacy tools—pragmatic ways to connect literacy with power, or lack of power—in hand.

Jessica: Looking back, I can see so many missed opportunities, for even small acts, small changes. I also draw on that experience to refute those who say that elementary-aged children are too young to "do" critical literacy, since they need to know "basic" skills first, and be older . . . I may not have engaged in critical literacy practices with them, but I can attest to the fact that my 5-year-old students would have, had I offered.[4]

JuliAnna: I feel the same way about missed opportunities, and often tell my teacher education students about all of the things I failed to do as a novice teacher. I did care about helping students and had the heart but lacked the tools. So, although I began my teaching career quite far from critical pedagogies, my efforts over the past several years to build upon critical literacies knowledge and prac-tice has had, at its core, a desire to empower students, an admittedly well-worn phrase; it has been this wish that has influenced me to put poetry in the hands of migrant students in an after-school program that I created as a graduate student, and digital storytelling tools in the way of youth who had been dislocated after Katrina (Ávila, 2008; Ávila, Underwood, & Woodbridge, 2008), and now chal-lenge English Education students to define critical literacy for themselves as they prepare for their own classrooms (Ávila, 2013). Along the way, I have tried to choose what seemed to me the most powerful resources I could to teach English Language Arts, the subject in which I work, learning all the while, as I observed what learners did in each setting. And just as skills workbooks are universal, criti-cal literacies, and individual interpretations of them, are not. It would be several years before I would learn about critical literacy in any sort of formal way in graduate school.

I can't recall the first class or time that some initial sort of comprehension of it began to develop. It started with Freire and has continued to become more nuanced over time and educational contexts (classroom teacher, literacy coach, and, most recently, with preservice and inservice English and literacy educators). It has become so nuanced, in fact, that when recent students ask me what exactly critical literacy "is," I have to pause and think. "It depends on the context," I will often say. "And the people and texts involved." "And the power relations." "And the purposes of whichever activity we are talking about." "And . . ." At that point, their eyes often glaze over. We do not always do a good job, in American education at least, preparing teachers to deal with messiness; after all, standards and standardized testing often seem to tie learning up with a neat bow.

Jessica: That's so funny; I too have trouble describing critical literacy in a cocktail party sound bite, even though I often visualize Peter Freebody and Allan Luke's (2003) four resources model as a list in my head, floating right alongside Hilary Janks' (2010) four-part list, when I try to explain it. My mental version of the four resources looks like this (also thanks to Stevens and Bean, 2007): children need to learn and use four different competences: coding, semantic, pragmatic, and critical. Or sometimes, I think of them as four roles that critically literate people enact: code breaker, meaning maker, text user, and text critic. Janks' model is a bit more complicated, because I start to visualize the graphics in her 2010 book, and as I try to explain, my listeners experience the same phenomenon you described. But in brief, there are four dimensions to critical literacy, and they all interact with one another: domination, access, diversity, and design. We've collected many other definitions of critical literacy in this volume—I think our readers will enjoy the variety.

Overall, it's true—our graduate school educations helped us to learn to make *more* complicated definitions, not to streamline things, and certainly not to tie things up in pretty packages. Like you I read Freire (2000) there, and Luke, Free-body, Janks, Comber, Vasquez (many of our contributors, in fact!). I didn't so much adopt critical literacy as a research platform or teaching model as I absorbed it into my academic identity, so that, also like you, I have trouble explaining why it's necessary because it's so *obvious* to me. In our writing it's fun to complicate critical literacies and think through the ramifications of their enactment, but in my work with preservice teachers, and yours with practicing teachers, we both seem to have felt the need to take some steps backwards, or to slow down a bit, don't you think?[5] We can blame our current national accountability fetish for that, I think.

JuliAnna: I agree. I maintain that critical literacy must be defined by individuals once they have learned about, and experienced, its central ideas and what the critical literacy communities, which have obviously shifted over time, have documented about their own efforts to make literacy critical.[6] I find that after reading a text like *Literacy with an Attitude* (Finn, 2009), students often have many experiences about how non-critical their own educations have been. These negative examples are much like my early experiences where I was told that students didn't need to read complex texts (a need that I still believe is a fundamental right). Once we have a sense of what our rights might include, we can then question, challenge, and perhaps demand additional opportunities, those that might free us—from reductive assumptions, from a normed and norming system of education, from being told what we are "able" to read and do.

In a chapter in 2004, Luke mentioned that, "As recently as a decade ago, for most language and literacy educators, the term *critical* referred to higher order reading comprehension and sophisticated personal response to literature" (p. 21); this is something I regularly find with my English Education students. In an effort to bring critical literacy into my English methods courses, after we've done other activities meant to encourage them "to understand that every text comes with social values implicit simply because it is representing the world in a particular way" (Misson & Morgan, 2007, p. 84), I ask students to identify a community/social issue that they find compelling and to craft a digital story that they will share with their future students. I do provide some basic requirements in terms of the minimum number of images or video footage they should include but try to leave as much of the decision making in their hands as possible. This causes them some amount of consternation and leads to questions of the "is this good enough or what you expect" variety. Of note is that the majority of them ignore my suggestion that their intended audience is their future middle or secondary school students; in their post-surveys, most write that they crafted their stories for a much wider audience. They define that aspect of the assignment for themselves and assert their agency in a way that transcends the limitations I, as the authority figure in the situation, impose. One student who made hers about the "cradle to prison pipeline" reported that she would show it to her students but also wanted to "aim it to teachers and people involved in education" to illustrate a need for change; in other words, she wanted to reach those with power to effect change regardless of whether it met my requirements or not. Even though it is was a directly defiant move, I find it striking since so much of the tenor of the course focuses on doing what it takes to attain a high grade; through the acts of composing and production, which Morrell (2008) reminded us are crucial in critical literacy praxis, they transcend that narrower focus.

Jessica: I also have a lot of students who want to get an "A" and I face challenges similar to yours when I teach about critical literacy, and teach critically, with them. The main issue for me, and probably for many others who do this kind of work, is in moving students and myself from (merely) *recognizing* that we operate in a banking education system to *making changes* in our own pedagogy and practice. It's actually relatively easy for me as a semi-independent professor to make changes, but that's only because I teach courses that are prerequisites to credential courses—courses whose content, assignments, and assessment methods, while standardized to some extent by those of us who teach them, are still malleable. For instance, in the course I teach most often (titled "Evaluating Literacy"), every time I teach, I can make changes to all assignments except the one assignment common to all sections of the course. I can also change the readings, as long as they support the overarching set of "student learning outcomes" that my colleagues and I created together. I can make and have made critical literacy the focus of the course, and I continuously work on augmenting my own critical literacy classroom approaches.

But my colleagues who teach methods courses (for preservice teachers, about different content areas) are much more constrained. The content of their courses, and sometimes the assessments they must give in them (i.e., the California Teacher Performance Assessment) severely limit professor agency. In turn, these professors have little room to foster teacher agency. The same strictures on teacher agency apply in most public schools in which my students will go on to get teaching jobs. Constrained by heavy testing systems and prepackaged language arts curricula, burdened by expectations of constantly increasing test scores, and by the knowledge that they will be evaluated based in part on their students' test scores (all of which I've written about [Zacher Pandya, 2011]), it's little wonder that it is hard for them to begin to imagine critical literacy in practice. In this context, I feel my job is to begin a dialogue about what critical literacy practices are and why we all need to engage with them. I also offer students spaces to enact aspects of critical literacy praxis in assignments, but, as you note, assigning critical literacy tasks can feel somewhat hypocritical. Vivian Vasquez, Stacie Tate, and Jerome Harste's new book is on this very subject: *Negotiating Critical Literacies with Teachers* (2013). I'm hoping that it and Hilary Janks' new book, written with Dixon, Ferreira, Granville & Newfield (2013), will offer some new starting points for me and my future preservice teachers.

JuliAnna: Can we go back to the question that you brought up earlier of teaching "the basics" before, and instead of, critical literacies? It has followed me from situation to situation, across state lines and in both urban and rural contexts. I've encountered so many students who think their future students need to learn "basic skills" before they learn more complex stances that will likely result in messier outcomes, not measurable by standardized assessments because that particular continuum of learning itself is not standardized.

I have traded discomforts (from contending with reductionist views of literacy to now being able to tell students what exactly critical literacy *is*) and believe that my feeling of uneasiness is a hallmark of critical literacies in practice, or perhaps this is simply part of what Freire calls "becom[ing] inserted in a permanent process of searching" (Horton & Freire, 1990, p. 11). Whereas as a high-school teacher I was uncomfortable teaching a remedial curriculum to students who had a right to better, I now dodge a feeling that requiring to complete what I deem to be a critical literacies activity is still a mandate, no matter how much choice my students have while meeting it. I continue to wonder how we can practice critical literacies when there are always unequal power relations, or at least as long as there is some sort of grading and "accountability" system in place. Horton and Freire (1990) mention the balancing act between authority and authoritarianism (p. 181), and, during a fairly recent semester, I tried to use digital tools and technology to shift some amount of power to students but found that to be a tricky and imperfect transfer (Ávila, 2013) and ran headfirst into what they discussed.

Jessica: I have also felt the lure of the empowerment potential of digital media. We've talked a lot lately about your and my efforts to bring participatory culture (Jenkins, Purushotma, Weigel, Clinton, & Robison, 2009) into the college classroom via digital projects, and we've certainly been thinking and writing a lot about critical digital literacy practices lately (Ávila & Zacher Pandya, 2012). I've been using digital video production in my literacy courses as a sort of critical participatory literacy, though as you note, it's not as easy as it sounds to make critical literacy assignments, or graded courses, "participatory." My students appreciate acquiring new digital literacy skills, and find the process of articulating their thoughts in a new mode challenging—one of them called the process of making a video in lieu of writing an essay "more than just writing"—but it's easy for them to get bogged down in what the final product "should" be rather than what the multimodal composing process allows them to do and say that an essay doesn't.

JuliAnna: Yes—I think it's easy for them to focus on what's required and getting an "A" and so they lose sight of the process we're trying to socialize them into, a process that is at odds with the schooling many are used to, which it makes them uncomfortable. They seem to want the expert to just tell them what to do and how to do it, a scenario Horton & Freire (1990) warn us about (p. 130). Just as I may need some level of discomfort to question my own assumptions and approaches in order to remain in the zone of critical literacies, I believe that we, as educators, need to keep critical literacies in the conversation in our curricula. Otherwise, I find that I, and my students, narrow our focus to just getting through assignments, lessons, units, objectives, in order to get through the day, without questioning the macro-contexts in which we teach and learn. We can be relentlessly caught up in what seems like an objective process: meeting standards and preparing for assessments, falling into what Alexander (2007) describes as an approach where "English is commodified and classified so that it is amenable to tick boxes" (p. 106); this is one underlying tension between my pre- and in-service teacher education students each term as, overwhelmed and overworked, they want the most efficient path to this process and I push them to consider ideas, topics and questions beyond standards and assessment. They do not always appreciate my invitation to dwell in an untidy, unstandardized place. When they submit lesson plans for evaluation, their templates often consist of rows upon rows of boxes upon boxes (which relates back to a comment I made at the beginning of our conversation), and so I tease them that teaching will not be nearly so containable.

Jessica: And teaching is where we have to walk the critical literacy walk, as you've said . . . I've been working for about 2 years now with a group of teachers at a local charter school that I call Esperanza. My research team and I have been helping third-, fourth-, and fifth-grade students make movies during the regular school day, and we've had a lot of fun with the kids and teachers. It's a multi-year project, and we're in this exciting overlapping cycle of data collection, data analysis, writing, and rethinking as we start new projects. Our goal has been to engage children with critical digital literacies—that is, to use multimodal composition to push children to question their worlds and design powerful texts to speak to injustices they perceive.[7] The school has a social justice focus—one of the reasons we chose to work there—and the teachers are quite comfortable using literacy activities to help children explore their worlds. The teachers have more flexibility and autonomy in their planning than those at non-charter schools in the same district. But, as you've noted, we don't teach or plan in a vacuum, and, since we wanted the teachers to decide where and when the video making would make sense, we've had to fit the projects into their curriculum. We've found (perhaps not surprisingly) that the more we constrain projects, the less room for child choice there is, and the fewer critical literacies skills we foster.

And it's messy! We've done well engaging children and teachers in the project, and are certainly learning a lot about multimodal composition in classrooms, as well as about the language and literacy choices bilingual children make. But we're only now approaching a project in which children can make inquiries into something they want to do to change in their worlds. We have been caught up, I'll freely admit, in putting "basic skills"—albeit powerful digital literacies basic skills—before critical literacies skills. I'm excited about our potential future findings, and I'm glad that I have the work of authors in this collection to guide me—people who have already struggled with this dilemma and have managed to enact critical literacies in elementary schools (Exley, Woods, & Dooley, Chapter 5; Flint & Laman, Chapter 6; Comber & Nixon, Chapter 7; and of course, Vasquez, Chapter 13). The combination of assessment pressures, planning constraints, and the assumptions we all make about young children's abilities to engage in critical literacies projects can really limit critical literacy teaching—with or without digital components—in elementary schools.

Since contextual constraints are sometimes brought up as reasons *not* to engage in critical literacy, I'm glad that so many of our contributors show critical literacies practices in less-than-privileged contexts, like the one in which I'm working, where critical literacies are arguably most necessary. There's no better way to understand critical literacy than to "do" it, really, and we're fortunate to be able to share the work of so many others who are thinking about it. We'll end this conversation with a brief introduction of the book's contents, and our reasoning for the arrangement, in the following section.

About the Book

We have structured this book in order to prove our larger argument that critical literacy is alive, well, and needed, at all age levels, and in all (educational) contexts. After Jerome Harste's foreword, Allan Luke, Hilary Janks, and Patrick Finn start off the book, in a section titled Theoretical Frameworks and Arguments for Critical Literacy. Luke gives an indispensable, concise definition of critical literacy, including its historical antecedents and inheritances. Janks presents her clearly delineated argument for the need for critical literacy in the South African context and around the world. Finn draws parallels between the Socialist Sunday schools in 1920s America and current efforts to foster critical literacy. These chapters should be useful reading for those who are new to critical literacy, and for those need a refresher about why critical literacy is still so important today.

The second, and largest section of the book, is entitled Critiquing Critical Literacy in Praxis. We have loosely organized its chapters by age level of the students involved in the projects under discussion. In the first, Beryl Exley, Annette Woods, and Karen Dooley explore the affordances of three different approaches to critical literacy teaching in an Australian early-years (prekindergarten) program. Amy Flint and Tasha Tropp Laman describe the ways elementary teachers use poetry in the writing workshop to come to realizations regarding critical literacy in their own classrooms. In their chapter, Barbara Comber and Helen Nixon define the place-based pedagogy that they and Marg Wells, a classroom teacher, have been using to offer critical literacy opportunities to elementary students in Australia. In the next two chapters in this section, Elisabeth Johnson and Lalitha Vasudevan detail the existing critical literacy practices of high-school students, and then Enid Rosario-Ramos and Laura Johnson highlight the role of communities as counter-storytelling contexts, drawing on their work with urban Puerto Rican youth and adults. While we have not included chapters explicitly about visual, artifactual, and digital literacies in relation to critical literacy, readers will see elements of these topics in this second section in particular.

We have titled the final section of the collection Revisions of Critical Literacy, trying to get at the ways in which critical literacies in practice shift, are embattled, and might be rethought. Its contents reflect some of the ways global flows of ideas—particularly about assessment—have created new contexts in which critical literacy is and is not enacted. In the first chapter, Michael Moore, Don Zancanella, and JuliAnna Ávila discuss the assumptions behind text complexity and the invisibility of critical literacy in the U.S. Common Core State Standards. Shinya Takekawa illustrates the problems with, and possibilities for, implementing critical literacy in the context of Japan's national curriculum, typical pedagogical approaches, and the Japanese government's sensitivity to international assessment rankings. Drawing on data from a recent research project, Jessica Zacher Pandya writes about failed attempts to mandate and standardize critical literacy in elementary school. In the last chapter, Vivian Maria Vasquez addresses her career-long journey in critical literacy via an "audit trail." Cynthia Lewis has written a conclusion in which she thought-provokingly argues that the chapters in the book can be viewed as primarily about three themes: embodiment/spatiality, digital technologies/globalization, and standardization.

We hope this book offers readers from all corners of the globe, and from all educational circles, a new and refreshing look at critical literacies in context. Most of all, though, we hope that the work presented here energizes teachers and researchers to begin, or continue, critical literacies practices, projects, and stances, even when resources are scarce and circumstances less than ideal. We wanted to move critical literacies forward, as our title suggests, and we happily anticipate reading and hearing about its future incarnations. We'd like to leave the reader with a comment from Freire, who reminds us that critical literacy "is not easy, but it's not impossible" (Horton & Freire, 1990, p. 219).

Notes

1 See Vasquez, Tate, and Harste (2013) for more positive portrayals of preservice teachers' engagement with critical literacies.

2 Elizabeth Dutro's work with children in diverse settings (Dutro, Kazemi, & Balf, 2005) offers some examples. Also read about Marg Wells, the teacher who collaborates with Barbara Comber (Comber & Nixon, this volume).

3 This is a good spot to cite some of the many recent articles detailing critical literacy projects in school: Comber (2013); Pahl and Rowsell (2011); Rogers, Mosely, and Folkes (2009); Wood and Jocius (2013).

4 Or, had I been reading Vivian Vasquez's work at the time (Vasquez [2004]; Vasquez, Muise, Nakai, Shear, & Heffernan [2003]; Marsh & Vasquez, [2012]; and see Vasquez's chapter in this volume for more reading), or Husbye et al. (2012) now.

5 See Lewison, Flint, and Van Sluys (2002) for an account of working on critical literacy issues with novice and experienced teachers.

6 Ernest Morrell's studies (cf. 2008) are relevant examples of such work, as is the work of the community centers described by Enid Rosario-Ramos and Laura Johnson (this volume).

7 We are certainly not the only researchers doing this. See Alvermann, Moon, and Hagood (1999); Garcia (2012), Haddix and Sealey-Ruiz (2012); Lewis, Doerr-Stevens, Tierney, and Scharber (2012); Parker (2013); Rogers, Winters, LaMonde, and Perry (2010); Schmier (2012); and Smith and Hull (2012) for more examples.

References

Alexander, J. (2007). 'The uncreating word': Some ways not to teach English. In V. Ellis, C. Fox, & B. Street (Eds.) *Rethinking English in schools: A new and constructive stage* (pp. 102–116). London, UK: Continuum.

Alvermann, D., Moon, J., & Hagood, M. (1999). *Popular culture in the classroom: Teaching and researching critical media literacy*. Newark, DE: International Reading Association.

Ávila, J. (2008). A desire path to digital storytelling. *Teachers college record*. http://www.tcrecord.org. ID Number: 15463.

Ávila, J. (2013). Participatory culture goes to school. *Teaching Education*, *24* (1), 97–111.

Ávila, J., Underwood, C., & Woodbridge, S. (2008). "I'm the expert now": Digital storytelling and transforming literacies among displaced children. In D. McInerney & A.D. Liem (Eds.) *Research on sociocultural influences on motivation and learning: Teaching and learning: International best practice* (Vol. 8). Charlotte, NC: Information Age Publishing.

Ávila, J. & Zacher Pandya, J. (2012). Traveling, textual authority, and transformation: an introduction to critical digital literacies. In J. Ávila & J. Zacher Pandya (Eds.) *Critical digital literacies as social praxis: Intersections and challenges* (pp. 1–12). New York, NY: Peter Lang.

Comber, B. (2013). Schools as meeting places: critical and inclusive literacies in changing local environments. *Language Arts*, *90* (5), 361–371.

Dutro, E., Kazemi, E., & Balf, R. (2005). The aftermath of 'you're only half': Multiracial identities in the literacy classroom. *Language Arts*, *83* (2), 96–106.

Finn, P. J. (2009). *Literacy with an attitude: Educating working-class children in their own self-interest* (2nd edn). Albany, NY: SUNY Press.

Freebody, P. & Luke, A. (2003). Literacy as engaging with new forms of life: the four resources model. In G. Bull and M. Anstey (Eds.) *The literacy lexicon* (pp. 51–66). Australia: Pearson Education.

Freire, P. (2000). *Pedagogy of the oppressed*. New York, NY: Continuum.

Garcia, A. (2012). Utilizing mobile media and games to develop critical inner-city agents of social change. In J. Ávila & J. Zacher Pandya (Eds.) *Critical digital literacies as social praxis: Intersections and challenges* (pp. 107–125). New York, NY: Peter Lang.

Haddix, M. & Sealey-Ruiz, Y. (2012). Cultivating digital and popular literacies as empowering and emancipatory acts among urban youth. *Journal of Adolescent & Adult Literacy*, *56* (3), 189–192.

Hull, G. & Stornaiuolo, A. (2010). Literate arts in a global world: Reframing social networking as cosmopolitan practice. *Journal of Adolescent and Adult Literacy*, *54* (2).

Husbye, N., Buchholz, B., Coggin, L., Powell, C., & Wohlwend, K. (2012). Critical lessons and playful literacies: digital media in PK–2 classrooms. *Language Arts*, *90* (2), 82–92.

Horton, M. & Freire, P. (1990). *We make the road by walking: Conversations on education and social change*. Philadelphia, PA: Temple University Press.

Janks, H. (2010). *Literacy and power*. London, UK: Routledge.

Janks, H., Dixon, K., Ferreira, A., Granville, S., & Newfield, D. (2013). *Doing critical literacy: Texts and activities for students and teachers*. London, UK: Routledge.

Jenkins, H., Purushotma, R., Weigel, M., Clinton, K., & Robison, A. (2009). *Confronting the challenges of participatory culture: Media education for the 21st century*. Cambridge, MA: The MIT Press.

Lewis, C., Doerr-Stevens, C., Tierney, J., & Scharber, C. (2012). Relocalization in the market economy: Critical literacies and media production in an urban English classroom. In J. Ávila & J. Zacher Pandya (Eds.) *Critical digital literacies as social praxis: Intersections and challenges* (pp. 179–196). New York, NY: Peter Lang.

Lewison, M., Flint, A. S., & Van Sluys, K. (2002). Taking on critical literacy: The journey of newcomers and novices. *Language Arts, 79*, 382–392.

Luke, A. (2004). Two takes on the critical. In B. Norton & K. Toohey (Eds.) *Critical pedagogies and language learning* (pp. 21–29). Cambridge, UK: Cambridge University Press.

Marsh, J. & Vasquez, V. (2012). Aligning instruction to developmental needs in critical and digital literacies. *Language Arts, 90* (2), 151–157.

Misson, R. & Morgan, W. (2007). 'The uncreating word': Some ways not to teach English. In V. Ellis, C. Fox, & B. Street (Eds.) *Rethinking English in schools: A new and constructive stage* (pp. 73–87). London, UK: Continuum.

Morrell, E. (2008). *Critical literacy and urban youth: Pedagogies of access, dissent and liberation*. New York, NY: Routledge.

New London Group (1996). A pedagogy of multiliteracies: Designing social futures. *Harvard Educational Review, 66*, 60–92.

No Child Left Behind Act of 2001, 107th Congress. (January 8, 2002).

Pahl, K. & Rowsell, J. (2011). Artifactual critical literacy: A new perspective for literacy education. *Berkeley Review of Education, 2* (2), 129–151.

Parker, J. (2013). Critical literacy and the ethical responsibilities of student media production. *Journal of Adolescent and Adult Literacy, 56* (8), 668–676.

Rogers, R., Mosely, M., & Folkes, A. (2009). Standing up to neoliberalism through critical literacy education. *Language Arts, 87* (2), 127–138.

Rogers, T., Winters, K., LaMonde, A. & Perry, M. (2010). From image to ideology: analysing shifting identity positions of marginalized youth across the cultural sites of video production. *Pedagogies: An International Journal 5* (4), 298–312.

Salinger, J.D. (1951). *The catcher in the rye*. Boston, MA: Little, Brown.

Schmier, S. (2012). Designing spaces for student choice in a digital media studies classroom. In J. Ávila & J. Zacher Pandya (Eds.) *Critical digital literacies as social praxis: Intersections and challenges* (pp. 15–39). New York, NY: Peter Lang.

Sleeter, C. & C. Grant. (2008). *Making choices for multicultural education: Five approaches to race, class and gender* (6th edn). Hoboken, NJ: Wiley & Sons.

Smith, A. & Hull, G. (2012). Critical literacies and social media; Fostering ethical engagement with global youth. In J. Ávila & J. Zacher Pandya (Eds.) Critical digital literacies as social praxis: Intersections and challenges (pp. 63–84). New York, NY: Peter Lang.

Stevens, L. P. & T. Bean. (2007). *Critical literacy: Context, research and practice in the K-12 classroom*. Thousand Oaks, CA: Sage Publications.

Vasquez, V. (2004). *Negotiating critical literacies with young children*. New York, NY: Routledge Press.

Vasquez, V., Muise, M., Nakai, D., Shear, J., & Heffernan, L. (2003). *Getting beyond I like the book: Creating spaces for critical literacy in K-6 classrooms.* Newark, DE: International Reading Association.

Vasquez, V., Tate, S., & J. Harste. (2013). *Negotiating critical literacies with teachers: Theoretical foundations and pedagogical resources for pre-service and in-service contexts.* New York, NY: Routledge.

Wood, S. & Jocius, R. (2013). Combating "I hate this stupid book!": Black males and critical literacy. *The Reading Teacher, 66* (8), 661–669.

Zacher Pandya, J. (2011). *Overtested: How high-stakes accountability fails English language learners.* New York, NY: Teachers College Press.

SECTION I

Theoretical Frameworks and Arguments for Critical Literacy

2

DEFINING CRITICAL LITERACY*

Allan Luke

The new information order is messing with governments', political parties', and corporations' longstanding domination of mass communications, honed and refined in the last century to control and mediate the printed word and traditional broadcast media. In the past year, the U.S. State Department critiqued the Chinese government for its censorship of web engines, arguing that freedom of (Google) access to information was a democratic right. Yet several months later, they declared the Wikileaks release of diplomatic cables a threat to national and geopolitical security. More recently, the new media have been used as a means for the dissent and revolution in the Middle East, with several governments attempting to shut down instant messaging and social networking, while maintaining longstanding control over traditional print and video reporting. This is, no doubt, occupying the time of U.S. government employees in Langley, Virginia—it has led to a growth in the work of censors and monitors in Singapore, Egypt, the United Kingdom and elsewhere. At the same time, their counterparts at media and technology corporations Google, Newscorp, Microsoft, Thomson-Reuters, Twitter, and Facebook are conceptualizing and developing strategies and technologies for maintaining the profiles of their brands, their influence, profits, and market share in response to dynamic new contexts of use and regulation.

The "global village" imagined by Marshall McLuhan (1968) is fact: a virtual and material world where traditional print and image, canonical genres and new modalities of information sit side by side—where new and old media build discourse communities and enable political and cultural action in historically

* This chapter is an expanded version of: Luke, A. (2012). Critical literacy: Foundational notes. *Theory Into Practice, 51* (1), 4–11. DOI: 10.1080/00405841.2012.636324. Reprinted by permission of Taylor & Francis (http://www.tandfonline.com).

unprecedented ways. New media are transforming relations of production and consumption, and, as the recent U.S. election showed, remaking democratic politics and electoral practices. Just as they are reshaping relations of work and leisure, production and consumption, new media are enabling new community formations and coalitions, new global and local social movements. This is altering longstanding social fields and relations, putting into question the viability of many twentieth-century institutions of print and TV popular culture: newspaper and magazine-based media empires, book publishers, television networks, and music labels.

Journalism The current uprisings across this village return us to the classical questions of critical literacy. What is "truth"? How is it presented and represented, by whom, and in whose interests? Who should have access to which images and words, texts and discourses? For what purposes? This isn't simply about reading or functional literacy. It never has been. *Brave New World* (Huxley, 1932), *1984* (Orwell, 1949), *Fahrenheit 451* (Bradbury, 1962), and *Oryx and Crake* (Atwood, 2003) should be required reading for all students and citizens. They remind us that civil society, human relationships, human agency and informed action are dependent upon access to flows of information and knowledge, text and discourse. These dystopian works teach about the centrality of memory and history, the dangers of autocratic control, and the moral and species-survival imperatives of dialogue, exchange, and critique. In so doing, they warn of the other dialectical effect of wall-to-wall digital culture: 24/7 surveillance, the loss of privacy, and, with it, the loss of individual and collective freedom of speech and expression. Despite the demonstrable limits of the Eurocentric ideals and achievements of the modern state, these remain aspirational human rights at the heart of the project of critical literacy.

Struggles over power are, *inter alia*, struggles over the control of information and interpretation, text and discourse. Wherever textual access, critique, and interpretation are closed down or centrally controlled and remediated, whether via corporate or state or religious control of the press, of the internet, of server access, of the archive of knowledge—from the first libraries of Alexandria to Google—human agency, political self-determination, cultural autonomy and, if we follow the vision of these writers, species survival itself are put at risk.

These are the core curriculum questions: about whose version of cultures, histories, sciences, and everyday life will count as official knowledge. They are questions about pedagogy and teaching: about which modes of information and cognitive scripts, which designs and genres shall be deemed worth learning, what kinds of tool for use with reading and writing will be taught, for what social and cultural purposes and interests. These are not disinterested or neutral, technical and "scientific" decisions—and where they are taken as such, they risk turning "history into nature," to paraphrase Roland Barthes' (1972) explanation of media and ideology.

The term *literacy* refers to the reading and writing of text. Unlike speech, it is not a "natural" and innate species behavior. Writing—whether in manuscript, print, or digital form—is a malleable human technology. As such, it has been invented and reinvented, shaped and reshaped for particular cultural and social functions and uses. Since the initial development of syllabary and cuneiform writing systems in Mesopotamia, its development has taken various forms and directions in the West and Anglo-European countries, in Middle Eastern and Asian cultures and societies, and, notably, in Indigenous cultures (e.g., Mayan logograms). Contrary to early, panegyric accounts of the history of Western literacy, this has not been a linear or uniform development, either in technological or cultural terms (cf. Bhattacharya, 2011). In each case, different systems of writing, inscription, and record keeping were enlisted for varied and often distinctive practical economic functions (e.g., crop and weather records, currency, debt, trade), for governance (e.g., currency, laws, kinship records), for history and cultural memory (e.g., sacred texts, poetry, epic poems, narrative), and, in instances, for the development of science and technology (Goody, 1986). These varying functions have set the contexts for distinctive orthographies, genres, specialist registers, and lexicogrammatical conventions.

The term *critical literacy* refers to the use of the technologies of print and other media of communication to analyze, critique, and transform the norms, rule systems, and practices governing the social fields of institutions and everyday life (Luke, 2004). Because the emergence of literacy in the West was defined by Luther's fifteenth-century theological and ideological insurrection against Papal control over the "word" (Luke, 1988), there is a strong historical case that the use of literacy to "decide for oneself," to paraphrase Luther and Phillip Melanthon, set key conditions for the emergence of the European nation state and "print capitalism" (Anderson, 1983).

Critical literacy is not new, the object of a half-century of theoretical debate and practical innovation in the field of education. Since Freire's (1970) educational projects in Brazil, approaches to critical literacy have been developed through feminist, postcolonial, poststructuralist and critical race theory, critical linguistics and cultural studies, and, indeed, rhetorical and cognitive models of writing and reading.

This is an introduction to models for schools. Critical literacy is an overtly political orientation to teaching and learning and to the cultural, ideological, and sociolinguistic content of the curriculum. It is focused on the uses of literacy for social justice in marginalized and disenfranchised communities. We can frame this focus in terms of Nancy Fraser's concepts of "redistributive," "recognitive," and "representative" social justice (Fraser, 1997, 2009):

(1) *Redistributive social justice*: the more equitable distribution and achievement of conventionally defined and measured literate practices;
(2) *Recognitive social justice*: shifts in the ideological content and uses of literacy to include cultural knowledges and texts of historically marginalized and excluded communities and cultures;
(3) *Representative social justice*: promotion of the uses of literacy to represent the interests, values, and standpoints of one's communities and cultures.

Critical literacy has an explicit aim of the critique and transformation of dominant ideologies, cultures and economies, institutions, and political systems. As a practical approach to curriculum, it melds social, political, and cultural debate and discussion with the analysis of how texts and discourses work, where, with what consequences, and in whose interests.

Different approaches reflect regional and local cultural and policy contexts. Over five decades, models have been developed in large-scale national literacy campaigns, informal and community education programs for women and migrants, adult and technical education, university literature and cultural studies, and teacher education. In schools, models of critical literacy have been applied in the fields of English, language arts, writing, teaching of English to speakers of other languages, social studies education, media and information technologies (e.g., Comber & Simpson, 2001; Morgan & Ramanathan, 2005). The chapters in this volume review and critique many of these approaches.

Historical Foundations

The term "critical" has a distinctive etymology. It is derived from the Greek word *kriticos*, the ability to argue and judge. Working in marginalized Indigenous and peasant communities in Brazil, Freire's (1970) approach was grounded in Marxist and phenomenological philosophies. He argued that traditional schooling was based on a "banking model" of education, where learners' lives and cultures were taken as irrelevant. He advocated a dialogical approach to literacy based on principles of reciprocal exchange. These would critique and alter binary relationships of oppressed and oppressor, teacher and learner. "Cultural circles" would begin with dialogue on learners' problems, struggles and aspirations. The focus would be on naming and renaming, narrating and understanding learners' life worlds, with the aim of framing and solving real problems. Reading and writing are about substantive lives and material realities, and they are goal- and problem-directed. "Reading the word," then, entails "reading the world" (Freire & Macedo, 1987), unpacking myths and distortions and building new ways of knowing and acting upon the world. In this regard, Freire conceptualized critical literacy as a form of ideology critique: a deliberate attempt to disrupt what Hegel and Marx referred to as the "false consciousness" achieved when the values, beliefs, and knowledges of dominant social groups were presented as true and incontestable. Technical mastery of written language, then, is a *means* to broader human social and cultural agency, individual and collective action—not an end in and of itself.

There are many antecedents to Freire's approach. Early twentieth-century exemplars of working-class and African-American community education were established in many cities (Shannon, 1998; Willis, 2008). Significant European treatises define language and literature as potential modes of political and social action. These range from Voloshinov's (1929/1986) analysis of "speech genres" as political acts to Brecht's experiments with political drama (Weber & Heinen,

2010). Work in postwar British cultural studies by Richard Hoggart (1957) and Raymond Williams (1977) set the directions for approaches to critical literacy: the expansion of education beyond canonical and literary texts to include works of popular culture; and a focus on critical analysis as *counter-hegemonic* critique that might, in turn, encourage recognition of marginalized communities' histories and experiences.

Poststructuralist models of discourse are a further major philosophical influence. Versions of social and material "reality" are built and shaped through linguistic taxonomy and categorization. Yet one of the principal unresolved issues in Freire's work was its dialectical technique of binary opposition (e.g., oppressor/oppressed, monologue/dialogue), derived from Hegel's and Marx's conception of the "master/slave dialectic," and the absence of an elaborated model of text and language. A central tenet of Foucault's (1972) analysis of discourse was that binary opposition has the potential to obscure the complexity and multiplicity of discourse. Discourse, he demonstrated, had historically been key to the assertion of power in the definition and positioning of human subjects, their actions and contexts. Poststructuralist theory critiqued the authority of the received literary and scientific canon and argued against the validity of any definitive interpretation or "truth" from a given text (Derrida, 1978).

Taken together, these diverse foundations set the stage for an exploration of critical literacy in this volume. This would include: (1) a focus on ideology critique, cultural and political analysis of texts as a key element of education against cultural exclusion and marginalization; (2) a commitment to the inclusion of working-class, cultural and linguistic minorities, Indigenous learners, and others marginalized on the basis of gender, sexuality, or other forms of difference; (3) an engagement with the significance of text, ideology, and discourse in the construction and reconstruction of social and material relations, everyday cultural and political life.

Educational Antecedents

In the late twentieth century, reading psychologists began to expand models of reading beyond prototypical behaviorist principles to emphasize meaning construction (e.g., vanDijk & Kintsch, 1983). Hence, American reading research now focuses on "comprehension" and "higher-order" skills, including prediction and inference. These versions of *critical reading* define literacy as an internal cognitive process reliant upon readers' background knowledge or "schemata" (Anderson & Pearson, 1984). There is a rationalist assumption at work here: that critique enables the identification of logical or factual error. The Enlightenment belief in the scientific falsification and verification of knowledge is central to the definition of higher-order thinking and, indeed, linguistic complexity and function (Halliday & Martin, 1995). Thus, in Anglo-American schooling, reading is affiliated with the developmental acquisition of complex forms of reasoning and cognitive processes (e.g., taxonomy, categorization) and developmental growth from narrative to expository genres (Olson, 1996).

In schools, critical reading is taught as a reasoned approach to identifying author bias; approaches to comprehension focus on the multiple possible meanings derived from the interaction of background knowledge and textual message. Yet there is typically little recognition that texts and curricula necessarily engage particular cultural and political standpoints, and little explicit recognition that texts are contestable media of sociocultural exchange and power. While there may be discussion of truthfulness, veracity, and dependability of texts, there is little emphasis on the ways that text selection and the shaping of what counts as "reading" and "writing" can serve cultural and social class-based interests (Luke, 1988).

Current models of critical reading also draw from postwar literary theory. Many 1960s university and secondary school English classrooms focused readers on the close reading of textual features and literary devices (e.g., Wellek & Warren, 1949). In U.S. English education, the shift from New Criticism to reader response theory (Rosenblatt, 1978) set the grounds for an increased emphasis on "personal response" to literature. A comparable move in the United Kingdom was the rise of "personal growth" models of literary study that emphasized individual voice and interpretation (Britton, 1970). The assumption was that literary texts produce diverse meanings, depending upon readers' affective responses. In more general terms, literature becomes a means for the moral and intellectual construction of the self (Willinsky, 1990).

These models of literacy as cognitive process, as textual analysis, and as personal response feature in current school curricula. These do set the grounds for a move beyond Freire's typification of schooling as a banking model. Cognitive models invoke readers' background knowledge, acknowledging the cultural basis of the resources children bring to school. Further, reader response model approaches share with Freire a focus on the possibilities of literacy for the critical analysis of self/other relations and the restoration of power to readers. These remain focal points in the development of cultural approaches to literacy (e.g., McNaughton, 2011) and in efforts to meld learner-centered models with social and political analysis (e.g., Edelsky, 1991).

Yet critical literacy approaches set the reshaping of political consciousness, material conditions, and social relations as first principles. They also differ from traditional cognitive and literary models in their understandings of the relative agency and power of readers and writers, texts and language.

Critical Pedagogies

Freire's principles are assembled in the broad project of "critical pedagogy" (Lankshear & McLaren, 1993). Freire draws from Marx the key concept that ruling-class ideology defines school knowledge and ideology. By this view, school literacy creates a *receptive* literacy, involving a passive reproduction of knowledge. The focus of critical literacy is on ideology critique of the world portrayed in media, literature, textbooks, and functional texts (Shor & Freire, 1987). The alternative is to begin from learners' worldviews, in effect turning them into inventors of the curriculum, critics and creators of knowledge. To apply a sociological description, critical pedagogy thus marks a deliberate weakening of relations of "classification" and "framing" (Bernstein, 1990), shifting control over curriculum content and social relations away from traditional teacher-centered education.

Critical analyses of economic conditions were central to literacy campaigns led by Freire in Africa and the Americas (Kukendall, 2010), and they are the focus of ongoing efforts at political education in the Americas (e.g., Darder, Baltodano, & Torres, 2003). Students are involved in analysis of the effects of capitalism, colonialism, and inequitable economic relations. This entails working with learners to question class, race, and gender relations through dialogic exchange. In such a setting traditional authority and epistemic knowledge relations of teachers and student shift: learners become teachers of their understandings and experiences, and teachers become learners of these same contexts. This might entail setting open dialogic conditions of exchange by establishing a cultural circle amongst adult learners. In school classrooms, it might entail establishing democratic conditions in classrooms where authentic exchange and text work can occur around social and cultural issues (Vasquez, 2004; Lewison, Leland, & Harste, 2008). In schools and universities, these approaches also focus literacy on community study, the analysis of social movements, engagement with repressed or silenced histories and cultures, service learning, and political activism. They also involve the development of a critical "media literacy," focusing on the analysis of popular cultural texts, including advertising, news, broadcast media, and the internet (e.g., Alvermann & Hagood, 2000; Kellner & Share, 2005). Finally, there is a broad focus in these models on competing versions of history and science, and the analysis of current ecological and environmental issues.

In the early 1990s, feminist scholars argued that the model risked an ideological imposition that was contrary to its ethos. In everyday practice, there was, and is, a parallel risk of pedagogic imposition given the complex forms of gendered and raced voice and power, identity, and subjectivity at work in classroom interaction (Luke & Gore, 1991). The critiques have had a continuing impact. Especially in Australia and Canada, approaches to school reading focus on textual and media representations of women and girls (Morgan, 1997; Mellor, O'Neill & Patterson, 2000; Cherland & Harper, 2007) and on gendered patterns of classroom interaction (Lee, 1996). Relatedly, there is a stronger focus on "standpoint" and agency, including a critique of patriarchy in critical pedagogy.

American approaches to critical literacy have developed a strong focus on the *politics of voice*, on engaging with the histories, identities, and struggles faced by groups marginalized on the basis of difference of gender, language, culture, and race, and sexual orientation (e.g., Kumishiro & Ngo, 2007). A critical approach to language and literacy education requires an explicit engagement with cultural and linguistic diversity (Norton & Toohey, 2004; Kubota & Lin, 2009). Hence, there is a strong emphasis on *recognitive* social justice; that is, on changing the subject of school literacy instruction, of deliberately altering curriculum contents, discourses, and ideologies. With the aforementioned shifts in classification and framing of classroom knowledge and interaction away from teacher-centered pedagogy, American models of critical pedagogy align with broad tenets of progressive education.

Discourse Analytic Approaches

Three decades of ethnographic research have documented the cultural, social, cognitive, and linguistic complexity of literacy acquisition and use. This raises two substantive educational challenges for critical pedagogies. First, they are largely synchronic, advocating particular approaches to literacy pedagogy without a broader developmental template. While Freirian models provide a progressivist pedagogical approach and a neomarxian political stance, they lack specificity on how teachers and students can engage with the complex structures of texts, both traditional and multimodal. The acquisition of language, text, and discourse in any language or system of writing requires the developmental engagement with levels of linguistic and discourse complexity and access to multiple discourses and affiliated linguistic registers (Gee, 1991; Lemke, 1996). Later models of critical literacy, particularly those developed in Australia and the UK, attempt to come to grips with these practical educational issues.

A major critique of critical pedagogy was that it overlooked the need for students to master a range of textual genres and registers, specialized ways with words used in science, social institutions, and further education (Halliday & Martin, 1995). Systemic functional linguists argue that the mastery of genre entails incrementally more sophisticated lexical and grammatical choice (Hassan & Williams, 1996). Equitable access to how texts work, they argue, is an essential step in redistributive social justice, and cannot be achieved through a principal focus on student voice or ideology critique. The affiliated approach to critical literacy, then, argues for explicit instruction and direct access to "genres of power" (Kalantzis & Cope, 1996). Yet there are unresolved issues about the balance of direct access required to canonical texts and registers, on the one hand, and ideology critique, on the other.

A practical approach is based upon critical discourse analysis, an explicitly political derivative of systemic functional linguistics (Fairclough, 1990; Janks, 2010). Bringing together ideology critique with an explicit instructional focus on teaching how texts work, Fairclough (1990) argues for the teaching of "critical language awareness." This entails teaching students the analysis of a range of texts—functional, academic, literary—attending to lexico-grammatical structure, ideological contents, and the identifiable conditions of production and use (Luke,

2000). Critical linguistics makes broad distinctions between ideological formations in texts, their social functions and their distinctive linguistic features, and the social fields where they have exchange value (Pennycook, 2001).

This enables teachers and students to focus on how words, grammar, and discourse choices are used to shape a version of material, natural, and sociopolitical worlds. It also enables a focus on how words and grammar attempt to establish relations of power between authors and readers, speakers and addressees. Models build from M.A.K. Halliday's (1978) analytic description of language functions in terms of "field" (representation of the world), "tenor" (social relations), and "mode" (textual conventions). Focusing on field, for example, students can analyze lexical choice, and sentence-level and text proposition-level grammatical transitivity to study how the agency and actions of human subjects, social institutions, and even natural forces are portrayed in texts. Focusing on tenor, they might study how pronominalization, grammatical modes (e.g., declaratives, imperatives, interrogatives) and modality (e.g., the use of modal auxiliaries and qualifiers) are used by writers and speakers to position themselves and their audiences in relations of power. An instructional focus on mode, further, can identify how specific genres have developed conventions in relation to specific social, cognitive, and cultural functions and purposes. Taken together, this approach enables a critical engagement with the question of how and where texts are used, by whom, and in whose interests. It also builds learners' resources for both encoding texts—that is, making deliberate and conscious genre, lexical and grammatical choices in how they construct the world and their social relations—and for critical reading and analysis of texts of everyday cultural life.

Critical literacy, by this account, entails the developmental engagement by learners with the major texts, discourses, and modes of information. It attempts to attend to the ideological and hegemonic functions of texts, as in critical pedagogy models. But it augments this by providing students with technical resources for analyzing how texts work (Wallace, 2003; Janks, 2010). For example, this might entail the analysis of a textbook or media representation of political or economic life. But in addition to questions of how a text might reflect learners' life worlds and experiences, it also aims to teach them how the selection of specific grammatical structures and word choices attempts to manipulate the reader. In these ways, the discourse analytic approach attempts to move beyond the principles of political "consciousness raising" and diasporic "voice" that feature in American critical pedagogy models to include deliberate foci on metalinguistic and metacognitive engagements with texts, discourses and media.

What is to be Done?

Taken together, critical literacy approaches view language, texts, and their discourse structures as principal means for representing and reshaping possible worlds. The aim is the development of human capacity to use texts to analyze social fields and their systems of exchange, with an eye to transforming social relations and material conditions. As a cultural and linguistic practice, then, critical literacy entails an understanding of how texts and discourses can be manipulated to represent and, indeed, *alter* the world. But this focus on "power," on "transformation" and change does not and cannot in itself resolve central issues around moral and political normativity (Muspratt, Luke, & Freebody, 1998; Pennycook, 2001): around the questions of whose values, texts, ideologies, and discourses should take center stage, and about the desired shapes and directions of social transformation. It places these on the table as necessary starting points—but it does not and cannot by definition provide a comprehensive and definitive approach to practical matters of curriculum and pedagogy. Because of its historical materialist roots, the ideational substance of critical literacy education necessarily is to be found in an analysis of specific political economic formations, specific social and discourse relations, and local cultural resources, communities, and contexts.

Freire's initial model was a significant statement in point-of-decolonization educational theory. That is, the silencing of the urban poor, of Indigenous minorities and of a subjugated peasantry in the context of liberationist theology and what was then referred to as "third world" politics set the grounds for an explicitly political educational agenda. Yet, while the Freirian model was based on binary analyses of "oppressed" and "oppressors," globalized "hypercapitalist" systems (Graham, 2006) have led to more complex economic and political forces, with the emergence of multiple forms of solidarity and identity, new political coalitions and social movements.

New media have created dynamic and enabling conditions for new cultures, social movements, and politics (Hammer & Kellner, 2009). Definitions of literacy have expanded to include engagement with texts in a range of semiotic forms: visual, aural, and digital multimodal texts (e.g., Coiro, Knobel, Lankshear, & Leu, 2008). As my initial comments on the current political contexts in the Middle East suggest, this isn't just a matter of the development of creative industries, new identities, and new technologies, as stated in contemporary curriculum policy. Much current policy is moving towards embracing models of design, multiliteracies, models of creativity, and critical thinking as principal components in the curriculum capacities for a new digital species of *Homo economicus*.

Instead, the project of critical literacy is about the possibility of using new literacies to change relations of power, both people's everyday social relations and larger geopolitical and economic relations. At the same time, digital engagement in itself does not constitute a critical literacy approach, for digital culture sits within a complex, emergent political economic order that, for many learners and adults, is well beyond comprehension and critique. Who understands structures of debt? The transnational division of labor and wealth? Derivatives and futures markets? This will require a new vocabulary to describe, analyze, and, indeed, critique current economic structures, flows and forces (Luke, Luke & Graham, 2007).

Critical literacies are, by definition, historical materialist works in progress. There is no "correct" or universal model. Critical literacy entails a process of naming and renaming the world, seeing its patterns, designs, and complexities, and developing the capacity to redesign and reshape it (New London Group, 1996). How educators shape and deploy the tools, attitudes, and philosophies of critical literacy is utterly contingent. This will depend upon students' and teachers' everyday relations of power, their lived problems and struggles, and, as the chapters in this volume demonstrate, on educators' professional ingenuity in navigating the enabling and disenabling local contexts of educational policy.

There are simple lessons from several decades of teachers' work with critical literacy in schools across the United States, Canada, the United Kingdom, South Africa, Australia, and New Zealand, but also in Africa, Brazil, and the Americas, and, in the last decade, Singapore, Hong Kong, Europe, and Japan. While it is difficult to mandate and implement in school systems and state ideological contexts which set out to control open access to and engagement with information, texts, and discourses, it has proven equally difficult to suppress. Discourse, Foucault (1972) would remind us, necessarily takes idiosyncratic shapes and turns in local contexts, often in the face of systematic attempts to monitor and control. Many teachers and students across these national and institutional contexts continue to explore and invent critical ways of engaging with texts, their cultural practices, and traditions—old and new, residual and emergent, global and local, print and digital.

References

Alvermann, D. & Hagood, M. (2000). Critical media literacy: Research, theory, and practice in "new times." *Journal of Educational Research, 93*, 193–205.

Anderson, B. (1983). *Imagined communities*. London, UK: Verso.

Anderson, R. C. & Pearson, P. D. (1984). A schema-theoretic view of basic processes in reading comprehension. In P. D. Pearson, R. Barr, M. Kamil, & P. Mosenthal (Eds.) *The handbook of reading research*, vol. 1 (pp. 255–291). New York, NY: Longman.

Barthes, R. (1972). *Mythologies*. Trans. A. Lavers. London, UK: Paladin.

Bernstein, B. (1990). *The structuring of pedagogic discourse*. London, UK: Routledge and Kegan Paul.

Bhattacharya, U. (2011). The 'West' in literacy. *Berkeley Review of Education, 2* (2), 179–199.

Britton, J. (1970). *Language and literacy*. London, UK: Allen Lane.

Cherland, M. & Harper, H. (2007). *Advocacy research in literacy education*. New York, NY: Routledge.

Coiro, J., Knobel, M., Lankshear, C., & Leu, D. (Eds.) (2008). *The handbook of research on new literacies*. Mahwah, NJ: Erlbaum.

Darder, A., Baltodano, M., & Torres, R. (Eds.) (2003). *The critical pedagogy reader*. New York, NY: Routledge.

Derrida, J. (1978). *Writing and difference*. Trans. A. Bass. Chicago, IL: University of Chicago Press.

Edelsky, C. (1991). *With literacy and justice for all*. London, UK: Taylor & Francis.

Fairclough, N. (Ed.) (1990). *Critical language awareness*. London, UK: Longman.

Foucault, M. (1972). *The archaeology of knowledge and the discourse on language*. Trans. A. Sheridan-Smith. London, UK: Tavistock.

Freire, P. (1970). *Pedagogy of the oppressed*. Trans. M.B. Ramos. New York, NY: Continuum.

Freire, P. & Macedo, D. (1987). *Literacy: Reading the word and the world*. South Hadley, MA: Bergin & Garvey.

Fraser, N. (1997). *Justus interruptus*. London, UK: Routledge.

Fraser, N. (2009). *Scales of justice*. New York, NY: Columbia University Press.

Gee, J.P. (1991). *Social linguistics and literacies*. London, UK: Taylor & Francis.

Goody, J. (1986) *The domestication of the savage mind*. Cambridge, UK: Cambridge University Press.

Graham, P. (2006). *Hypercapitalism*. New York, NY: Peter Lang.

Halliday, M.A.K. (1978). *Language as social semiotic*. London, UK: Arnold.

Halliday, M.A.K. & Martin, J.R. (1995). *Writing science*. London, UK: Taylor & Francis.

Hammer, R. & Kellner, D. (Eds.) (2009). *Media/cultural studies: A critical approach*. New York, NY: Peter Lang.

Hassan, R. & Williams, G. (Eds.) (1996). *Literacy in society*. London, UK: Longman.

Hoggart, R. (1957). *The uses of literacy*. Harmondsworth, UK: Penguin.

Kalantzis, M. & Cope, B. (Eds.) (1996). *The powers of literacy*. London, UK: Taylor & Francis.

Kellner, D. & Share, J. (2005). Toward critical media literacy: Core concepts, debates, organisation and policy. *Discourse, 3*, 369–386.

Kubota, R. & Lin, A. (Eds.) (2009). *Race, culture and identities in second language learning*. New York, NY: Routledge.

Kukendall, A.J. (2010). *Paulo Freire and the cold war politics of literacy*. Chapel Hill, NC: University of North Carolina Press.

Kumishiro, K. & Ngo, B. (Eds.) (2007). *Six lenses for anti-oppressive education*. New York, NY: Peter Lang.

Lankshear, C. & McLaren, P. (Eds.) (1993). *Critical literacy*. Albany, NY: State University of New York Press.

Lee, A. (1996). *Gender, literacy, curriculum*. London, UK: Taylor & Francis.

Lemke, J. (1996). *Textual politics*. London, UK: Taylor & Francis.

Luke, A. (1988). *Literacy, textbooks and ideology*. London, UK: Falmer Press.

Luke, A. (2000). Critical literacy in Australia: A matter of context and standpoint. *Journal of Adolescent & Adult Literacy, 43*, 448–461.

Luke, A. (2004). Two takes on the critical. In B. Norton & K. Toohey (Eds.) *Critical pedagogies and language learning* (pp. 21–31). Cambridge, UK: Cambridge University Press.

Luke, A., Luke, C., & Graham, P. (2007). Globalisation, corporatism and critical language education. *International Multilingual Research Journal, 1*, 1–13.

Luke, C. & Gore, J. (Eds.) (1991). *Feminisms and critical pedagogy*. London, UK: Routledge.

McLuhan, M. (1968). *War and peace in the global village*. New York, NY: Bantam.

McNaughton, S. (2011). *Designing better schools for culturally and linguistically diverse children*. London, UK: Routledge.

Morgan, B. & Ramanathan, V. (2005). Critical literacies and language eduation: Global and local perspectives. *Annual Review of Applied Linguistics, 25*, 151–169.

Morgan, W. (1997). *Critical literacy in the classroom*. London, UK: Routledge.

Muspratt, S., Luke, A., & Freebody, P. (Eds.) (1998). *Constructing critical literacies*. New York, NY: Hampton Press.

New London Group (1996). A pedagogy of multiliteracies: Designing social futures. *Harvard Educational Review*, *66*, 60–92.

Norton, B. & Toohey, K. (Eds.) (2004). *Critical pedagogies and language learning*. Cambridge, UK: Cambridge University Press.

Olson, D.R. (1996). *The world on paper*. Cambridge, UK: Cambridge University Press.

Pennycook, A. (2001). *Critical applied linguistics*. Mahwah, NJ: Erlbaum.

Rosenblatt, L. (1978). *The reader, the text, the poem: The transactional theory of the literary work*. Carbondale, IL: Southern Illinois University Press.

Shannon, P. (1998). *Broken promises: Reading instruction in 20th century America*. South Hadley, MA: Bergin & Garvey.

Shor, I. & Freire, P. (1987). *A pedagogy for liberation*. South Hadley, MA: Bergin & Garvey.

vanDijk, T.A. & Kintsch, W. (1983). *Strategies of discourse comprehension*. New York, NY: Academic.

Voloshinov, V.N. (1929/1986). *Marxism and the philosophy of language*. Trans. L. Matejka & I.R. Titunik. Cambridge, MA: Harvard University Press.

Weber, B. & Heinen, H. (Eds.) (2010). *Bertolt Brecht: Political theory and literary practice*. Athens, GA: University of Georgia Press.

Wellek, R. & Warren, A. (1949). *Theory of literature*. New York, NY: Harcourt, Brace.

Williams, R. (1977). *Marxism and literature*. Oxford, UK: Oxford University Press.

Willinsky, J. (1990). *The new literacy*. London, UK: Routledge.

Willis, A.I. (2008). *Reading comprehension research and testing in the US: Undercurrents of race, class and power in the struggle for meaning*. Mahwah, NJ: Erlbaum.

Classroom Resources for Teachers

Atwood, M. (2003). *Oryx and Crake*. Toronto, Canada: McClelland & Stewart.

Bradbury, R. (1962). *Fahrenheit 451*. New York, NY: Ballantine.

Comber, B. & Simpson, A. (Eds.) (2001). *Negotiating critical literacies in classrooms*. Mahwah, NJ: Erlbaum.

Huxley, A. (1932). *Brave new world*. London, UK: Chatto & Windus.

Janks, H. (2010). *Literacy and power*. London, UK: Routledge.

Lewison, M., Leland, C., & Harste, J. (2008). *Creating critical classrooms*. Mahwah, NJ: Erlbaum.

Luke, A. (2000). Critical literacy in Australia: A matter of context and standpoint. *Journal of Adolescent & Adult Literacy*, *43* (5), 448–461.

McNaughton, S. (2002). *Meeting of minds*. Auckland, NZ: Learning Media.

Mellor, B., O'Neill, M., & Patterson, A. (2000). *Reading stories*. Perth, WA: Chalkface Press/National Council of Teachers of English.

Morgan, W. (1997). *Critical literacy in the classroom*. London, UK: Routledge.

Orwell, G. (1949). *1984*. London, UK: Secker & Warburg.

Vasquez, V. (2004). *Negotiating critical literacies with young children*. Mahwah, NJ: Lawrence Erlbaum.

Wallace, C. (2003). *Critical reading in language education*. London, UK: Palgrave Macmillan.

3

THE IMPORTANCE OF CRITICAL LITERACY*

Hilary Janks

Introduction

This chapter makes an argument for the ongoing importance of critical literacy at a moment when there are mutterings about its being passé. Foucault argues that "discourse is the power which is to be seized" (1980) because he recognizes its ability to produce us as particular kinds of human subjects. In an age where the production of meaning is being democratized by Web 2.0, social networking sites, and portable connectivity, powerful discourses continue to speak to us and to speak through us. We often become unconscious agents of their distribution. At the same time, these new media have been used for disseminating counter-discourses, for mobilizing opposition, for questioning and destabilizing power and, in the Syrian war, for publicizing acts of atrocity. This is the context within which we need to consider the role of critical literacy in education. The second part of the chapter formulates the argument. The 2010 World Press award photograph, together with Said's (1978) analysis of Orientalism as examples of the power of image and discourse, and the "Mountains of Kong" as a metaphor for the power of text and the force of images are all used as evidence that an ability to understand the social effects of texts is important. The last part of the chapter draws on new materials (Janks, Dixon, Ferriera, Granville, & Newfield, 2013), as examples of the kind of work that, I would argue, is still necessary in classrooms around the world.

In a peaceful world without the threat of global warming or conflict or war, where everyone has access to education, health care, food and a dignified life, there would still be a need for critical literacy. In a world that is rich with difference,

* Originally published as Janks, H. (2012). The importance of critical literacy. *English Teaching: Practice & Critique, 11* (1), 150–163. http://edlinked.soe.waikato.ac.nz/research/files/etpc/files/2012v11n1dial1.pdf. Reprinted with permission.

there is still likely to be intolerance and fear of the other. Because difference is structured in relation to power, unequal access to resources based on gender, race, ethnicity, nationality, and class will continue to produce privilege and resentment. Even in a world where socially constructed relations of power have been flattened, we will still have to manage the politics of our daily lives. I have called these politics little *p* politics to distinguish them from big *P* politics (Janks, 2010, p. 186).

Politics with a capital *P* is about government and world trade agreements and the United Nations peace-keeping forces; it is about ethnic or religious genocide and world tribunals; it is about apartheid and global capitalism, money laundering, and linguistic imperialism. It is about the inequities between the political North and the political South. It is about oil, the ozone layer, genetic engineering, and cloning. It is about the danger of global warming. It is about globalization, the new work order, and sweat shops in Asia.

Little *p* politics, on the other hand, is about the micro-politics of everyday life. It is about the minute-by-minute choices and decisions that make us who we are. It is about desire and fear; how we construct them and how they construct us. It is about the politics of identity and place; it is about small triumphs and defeats; it is about winners and losers, haves and have nots, school bullies and their victims; it is about how we treat other people day by day; it is about whether or not we learn someone else's language or recycle our own garbage. Little *p* politics is about taking seriously the feminist perspective that the personal *is* the political.

This is not to suggest that *politics* has nothing to do with *Politics*. On the contrary, the socio-historical and economic contexts in which we live produce different conditions of possibility and constraint that we all have to negotiate as meaningfully as we can. While the social constructs who we are, so do we construct the social. This dialectic relationship is fluid and dynamic, creating possibilities for social action and change.

The Arguments for and Against Critique

I take the position that a critical stance to language, text, and discourse cannot be dismissed as no longer relevant and I have taken some trouble to understand the arguments that suggest that it is no longer important. Kress (2010) in his theory of design rejects theories of both communicative competence and theories of critique: *competence* because it "anchors communication in convention as social regulation" (p. 6) and *critique* because of its engagement "with the past actions of others and their effects" (p. 6). For him "competence leaves arrangements unchallenged." This is not a new idea. Fairclough's article on "The appropriacy of appropriateness" (1992) showed that what counts as appropriate and who decides are questions of power, thus providing a fundamental challenge to Dell Hymes' theory of communicative competence. "Appropriateness," like other language and text conventions, was shown to be tied to the social order and subject to challenge and change.

Critique, on the other hand, is rejected by Kress because it is: "oriented *back-wards* and towards superior power, concerned with the *present* effects of the past actions of others" (p. 6, my italics). Not only is this internally contradictory—how can it be oriented backwards if it is concerned with present effects?—he also contradicts himself when two lines later he says that, "The understanding developed through critique is essential in the practices of design" (p. 6).

His arguments rest on his sense that current forms of knowledge production, of text making, and of social and semiotic boundaries are unstable (Kress, 2010, p. 23). The move from knowledge consumption to knowledge production evident in Web 2.0 has removed previous forms of authorization and ownership. (Wikipedia is a good example.) Authorship is further challenged by new forms of text making: mixing, mashing, cutting, pasting, and recontextualizing are taken-for-granted practices of the net generation. These processes result in easy and ongoing textual transformation that destabilizes the very notion of "a text." Finally, Kress points to the social and semiotic blurring of frames and boundaries. Conventions, grammar, genres, semiotic forms are all in a state of flux and the boundaries between information and knowledge, fact and fiction, are fluid. For Kress,

> The rhetor as the maker of a message *now* makes an assessment of all aspects of the communicational situation: of his or her interest; of the characteristics of the audience; the semiotic requirements of the issue at stake; and the resources available for apt representation; together with establishing the best means of dissemination.
>
> *(Kress, 2010, p. 26, my italics)*

Kress goes on to say that, once the message has been designed and produced, it is open to remaking and transformation by those who "review, comment and engage with it" (Kress, 2010, p. 27).

I would argue that Kress' description of the rhetor has always been the case, with different modes assuming prominence at different moments in history. Nevertheless, there are important aspects of this description that it is important to challenge in defense of critique. First is the assumption that the rhetor's choices are both conscious and freely made, when there is evidence to suggest that our choices are circumscribed by the ways of thinking, believing, and valuing inscribed in the discourses that we inhabit. Without critique, the possibility of disrupting these discourses is reduced. In addition, convention, genre, grammar have always been subject to change; this does not mean that they no longer constrain our semiotic choices in all domains of communication. Equally important are the resources needed for "review." Engagement is not enough. The interest of the interpreter is not enough. Recognition of the rhetor's interest and estrangement are also necessary for redesign. One has to have a sense of how the text could be different and this requires something in addition to engagement. One has to be able to read the content, form, and interests of the text, however unconsciously, in order to be able to redesign it.

Critical literacy has for some time focused on the relationship between text consumption and text production. And critique figures as an aspect of both. This can be represented by the redesign cycle (Janks, 2010) (Figure 3.1).

It is not possible to deconstruct a text without looking backwards to the text and without considering how it could be different, thus also looking forward to redesign (Figure 3.2).

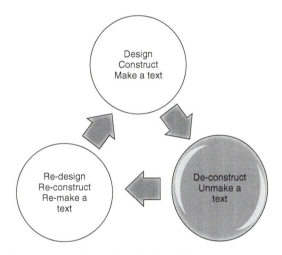

FIGURE 3.1   The redesign cycle (Janks, 2010, p. 183).

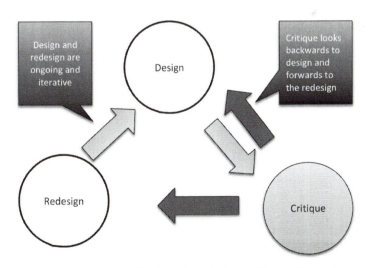

FIGURE 3.2   Critique is oriented backwards to design and forwards to redesign.

Critique enables participants to engage *consciously* with the ways in which semiotic resources have been harnessed to serve the interests of the producer and how different resources could be harnessed to redesign and reposition the text. It is both backward- and forward-looking.

It is important to recognise that redesign, like design, can be used ethically or unethically to advance the interests of some at the expense of others. The democratization of text production reinforces Foucault's (1980) notion of power as something that circulates rather than the Marxist notion of power as a form of domination and subordination. I believe that both forms of power are evident in the world in which we live and that both should be subject to critique. What matters is that critique is not the endpoint; transformative and ethical reconstruction and social action are.

The 2010 World Press Award as an Example of Orientalism

The photograph of Bibi Aisha taken by Jodi Bieber won the 2010 World Press award and can be viewed on Google images. Bibi Aisha is an Afghan woman whose eyes and ears were cut off for running away from her husband's home, where she suffered from abuse, and the photograph confronts you with the reality of her disfigurement. Bieber explains that she did not want to portray Bibi Aisha as a victim but as a beautiful woman (http://www.time.com/time/video/player /0,32068,294175100001_ 2007267,00.html).

Mutilation is a violation of a woman's human rights. Would the mutilation have been less reprehensible if Aisha had not been young and beautiful? How does the photograph use and reproduce discourses of youth and women's beauty to make its point? Because Aisha has been photographed looking at the viewer, the image demands that we engage with her and do not see her as simply a victim-object. While this has, in my view, been achieved in the original photograph, this is not true of its use on the cover of *Time*, August 9, 2010. It is important to consider the effects of the recontextualization of the photograph.

Here the photograph is anchored by the caption "What Happens if we Leave Afghanistan" offered as a statement, not a question. This caption constructs Aisha as an iconic victim of the Afghan-other, with the United States as the defender against barbarism. The United States as savior is further developed by her being moved to the United States for reconstructive surgery. David Campbell argues that the individual portrait:

> more often than not decontextualizes and depoliticises the situation being depicted, leaving it to accompanying headlines and texts to temporarily anchor meaning.
>
> *(http://www.david-campbell.org/wp-content/uploads/*
> *2011/02/Time-and-fake-cover-590x391.jpg)*

Campbell (with reference to Jim Johnson) shows how this works by contrasting the *Time* cover with a fake one. The fake cover appropriates the original *Time* cover and remixes it to produce a critique of the original. This is achieved simply by changing the caption to "What Still Happened Despite 10 Years of Occupying Afghanistan." The fake cover is authorless, it breaches normal conventions of copyright, it is disseminated easily on the internet, and it reaches an audience larger than that of the original *Time* cover (http://zeroanthropology.net/2010/08/05/is-time%E2%80%99s-afghan-%E2%80%9Ccover-girl%E2%80%9D-really-a-victim-of-mutilation-by-the-taleban/).

The *point* about recontextualisation is that the new context changes the meaning of the original. While Jodi Bieber was the author of the original portrait, the moment she sold it to *Time*, she lost ownership. This raises interesting critical literacy questions:

- How much control do photographers have over how their images are used? How much power does a photographer have in relation to a media giant like *Time*?
- Should photographers refuse to comment on the politics of use?
- How much control does anyone have over how their texts are remashed, redesigned, remixed?
- Should critique be about the author's position or about the effects of the text in different contexts of production and reception?
- Why is a discussion of effects backward looking, when they continue into the future? Will Aisha's life ever be the same?
- What are the ethical considerations of this kind of photography? Is Aisha's consent to being photographed informed consent? Could this young rural woman have imagined or really understood how the photograph would change her life?

David Campbell agrees with John Johnson that the:

> World Press Award has performed another decontextualisation and depoliticisation of the Bieber photograph. The award process has extracted the image from the political issues it became associated with, re-constituted the picture as a discrete object, and reattached it to Jodi Bieber as the author.
>
> *(http://www.david-campbell.org/2011/02/14/*
> *thinking-images-v10-bieber-afghan-portrait/)*

Is this in fact so? Can a text be divorced from its intertextual connections with other contexts of use or does each redesign carry traces of its history? Unlike Kress, I would argue that an understanding of the power of texts to shape identities and construct knowledge is perhaps even more pressing in an interconnected globalized world with ever more complex forms of text production and dissemination.

The *Time* magazine cover can be read as an instantiation of Orientalism. For Said, Orientalism is a discourse for dealing with the Orient by:

making statements about it, authorizing views of it, describing it, teaching it, settling it, ruling over it: in short, Orientalism is a Western style for dominating, restructuring and having authority over the Orient.

(Said, 1978, p. 3)

It is predicated on "the idea of European identity as a superior one in comparison to all non-European peoples and cultures" (Said, 1978, p. 3).

Said's (1978) study focused specifically on Western constructions of the Near East, Arabs and Islam. He is able to show a continuity in the way Orientals are represented that goes back to the earliest European scholars, writing to guard against the threat that fanatical Muslim hordes posed to Christianity and civilization (p. 344). Scholarship pertaining to the Orient was extended to the people of the Orient, their beliefs and their culture, producing in the late nineteenth century an essentialized and racist discourse of the Other as backward and degenerative (p. 206), irrational (p. 38), primitive (p. 231), and generally inferior to "white men" (p. 226). This was an instance of what came later to be described as the Great Divide theory in anthropology (Street, 1984).

What is remarkable about this discourse is its durability. Supporting a politics of European dominion, knowledge was necessary for the containment and rule of the colonized Other, particularly as, until the end of the seventeenth century, Islamic control over large parts of the Near and Far East, North Africa, Turkey, and Europe meant that Islam was feared and had come "to symbolize terror, devastation, the demonic, hordes of hated barbarians" (Said, 1978, p. 59) and a constant threat to Western civilization. Little has changed three centuries later. It's as if this discourse was waiting fully formed to be mobilized after 9/11. This explains the paternalism and sense of superiority made manifest in the caption on the *Time* cover. This paternalism has been called into question by recent events in the Middle East, now referred to as the Arab Spring, during which young people living in Tunisia, Algeria, Jordan, Yemen, Egypt, Sudan, Palestine, Iraq, Bahrain, Iran, and Libya have taken liberation into their own hands. And it is in danger of being reinstated by videos of atrocities in the civil war in Syria posted on YouTube by the perpetrators and reported in *Time*, 27 May 2013.

Another example, this time from Critical Geography, shows the power of both discourse and text. In a fascinating article titled "From the best authorities: the Mountains of Kong in the cartography of West Africa," Bassett and Porter (1991) investigate the representations of mountains in West Africa in maps dating back to the sixteenth century. Named the Mountains of Kong in Rennell's 1978 map,

they subsequently appear on nearly all the major commercial maps in the nineteenth century . . . ending in the early twentieth century. The Kong Mountains were popularly viewed as a great drainage divide separating streams flowing to the Niger River and the Atlantic . . . and an "insuperable barrier" hindering commerce between the coast and the interior. What is intriguing about the Kong Mountains is that they never existed except in the imaginations of explorers, mapmakers and traders.

(Bassett and Porter, 1991, p. 367)

The existence of these mountains was confirmed by the accounts of subsequent explorers and merchants, who believed that they had found this chain of mountains. Expecting to find them, they did. Bassett and Porter take this as confirmation of the "extraordinary authority of maps" (1991, p. 370), which is based on the "public's belief that these images are accurate representations of reality" (Robinson, 1978 in Bassett and Porter, 1991). Both the map as visual text and the scientific discourses which authorizes it shape our knowledge of the landscape. Backed by the African Association, established to extend European knowledge of Africa, this construction of the terrain held sway until Binger's expedition in 1888 which could not find even a "ridge of hills" (Bassett and Porter, 1991, p. 395). Binger's new map of the region opened the area to trade and colonization, by removing an impassable physical obstacle "that existed only in the mind of Europeans" (Bassett and Porter, 1991, p. 398).

In their article, Bassett and Porter (1991) include 48 different maps from 1798 to 1892 with their depictions of the varied width, height, and extent of the Mountains of Kong (pp. 387–389). They comment wryly that the variation "might be expected for imaginary mountains" (p. 390). These maps serve as a nineteenth-century example of Kress' contention that, once a message has been designed and produced, it is open to remaking and transformation by those who review, comment, and engage with it (Kress, 2010, p. 27). It also shows that text transformation is not a new phenomenon. It is also an extremely good example of how the transformations are subject to the underlying assumption that the mountains exist, an assumption that proved to be both wrong and remarkably durable.

In case one thinks that the authority of maps is a historical curiosity, we should remember that when the Peters projection map of the world was introduced in 1974, it was met with fierce controversy. The more familiar Mercator projection is a good representation of the shape of the continents, but because it is a flat representation of a round earth, it distorts size. The Peters projection, on the other hand, is an accurate representation of area, but it distorts shape. It is not possible to show shape and size accurately in one cartographic representation. Figure 3.3 shows this controversy translated into critical literacy classroom materials.

Foucault (1970) is interested in the procedures which constitute discourses, and the means by which power constitutes them as knowledge, that is, as truth. Conversely, he is interested in the ways in which these discourses of truth then bolster power. It is his theory that informs the work of Said. It is precisely the discourse/knowledge relation, combined with the power of discourse to produce us as particular kinds of human subjects, that necessitates critique. Notice how the dominant representation of West Africa caused grown men to find and report with exquisite detail on non-existent mountains that were "of stupendous height" (p. 378), "blue," "barren," "lofty," "snow covered," and "gold rich" (p. 384).

MAPS ARE TEXTS – TEXTS ARE REPRESENTATIONS

1 What is the difference between the next two maps? Which is more accurate?

This map is known as the Mercator projection. It is the representation that is most familiar to us. This map maintains the shape of the continents but distorts their size.

This map, known as the Peters projection, first appeared in 1974. This map maintains the relative size of the continents but distorts their shapes.

The earth is round. The challenge of any world map is to represent a round earth on a flat surface ... The Mercator projection creates increasing distortions of size as you move away from the equator. Mapmakers call this "the Greenland Problem" because Greenland appears to be the same size as Africa, yet Africa is fourteen times larger. Because the Mercator distortion is worst at the poles it is common to leave Antarctica off the map. This results in the Northern Hemisphere appearing much larger than it really is. The equator appears about 60% of the way down the map, diminishing the size and importance of the developing countries.
http://www.diversophy.com.images/peters

Hmm... Two maps. More than one valid point of view...

2 Peters' projection created a great deal of controversy when it was first published. Why do you think this was so? What do you think people argued about? Who would lose if Peters' map was recognized? Who stood to gain? Why?

FIGURE 3.3 Courtesy of Janks et al. (2014).

In the final chapter of *Literacy and Power* (Janks, 2010), I provide an argument which both defends the need for critical literacy and argues that, in a world where the only thing that is certain, apart from death and taxes, is change itself, critical literacy has to be nimble enough to change as the situation changes. The argument assumes a critical literacy agenda that is responsive to the changing socio-historical and political context, the changing communication landscape, teachers' and students' investments, and shifts in theory and practice. Rather than repeat that argument here, I have chosen to give you a taste of *Doing Critical Literacy* (Janks et al., 2014), new classroom materials that I have been working on with colleagues, some of whom worked with me on the 1993 *Critical Language Awareness Series* (Janks, 1993).

1. Figure 3.4 focuses on the need for critical literacy in understanding texts in relation to their socio-political contexts. This page from *Doing Critical Literacy* provides an example from the United States.

THE SPEAKER'S OR WRITER'S POSITION AND THE READER'S POSITION

Andre Bauer, the lieutenant governor of South Carolina

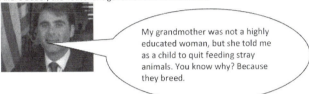

My grandmother was not a highly educated woman, but she told me as a child to quit feeding stray animals. You know why? Because they breed.

1   How does Bauer construct a position for his grandmother? Why does he do this?
2   What is Bauer's grandmother's position on stray animals?
3   Does Bauer agree with his grandmother?
4   Do you agree with Bauer and his grandmother?

When you read what Bauer has said. If you
*   agree with everything he has said you are the *ideal reader* who is reading *with* the text.
*   disagree with what he says you are a *resistant reader* who is reading *against* the text.

If we place this quote in context, the story gets more interesting. According to *Time* (Verbatim, 8 February 2010), Bauer said this when he was 'criticizing policies that extend welfare benefits to the poor'.

5   How does Bauer use language to position poor people?
6   Do you agree with his position on welfare?
7   Why is an understanding of context important?

When we listen to, read or view texts, it is important to *engage* with them. As critical readers we need to work out what the text is saying and to think about that in relation to our own beliefs and values.
      But we also have to step back from the text to ask critical questions.
What positions is the writer constructing? What does he want us to think? Who is the *ideal reader*? What is the ideal reading position? Then we have to ask ourselves whose interests are being served? Who benefits? Who does not? If we do this we become *resistant readers* who do not blindly buy into the meanings text offer us.

FIGURE 3.4   Courtesy of Janks et al. (2014).

2. Figure 3.5 is an example of material that focuses on the changing communication landscape.
3. The activities in Figure 3.6 work with identity investments.

Perhaps what I mean by critique—the ability to recognize that the interests of texts do not always coincide with the interests of all and that they are open to reconstruction; the ability to understand that discourses produce us, speak through us, and can nevertheless be challenged and changed; the ability to imagine the possible and actual effects of texts and to evaluate these in relation to an ethics of social justice and care—is not the same as those who believe that critical

http://cuip.uchicago.edu/~cac/ids/web2.0.jpg

1. Which of these sites do you use?
2. Choose 5 of these sites that are new ones for you. What do they enable you to do? What are their limitations?
3. Can you find one that no longer exists and suggest why.
4. What have you up-loaded on Web 2.0?

In 2011, social networking sites such as Facebook and twitter played an important part in what *Time* magazine is calling 'the Arab spring' (4 April 2011). Use the internet to understand the part played by the new communication landscape in uprisings in Tunisia, Algeria, Jordan, Yemen, Egypt, Sudan, Palestine, Iraq, Bahrain, Iran, Libya.

FIGURE 3.5 Web 2.0 (Courtesy of Janks et al., 2014.)

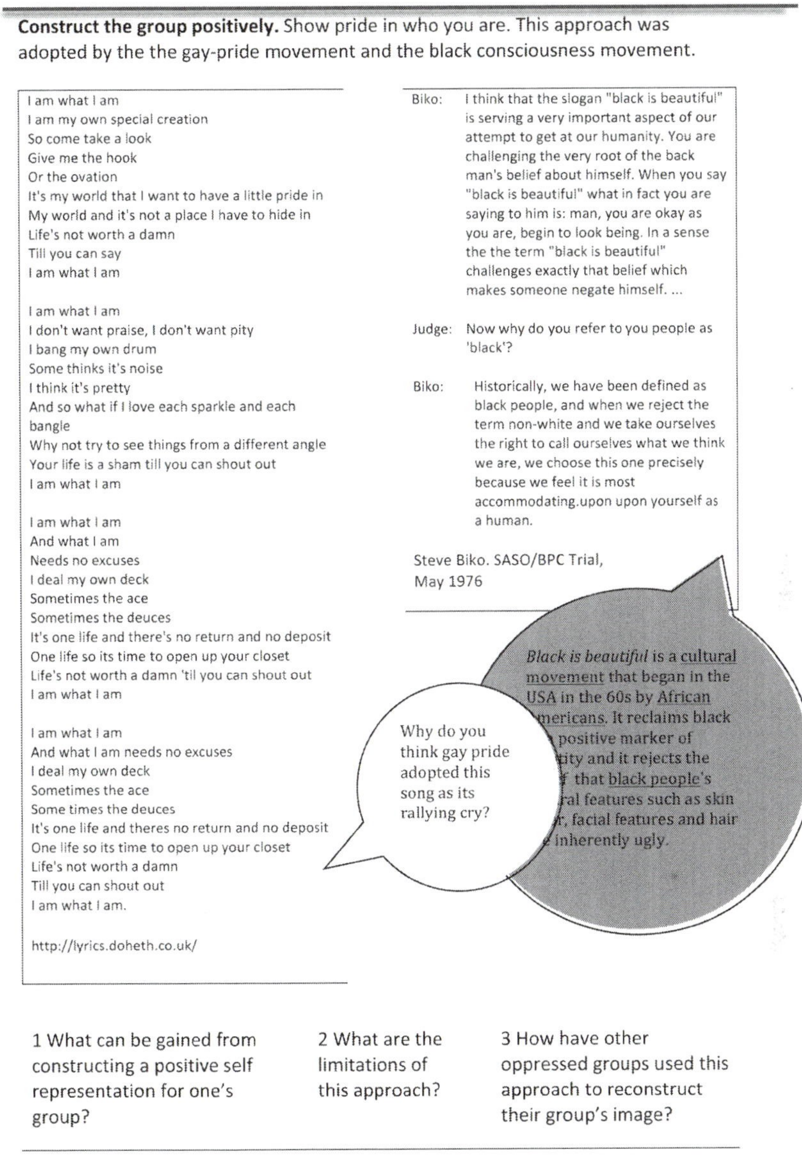

Construct the group positively. Show pride in who you are. This approach was adopted by the the gay-pride movement and the black consciousness movement.

I am what I am
I am my own special creation
So come take a look
Give me the hook
Or the ovation
It's my world that I want to have a little pride in
My world and it's not a place I have to hide in
Life's not worth a damn
Till you can say
I am what I am

I am what I am
I don't want praise, I don't want pity
I bang my own drum
Some thinks it's noise
I think it's pretty
And so what if I love each sparkle and each bangle
Why not try to see things from a different angle
Your life is a sham till you can shout out
I am what I am

I am what I am
And what I am
Needs no excuses
I deal my own deck
Sometimes the ace
Sometimes the deuces
It's one life and there's no return and no deposit
One life so its time to open up your closet
Life's not worth a damn 'til you can shout out
I am what I am

I am what I am
And what I am needs no excuses
I deal my own deck
Sometimes the ace
Some times the deuces
It's one life and theres no return and no deposit
One life so its time to open up your closet
Life's not worth a damn
Till you can shout out
I am what I am.

http://lyrics.doheth.co.uk/

Biko: I think that the slogan "black is beautiful" is serving a very important aspect of our attempt to get at our humanity. You are challenging the very root of the back man's belief about himself. When you say "black is beautiful" what in fact you are saying to him is: man, you are okay as you are, begin to look being. In a sense the the term "black is beautiful" challenges exactly that belief which makes someone negate himself. ...

Judge: Now why do you refer to you people as 'black'?

Biko: Historically, we have been defined as black people, and when we reject the term non-white and we take ourselves the right to call ourselves what we think we are, we choose this one precisely because we feel it is most accommodating.upon upon yourself as a human.

Steve Biko. SASO/BPC Trial, May 1976

Why do you think gay pride adopted this song as its rallying cry?

Black is beautiful is a cultural movement that began in the USA in the 60s by African mericans. It reclaims black positive marker of tity and it rejects the f that black people's al features such as skin r, facial features and hair inherently ugly.

1 What can be gained from constructing a positive self representation for one's group?

2 What are the limitations of this approach?

3 How have other oppressed groups used this approach to reconstruct their group's image?

FIGURE 3.6   Identities. (Courtesy of Janks et al., 2014.)

literacy has had its day. In the world in which I live, critical engagement with the ways in which we produce and consume meaning, whose meanings count and whose are dismissed, who speaks and who is silenced, who benefits and who is disadvantaged—continue to suggest the importance of an education in critical literacy, and indeed critique.

References

Bassett, T. and Porter, P. (1991). From the best authorities: the Mountains of Kong in the Cartography of West Africa. *Journal of African History*, *32* (3), 367–413.

Fairclough, N. (1992). The appropriacy of appropriateness. In Fairclough, N. (Ed.) *Critical language awareness*. London, UK: Longman.

Foucault, M. (1970). The order of discourse. Inaugural lecture at the Collège de France. In M. Shapiro (Ed.) *Language and politics*. Oxford, UK: Basil Blackwell.

Foucault, M. (1980). *Power/knowledge: Selected interviews and other writings 1972–1977*. New York, NY: Pantheon Books.

Janks, H. (1993). *The critical language awareness series*. Johannesburg, South Africa: Wits University Press and Hodder & Stoughton.

Janks, H. (2010). *Literacy and power*. London, UK: Routledge.

Janks, H., Dixon, K., Ferreira, A., Granville, S., & Newfield, D. (2014). *Doing critical literacy: Texts and activities for students and teachers*. London, UK: Routledge.

Kress, G. (2010). *Multimodality*. London, UK: Routledge.

Said, E. (1978). *Orientalism: Western conceptions of the Orient*. London, UK: Penguin Books.

Street, B. (1984). *Literacy in theory and practice*. Cambridge, UK: Cambridge University Press.

4

UNREST IN GROSVENOR SQUARE*

Preparing for Power in Elite Boarding Schools, Working-Class Public Schools, and Socialist Sunday Schools

Patrick J. Finn

> Education produces no effect whatsoever. If it did it would prove a serious threat to
> the upper classes, and probably lead to . . . [unrest] in Grosvenor Square.
>
> *(Oscar Wilde, The Importance of Being Earnest)*

Meritocracy and Individualism

Most American teachers are firmly committed to the concept of meritocracy. In an ideal meritocracy, students who are smart and work hard earn good grades, are placed in high-status school programs, enter high-status, high-paying professions, and end up with more money, status, and political power than the average citizen *regardless of the social status of their parents*. Students who are not smart and/or do not work hard earn poor grades, are placed in low-status school programs, enter low-status, low-paying occupations, and end up with less money, status, and political power than the average citizen *regardless of the social status of their parents*.

One cannot accept the concept of meritocracy without believing that children of elite parents tend to become elite adults, not because of structural injustice (injustices built into the structure of society), but because they are intelligent and hard-working, while children of working-class parents tend to become working-class adults, not because of structural injustice, but because they are intellectually deficient and/or lazy. This is the "logic of deficit" (Oakes and Rogers, 2006). Without the logic of deficit the concept of meritocracy does not work.

* This chapter is an expanded version of: Finn, P. (2012). Preparing for power in elite boarding schools and in working-class schools. *Theory Into Practice, 51* (1), 57–63. DOI: 10.1080/00405841.2012.636339. Reprinted by permission of Taylor & Francis (http://www.tandfonline.com).

Because most teachers of working-class students believe that our school system is a reasonably well-functioning meritocracy (Ladd, 1994), they focus on the problem of educating working-class children at the level of the individual rather than focusing on inequalities built into the structure of society. They try to motivate *individual* working-class students to cooperate with their teachers and acquire the knowledge and skills that will enable them to join the middle class *individually*—that is, to become *border crossers*—working-class students who cross the social class divide, adopt middle-class values, tastes, and attitudes, and vigorously defend the status quo.

Border crossers are proffered as proof that meritocracy "works." Never mind that *students who are very smart but poor* (in the top quartile on SATs but in the bottom quartile for family income) do not have as good a chance at getting a college degree from a high-status 4-year institution as *students who are not very smart but rich* (in the bottom quartile on SAT scores but in the top quartile in terms of family income) (Symonds, 2003).

Structural Inequality, Critical Literacy, and Critical Education

But unequal outcomes in school performance are, in fact, related to the social class of the students, and so one can explain unequal outcomes at a *structural level*. School outcomes are attributable in large part to the advantages afforded by the wealth, status, and power (or lack thereof) of students' social classes. Therefore, educational outcomes between social classes can only be made more equal by working to make the wealth, status, and power of the working class more equal to those of more affluent classes (Finn, 2007; Kincheloe, 2008; Oakes & Rogers, 2006).

Teachers of working-class students who focus on structural inequality encourage their students to become class-conscious, to feel confidence and pride in working-class values, knowledge, and beliefs; to feel important and entitled as members of the working class; and to strive for working-class solidarity. Their goal is to teach working-class students to use the same tools that those from more affluent classes use *to gain and defend their status, power, and economic well-being, not as individuals, but as a class*. Those tools are: high-status knowledge (not business arithmetic, but algebra; not "adolescent literature," but Shakespeare), cultural capital (*high-status* art, music, theater, dance, literature, and sports), social capital (networks of friends and acquaintances whose collective resources can be mobilized to protect and assert individual and group interests [Bourdieu, 1986]), and high levels of literacy.

This structural analysis and class-based approach to educating working-class students is widely referred to as *critical literacy*; those who engage in it are referred to as *critical literacy educators*; and the practice of it is referred to as *critical literacy education*.

Critical literacy is an overtly political classroom agenda for the education of working-class and other disenfranchised students. It is devoted to changing the relationship between the working class and the rest of society in ways that are advantageous to the working class (Luke, 2012). Critical literacy does not prioritize individual advancement through individual effort (border crossing), although this is often an acceptable outcome, especially if the border crossers remain committed to social justice.

When Lady Bracknell says in *The Importance of Being Earnest* that, "Education produces no effect whatsoever. If it did, it would prove a serious danger to the upper classes, and probably lead to . . . [unrest] in Grosvenor Square," she must have been assuming that an effective working-class education would be a critical education, part of which would be critical literacy.

In this paper I will compare the ways the concepts of social-class consciousness, meritocracy, and structural inequality are treated in three kinds of schools:

1. elite boarding schools that encourage social class consciousness, endorse meritocracy (which reflects well on most of their students), and deny or ignore structural inequality;
2. working-class public schools that valorize individualism and individual effort, deny the existence of social class as un-American, endorse the concept of meritocracy (which stigmatizes most of their students), and largely ignore structural inequality;
3. socialist Sunday schools of the early twentieth century that encouraged social class consciousness, refuted the concept of meritocracy (thereby not stigmatizing any of their students), adopted a structural analysis of inequality of school achievement, and engaged in critical literacy.

And I will propose that if our working-class schools were to engage in critical literacy—an overtly political classroom agenda devoted to changing the relationship between the working class and the rest of society in ways that are advantageous to the working class—they would look very much like the Socialist Sunday schools I describe below.

Elite Boarding Schools

Cookson and Persell (1985, 2010) argue that an unstated but clear objective of elite boarding schools (e.g., The Groton School and Phillips Exeter Academy) is to prepare students to maintain the status of their social class and assert their class interests when those interests come into conflict with the interests of other classes.

The student body of elite boarding schools has changed in the past 25 years (Khan, 2011). There are still a number of students from families whose wealth and status are derived from inherited wealth, and there are a small number of "scholarship students," but most of today's elite boarding-school students are children of "the one percent"—highly successful managers, journalists, lawyers, politicians, brokers, and bankers, for example. And so today's student bodies are more racially, ethnically, and culturally diverse than yesterday's children of the "power elite" (Mills, 1956), but one thing remains the same: They are overwhelmingly children of the very wealthy (Khan, 2011).

In elite boarding schools, for the most part, social class is accepted as a fact of life, and class consciousness is encouraged in students. Parents understand and approve the mission of the school, which is to produce leaders who are confident that what they know is correct and worthy of knowing, that what they believe is unimpeachable, and that what they admire is worthy of admiration.

The stately buildings and grounds of such schools nurture feelings of importance, privilege, and entitlement not only as individuals but also as a collective identity (Cookson & Persell, 1985, 2010; Gaztambide-Fernández, 2009). Expansive course offerings and extracurricular activities enable students to acquire cultural capital. School friendships and campus visits from important people (often alumni) provide graduates with social capital.

Students are expected to do hours of homework each school night. Assignments demand higher-order thinking, and students are expected to complete them with little guidance from their teachers. Students are expected to be inquisitive and assertive. They are permitted, even encouraged, to negotiate with teachers regarding their conduct and class requirements, and they are not always held fully accountable for their behavior. In fact, when done with wit and style, breaking rules can become a mark of distinction (Cookson & Persell, 1985, p. 138).

Teachers demand essay text literacy, the ability to comprehend, evaluate, analyze, and synthesize written texts (Gee, 1994) from students. It is the ability to make assertions in writing and to examine, develop, and defend them, to ferret out the assumptions upon which they are based, and to state them explicitly. Essay text literacy is the foundation of rational inquiry and the bedrock upon which powerful institutions such as universities, government, corporations, and professions are built. It is the literacy of argument and negotiation (Gee, 1994).

Students learn that the exercise of power sometimes requires the sacrifice of innocence; right should prevail, but sometimes it does not. At the same time, they learn to cloak power relations in moral authority. Anyon (2006) reported that in the "executive elite" schools she observed,

> [S]tudents were provided a more honest view of a society that sometimes involved [acknowledging] stark dishonesty. The executive elite children could be seen as developing a consciousness of themselves as a social class that could, and should, act in its own interest (p. 41).

The concepts of meritocracy and the logic of deficit are fully accepted. These attitudes, skills, and dispositions are entirely compatible with the self-interest of elite boarding-school students, including "scholarship students" who are eager to join the elite class and maintain the status quo.

Cookson and Persell (1985) observed that the quintessential elite boarding-school graduate is one who speaks like a man or woman of God but will settle a score without flinching—one who can simultaneously enunciate high ideals and practice realpolitik (politics based primarily on power and practical considerations, rather than ideology or ethics) with a refined vengeance (p. 14).

Freire (1970) referred to the kind of education provided to elite boarding-school students as "education for empowerment" as opposed to "education for domestication." If such education were offered to working-class students, it would be critical literacy education (P. J. Finn, 2009a).

Working-Class Public Schools

Following Anyon (1981), I define working-class public schools as ones where students come from households whose breadwinners are employed (or at least not chronically unemployed) and make less than the national median household income, which was about $50,000 in 2010 (U.S. Census, 2010). This demographic accounts for approximately half of the population of the United States. For the most part these schools have clean, well-maintained physical plants. Supplies may be short and are often supplemented by teacher purchases. They often lack the sort of support for music and sports programs that are common in middle-class schools. Compared to more affluent schools, a greater percentage of teachers are not certified, or are not teaching in the field for which they are certified.

A fundamental difference between more affluent schools and working-class public schools is what Willis (1977, 2004) described as "the basic teaching paradigm" versus "the modified teaching paradigm." The basic teaching paradigm is one where teachers have something students want—high-status knowledge and cultural capital. These are sometimes valued for themselves, but more typically they are valued for what they can buy—high grades, diplomas, degrees, qualifications, and licenses that can be exchanged for well-paying jobs, status, and power.

For their part, students cooperate in order to get the high-status knowledge and cultural capital that the teachers offer. The basic teaching paradigm operates, more or less, in most middle-class and more affluent public and private schools.

But many working-class students see high-status knowledge as useless and even antithetical to their working-class identity. They tend to develop "oppositional identity" (Ogbu, 1991) and define themselves in part as *not like schoolteachers and not like the social class that teachers represent to them*. And so, they do not cooperate. They resist teachers' attempts to teach. It is not uncommon for working-class students to find affirmation for their resistance from their homes and communities (Willis, 1977, 2004; Weiss, 1990).

When student resistance runs high, teachers tend to stop attempting to teach high-status knowledge and stop asking for real effort from most of their students.

In return, the students offer just enough cooperation to maintain the appearance of conducting school. That is the modified teaching paradigm (Willis, 1977, 2004). Under these circumstances, "good students" are defined as ones with a "good attitude"—those who are docile and obedient rather than inquisitive and assertive (Anyon, 1981; Weis, 1990).

In working-class public schools:

- Individualism and individual achievement are held up as American ideals. Class consciousness is deemed un-American.
- Teachers tend to be authoritarian. Rules are enforced legalistically. Many teachers believe that negotiating with students regarding assignments or student conduct will be seen by students as a sign of weakness and a threat to their authority.
- Assignments are simple and there is step-by-step direction from the teacher.
- Because of their resistance, students tend to acquire little cultural capital.
- Students have little to no experience with essay text literacy. All that is usually required is functional literacy—the ability to meet the minimal reading and writing demands of an average day for an average person. At best informational literacy is required—the ability to read and recall the kind of knowledge that is associated with school textbooks and to write answers to questions based on such knowledge (Gee, 1994). Even then, textbooks written for students at lower grade levels are often used (Anyon, 1981).
- Students are almost always presented with an idealistic, meritocratic, Disneyland picture of democracy in America. To question this vision is considered unpatriotic.
- Realistic histories of the working class and of labor movements are absent. Most teachers believe that these are not appropriate topics for public schools because they are too political (Anyon, 1981; P. J. Finn, 2009a).
- The schools tend to ignore, if not denigrate, any sense of importance or entitlement students may have as working-class children and young adults.
- The concept of meritocracy and the logic of deficit are fully endorsed.
- The few border crossers who will join the middle class and defend the status quo are considered ideal graduates.
- In brief, most students are offered education for domestication rather than education for empowerment (critical literacy education) (P. J. Finn, 2009a).

None of these characteristics are compatible with the self-interest of the vast majority of working-class public school students.

Socialist Sunday Schools

Because *socialism* and *capitalism* mean different things to different people, and because *socialism* is often stigmatized as un-American, some definitions and a brief discussion of the American Socialist Party are in order.

In many modern Western democracies, socialism is predicated on the belief that citizens have not only civil and political rights; they also have social rights—rights to livable wages, a decent education, and adequate housing and health care. These rights are obtained by collective action—unionism, community organizing, and political party politics. On the other hand, capitalism is predicated on the belief that citizens have civil and political rights but not social rights. Access to livable wages, a decent education, adequate housing, and health care should be determined solely by market forces: Those who acquire marketable skills and work hard at their jobs will have good wages and can buy decent education, housing, and health care on the open market. There is an affinity between the concepts of *individualism*, *meritocracy*, and *capitalism*, just as there is between the concepts of *collective action*, *critical literacy*, and *socialism*.

The American Socialist Party was founded in 1901 at a time when socialism was not the bogeyman that it is today in the United States. During its heyday, the American Socialist Party elected two U.S. congressmen and about 1,200 candidates to public office in 340 municipalities in 24 states. It published daily newspapers in Milwaukee and New York City. It ran its last major presidential campaign in 1920 (Teitelbaum, 1993). Socialist parties such as the Labour Party in Britain, the New Democratic Party in Canada, and the Social Democratic Party in Germany are major, often ruling, parties in many Western democracies today. A current member of the U.S. Senate, Bernie Sanders of Vermont identifies himself as a socialist.

Champions of the working class have attempted to provide critical literacy to working-class *adults* in taverns, church basements, and union halls since the beginning of the Industrial Revolution (Thompson, 1991). Calls for critical education in public elementary and high schools were heard as long as 80 years ago (Counts, 1932; Counts & Brameld, 1941) and continue today (Kincheloe, 2008; M. E. Finn, 2009), but the operation of Sunday schools for children between ages five and 14 by the American Socialist Party in many cities in the United States between 1900 and 1920 was perhaps the most unapologetic and enduring experiment in critical literacy for school-aged children in American history (Teitelbaum, 1993).

Socialist Sunday schools were started in order to present school-age students with a point of view that was not found in their public schools. Their curriculum was not meant to supplant the public school education. On the contrary, students were urged to cooperate and work hard in public school to acquire high-status knowledge, cultural capital, and high levels of literacy, perhaps for their intrinsic value but more importantly, as sources of power in the social-political-economic arena. The latter goal has been referred to as Machiavellian motivation (Oller & Perkins, 1978) and as Freirean motivation (P. J. Finn, 2009b)

Generally, the aim of Socialist Sunday schools was to produce intelligent champions for the workers' cause. Teachers were either working class or they had a strong allegiance to the working class. Not surprisingly, classes resembled

Freire's (1970) culture circles. Provocative questions like the following were often the basis of discussion: *Are strikebreakers bad men? What forces men to cross picket lines? Would you ever be a strikebreaker?* Such lessons were meant to teach students not to hate strikebreakers but to blame the economic and political systems that produce strikebreakers, and never to be strikebreakers themselves (Teitelbaum, 1993).

Students were asked to consider "home destroyers" like unemployment, poverty, and alcohol abuse and how they could be ameliorated. The objective of this lesson was to understand that, while temperance could help individual families, healthy families are fostered by adequate resources. Capitalism without an organized, powerful working class produces unemployment and poverty, and contributes to alcohol abuse—conditions that destroy healthy families. They were taught to take pride in being part of the working class that contributed so much to building the nation, to democracy and democratic thought, and to establishing universal civil, political, and social rights (Teitelbaum, 1993).

There were frequent lessons on why it's preferable to solve social problems working with others rather than working alone. The schools celebrated important contributors to our history like Thomas Paine, Mother Jones, and Eugene Debs, who are ignored in public schools or treated like super heroes (or heroines) who arose out of nowhere to fix social ills (valorizing individualism). Socialist Sunday schools introduced them as leaders who arose out of mass movements that changed the course of history (valorizing collective responses to social ills). Students were exposed to and took part in an abundance of working-class poetry, music, theater, and dance, providing them with a kind of cultural capital.

Students were introduced to the community of organized labor and reform movements through discussion and lecturers. They learned that poverty, unemployment, unhealthy and unsafe work, child labor, poor housing, poor sanitation, the destruction of nature, and disease are not isolated phenomena that can be resolved by well-meaning reformers; they are not caused by individual behavior and cannot be solved through individual effort. They are societal/structural problems that demand societal solutions.

Students learned that the working class can find allies outside of their ranks, but it would be primarily up to them—those who are hurt by unfair policies—to demand change. While many present-day conservatives seem to view the working class as individuals who want to whine about their privations and beg for unearned rewards ("takers," not makers), Socialist Sunday schools subscribed to Frederick Douglass's understanding that "power concedes nothing without a demand" (1857). They educated their students to understand structural injustice and how it affected them, and they prepared them to organize and seize the power needed to demand a just share of the nation's wealth and the fruits that accompany it, such as healthy families and healthy communities.

While they were different from today's working-class public schools in almost every regard, Socialist Sunday schools were to the early twentieth-century working class what elite boarding schools are to today's most affluent class. As in elite boarding schools, in Socialist Sunday schools:

- Social class was acknowledged and the interests of the class from which their students were drawn and where most of their students would remain were self-consciously served.
- Students came from homes where the mission of the school was well understood and supported.
- Teachers identified with the social class of the students.
- Students were encouraged to reflect on the structure of society, their place in it, and the relationship between their class and other classes.
- Students were encouraged to take pride in working-class contributions to building the nation and establishing universal civil, political, and social rights.
- Students were instilled with feelings of power, importance, and entitlement and with class consciousness, class solidarity, and the essential rightness of defending and advancing their individual and class interests.
- Students' parents tended to make up a kind of elite, but in this case it was a working-class elite. Friendships among students offered them the kind of social capital relevant to their cause.
- Campus visits from important people provided students with social capital and feelings of importance, but in this case the visitors were labor leaders and progressive community leaders.
- As stated earlier, schools insisted on the value of high-status knowledge, cultural capital, and high levels of literacy both for their intrinsic value, but more to the point, as sources of power in the social-political-economic arena.

Socialist Sunday schools were like elite boarding schools in every way but two:

1. While elite boarding schools wholeheartedly endorsed the concept of meritocracy, Socialist Sunday schools challenged every part of it. They challenged the belief that individual social class mobility should be the primary purpose of education in a democracy. They challenged the belief that students' success in school was primarily dependent on intelligence and hard work. They maintained that students' success depended in large part on eliminating societal problems such as unemployment, low wages, inadequate health care and housing, and poorly funded schools. These are problems that cannot be fixed by individual effort alone. Collective action is needed on the part of unions, community organizations, and political parties.

2. Elite boarding-school students are motivated to work hard to acquire high-status knowledge, cultural capital, and essay text literacy in order to maintain the status quo. That is, of course, education for empowerment. Socialist Sunday

school students were motivated to work hard in public school to acquire high-status knowledge, cultural capital, and essay text literacy in order to challenge the status quo and change the relationship between the working class and the rest of society. That too is education for empowerment but, when offered to working-class students, it is critical literacy education.

If critical literacy is to succeed in working-class public schools, they will need to produce the kinds of graduates that Socialist Sunday schools endeavored to produce:

1. Working-class men and women who are prepared to participate in collective action to change the relationship of the working class to other classes—ones who understand that "power concedes nothing without a demand" (Douglass, 1857).

2. Particular kinds of border crossers—ones who originate in the working class and acquire middle-class status as adults but do not abandon their working-class loyalties or commitment to social and economic justice.

3. Organic intellectuals—men and women who are prepared to do intellectual work, and who have working-class sensibilities. They can out-strategize and win an argument with a corporation lawyer and at the same time communicate with workers who tend to disparage intellectual work. Many giants in labor, civil rights, and community organizing such as Mary McLeod Bethune (National Council of Negro Women), Walter Reuther (United Automobile Workers of America (UAW) and Congress of Industrial Organizations (CIO)), and John Lewis (Student Nonviolent Coordinating Committee and present member of Congress) might be considered organic intellectuals. The quintessential graduates of critical literacy programs in working-class public schools will be men and women who can simultaneously enunciate high ideals and practice realpolitik with a refined vengeance.

This will, of course, lead to unrest, not in Grosvenor Square, but on the Washington Mall.

References

Anyon, J. (1981). Social class and school knowledge. *Curriculum Inquiry, 11* (1), 3–42.

Anyon, J. (2006). Social class, school knowledge, and the hidden curriculum: Retheorizing reproduction. In L. Weis, C. McCarthy & G. Dimitriadis (Eds.) *Ideology, curriculum, and the new sociology of education* (pp. 37–46). New York, NY: Routledge.

Bourdieu, P. (1986). The forms of capital. In J. Richardson (Ed.) *Handbook of theory and research for the sociology of education* (pp. 241–258). New York, NY: Greenwood.

Cookson, P. W. & Persell, C. H. (1985). *Preparing for power: America's elite boarding schools.* New York, NY: Basic Books.

Cookson, P. W. & Persell, C. H. (2010). Preparing for power: Twenty-five years later. In A. Howard & R. Gaztambide-Fernandez (Eds.) *Educating elites: Class, privilege, and educational advantage* (pp. 13–30). Lanham, MD: Rowman and Littlefield Education.

Counts, G. (1932). Dare progressive education be progressive? *Progressive Education, 9* (4), 257–263.

Counts, G. & Brameld, T. (1941). Relations with public education: Some specific issues and proposals. In T. Brameld (Ed.) *Worker's education in the United States* (pp. 249–277). New York, NY: Harper & Brothers Publishers.

Douglass, F. (1857). http://www.brainyquote.com/quotes/quotes/f/frederickd134371.html. Accessed 10/8/2013.

Finn, M. E. (2007). For further thought. In P.J. Finn & M.E. Finn (Eds.) *Teacher education with an attitude: Preparing teachers to educate working-class students in their collective self-interest* (pp. 231–246). Albany, NY: SUNY Press.

Finn, M. E. (2009). Grassroots organizing and teacher education. In R. Linne, L. Benin, & A. Sosin (Eds.) *Organizing the curriculum: Perspectives on teaching the US labor movement* (pp. 249–266). Rotterdam, The Netherlands: Sense Publishers.

Finn, P. J. (2009a). *Literacy with an attitude: Educating working-class children in their own self-interest* (2nd edn). Albany, NY: SUNY Press.

Finn, P. J. (2009b). A paradigm shift in the making for teachers of working-class students: From intrinsic motivation and border crossing to Freirean motivation and collective advancement. In R. Linne, L. Benin & A. Sosin (Eds.) *Organizing the curriculum: Perspectives on teaching the US labor movement* (pp. 75–86). Rotterdam, The Netherlands: Sense Publishers.

Freire, P. (1970). *Pedagogy of the oppressed.* New York, NY: Seabury Press.

Gaztambide-Fernández, R. A. (2009). *The best of the best: Becoming elite at an American boarding school.* Cambridge, MA: Harvard University Press.

Gee, J. (1994). Orality and literacy: From the savage mind to ways with words. In J. Maybin (Ed.) *Language and literacy in social practice* (pp. 168–192). Clevedon, UK: Multilingual Matters.

Khan, S. R. (2011). *Privilege: The making of an adolescent elite at St Paul's School.* Princeton, NJ: Princeton University Press.

Kincheloe, J. (2008). *Critical pedagogy* (2nd edn). New York, NY: Peter Lang.

Ladd, E. C. (1994). *The American ideology.* Storrs, CT: The Roper Center for Public Opinion Research.

Luke, A. (2012). Critical literacy: Foundational notes. *Theory into Practice, 51* (1), 4–11.

Mills, C. W. (1956). *The power elite.* London, UK: Oxford University Press.

Oakes, J. & Rogers, J. (2006). *Learning power: Organizing for education and justice.* New York, NY: Teachers College Press.

Ogbu, J. (1991). Cultural diversity and school experience. In C. E. Walsh (Ed.) *Literacy as praxis: Culture language and pedagogy* (pp. 25–50). Norwood, NJ: Ablex Publishing Corporation.

Oller, J. & Perkins, K. (1978). Intelligence and language proficiency as sources of variance in self-reported affective variables. *Language Learning, 28,* 85–97.

Symonds, W. (2003). College admissions: The real barrier Is class. *Business Week,* April 14, 68–69.

Teitelbaum, K. (1993). *Schooling for good rebels: Socialist education for children in the United States, 1900–1920.* Philadelphia, PA: Temple University Press.

Thompson, E. P. (1991). *The making of the English working class.* Toronto, CA: Penguin Books.

U.S. Census (2010). Retrieved from http://www.census.gov/prod/2010pubs/acsbr09-2.pdf.

Weis, L. (1990). *Working class without work: High school students in a de-industrializing economy.* New York, NY: Routledge.

Willis, P. E. (1977). *Learning to labor: How working class kids get working class jobs.* Westmead, UK: Saxon House.

Willis, P. E. (2004). Twenty-five years on: Old books, new times. In N. Dolby, G. Dimitriadis & P.E. Willis (Eds.) *Learning to labor in new times* (pp. 144–168). New York, NY: Routledge.

SECTION II

Critiquing Critical Literacy in Practice

5

THINKING CRITICALLY IN THE LAND OF PRINCESSES AND GIANTS

The Affordances and Challenges of Critical Approaches in the Early Years

Beryl Exley, Annette Woods, and Karen Dooley

Introduction

During the last four decades, educators have created a range of approaches for developing critical literacies for different contexts, including compulsory schooling (Luke & Woods, 2009) and second-language education (Luke & Dooley, 2011). Despite inspirational examples of critical work with young students (e.g., O'Brien, 1994; Vasquez, 1994), Comber (2012) laments the persistent myth that approaches for developing critical literacies are not viable in the early years. Assumptions about childhood innocence and the priorities of the back-to-basics movement seem to limit the possibilities for literacy teaching and learning in the early years. Yet, teachers of young students need not face an either/or choice between the basic and critical dimensions of literacies. Systematic ways of treating literacy in all its complexity exist. We argue that the integrative imperative is especially important in schools that are under pressure to improve technical literacy outcomes. In this chapter, we document how approaches to critical literacies were addressed in a fairytales unit taught to 4.5–5.5-year-olds in a high-diversity, high-poverty Australian school. We analyze the affordances and challenges of these different approaches to critical literacies, concluding they are complementary rather than competing sources of possibility. Furthermore, we make the case for turning familiar classroom activities to critical ends.

In the Australian context, versions of critical literacies taken up in the compulsory and postcompulsory school years under the banner of text analytic approaches are genre pedagogy, critical language awareness, and poststructuralist, postcolonial, and feminist deconstruction. Genre pedagogy is derived from systemic functional linguistics and seeks to equip students with mastery of educationally and socially powerful textual genres. The intent is that students will be able to turn their technical mastery to self-generated critical ends (e.g., Martin, 1999). At one end of the continuum, the robotic posturing of genre pedagogy is entrenched in Australian schools, and since 2008 has featured in the stimulus–response tasks of national literacy benchmarking tests throughout the years of schooling. In contrast, critical language awareness equips students more directly for critical work. It shows how language works to naturalize ideology to the advantage of some over others (e.g., Janks, 1993). Deconstructive approaches likewise foreground critical moves. They focus not so much on the syntax of grammar, but on the work of representation in excluding, omitting, and silencing perspectives (e.g., O'Brien, 1994).

Text analytic critical literacies were enshrined in curriculum in Queensland, Australia, the state from which we write, through a Years 1–10 English syllabus in the mid-1990s. This was consistent with developments across the nation. The text analytic approaches taken up at that time were notable for addressing two key issues that were not tackled by critical pedagogic approaches: (1) developmental aspects of the acquisition of critical capabilities; and (2) ways of engaging systematically with the features of texts (Luke & Woods, 2009). Two decades on, the roll-out of Australia's first national curriculum, the *Australian Curriculum: English* (Australian Curriculum, Assessment and Reporting Authority, 2012), offers new possibilities for critical literacies (Exley & Dooley, in press), but it also brings new pedagogic challenges. Specifically, formal study of grammar was not previously expected of 4.5–5.5-year-olds, yet it is the foundation for knowledge about language in the new curriculum. There is little in the way of research illustrating how to use functional systemic linguistic understandings to critical ends in the early years. In contrast, deconstructive pedagogy for young readers of fairy tales has been documented (Bourke, 2008). That work came out of a situation where children loved traditional fairy tale books—a point of difference from the unit we describe throughout this chapter.

The Classroom Context

Ms. Sue Porter (pseudonym), an experienced early years teacher, teaches a Preparatory (Prep) class in a mid-sized government (public) school serving the linguistically and culturally diverse population of a high-poverty outer suburban area. Prep is officially a noncompulsory year of education offered to all children in the state of Queensland prior to the first year of compulsory schooling. However, over the past few years the Prep curriculum has been brought under the umbrella of the "early years phase" of schooling. Since the implementation of the Australian Curriculum began in Queensland in 2012, Prep has been governed by the Foundation–Year 10 Australian Curriculum documents.

In Ms. Porter's class, as throughout the school, approximately 15% of the students identify as Indigenous[1] and approximately 10% live in homes where English is an additional language. Moreover, the level of significant educational problems, including difficulties with receptive and expressive language, is high in comparison to other schools (Luke, Dooley, & Woods, 2011). This is the type of school where pedagogy is being most impacted by current literacy reform in Australia. Since the imposition of a high-stakes national testing program, and provision of special federal government funding to "Close the Gap," Ms. Porter and her colleagues have been under considerable pressure to improve the literacy outcomes promoted by successive rounds of education policy making. As in many other schools in receipt of "equity funding," the press for achievement has prompted increased instruction in phonics, comprehension strategies, knowledge of parts of speech, and on-demand composition. Additionally, in 2012 the State Government Education System which controls Ms. Porter's school introduced a new set of resources as part of its response to the Australian Curriculum, known as *Curriculum into the Classroom* or *C2C*. The *C2C* resources provide unit content, including dialogue, worksheets, and flashcards for individual lessons and assessment items for formative and summative assessment for each five-week unit. Thus, in many early childhood classrooms in Queensland, these resources have become the privileged texts.

This is not the case in Ms. Porter's class. She believes in providing access to a great variety of texts, modes, ways of working, and a full and varied curriculum while improving technical literacy outcomes. As opposed to what is commonly described as narrowing of the curriculum, over the past 5 years that we have been working collaboratively with Ms. Porter, her approach to literacy teaching and learning has become both broader and more critical. Crucially, the outcomes of her students have improved over this time and expectations of student achievement are much higher across the school than was evidenced in the past.

Given the student population, Ms. Porter sought to ameliorate the mismatch between the language of the home and that of the school (Heath, 1983) by promoting talk as a means of developing understanding (Vygotsky, 1962). In addition, she took up some tenets of multiliteracies education (New London Group, 1996), in particular the need to explore the design elements of multimodal text overtly. Ms. Porter immersed students in a range of texts with linguistic, visual, auditory, spatial, gestural, and multimodal design elements. Further, over this time, we were able to document how she drew on a technical metalanguage or grammar for describing textual designs (although students were not required to use the technical metalanguage) and infuse various units of work with text analysis skills.

In the next three sections, we trial and document three approaches to the development of critical literacies in the early years, noting the affordances and challenges of each:

- *Approach 1: Business as usual*—Exploring generic structure of traditional fairy tales and exploring identity and reading "others" in reinterpreted fairy tales;
- *Approach 2: Shifting the pedagogical strategy*—Using process drama to develop critical language awareness;
- *Approach 3: Returning to the known to investigate new ways of thinking*—Using standard early childhood literacy strategies to get students thinking differently.

Analyzing the Research Data

In analyzing these three approaches we draw on Bernstein's (1996) notions of the classification and framing of pedagogic discourse. Pedagogic discourse is the embedding of an instructional discourse of skills and knowledge within a regulative discourse of character, manner, behavior, and so forth. Pedagogic discourse entails relations of power and control. "Power" refers to the classification of categories. Classification is stronger when category boundaries are strongly bounded, for example, when there is little connection between what is learnt at home and in school. "Control" refers to the framing of pedagogic discourse. Framing is stronger when the teacher overtly controls the selection, organization, and evaluative criteria of knowledge and skill. In developing critical literacies, educators continually weave a range of stronger and weaker classification and framing values to achieve different learning outcomes. For example, classification between home and school is often weakened to legitimize the knowledge within students' life worlds, whilst framing is also weakened to enable a degree of student control, an oft-used strategy for re/connecting disconnected students (e.g., Exley & Luke, 2010; Dooley & Thangaperumal, 2011).

Approach 1: Business as Usual—Learning About Fairytales and Looking for Resistant Readings

The original plans for the unit were developed by Ms. Porter and her Prep colleagues. This was usual practice in the school and a deliberate strategy for improving curriculum and pedagogy. It involved teachers working across the same year level collaborating on term-long curriculum plans and then producing weekly and daily plans to fit the needs of their individual classes. As planned by the teachers, the unit focused on generic knowledge of fairy tales, comprehension of particular fairy tales, and deconstruction of perspectives carried by fairy tales. The lesson sequence made use of both traditional fairy tale picture books and picture books that "twist" and reinterpret the original.

In tailoring the unit to her class, Ms. Porter began from her students' knowledge of Walt Disney DVDs. In doing so, she blurred the boundaries between home and school knowledge. This weaker classification of knowledge is a common move of critical educators and is usually accompanied by relatively weaker framing of the teacher–student relation as students are granted some control of the instructional and regulative discourse at the outset (e.g., Martin, 1999).

Traditional fairy tale picture books such as *The Three Little Pigs* and *The Three Billy Goats Gruff* were then introduced into the classroom. Reading and writing activities involving these books targeted both technical and critical outcomes. Ms. Porter built students' decoding and comprehension skills, as well as their knowledge of generic structure. In dealing with the structure of the texts, Ms. Porter strengthened the classification of school knowledge through the use of a grammatical metalanguage focused on the staging features of genre (e.g., "orientation," "complication," "resolution"). Framing was also strengthened as Ms. Porter assumed more control of the activities in order to build and transmit the technical metalanguage. These classification and framing values are typical of genre pedagogy (Martin, 1999). One of our observations about the lessons was that the critical possibilities of text analysis were somewhat lost to the focus on development of the technical metalanguage. This constraint on realization of the critical potential of genre pedagogy was identified by early proponents of critical literacies and, as noted by Luke and Dooley (2011), remains unresolved in practice.

Overtly critical lessons began when Ms. Porter provided sentence starter worksheets focusing on the identity stereotypes common in fairy tales. This activity exposed textual ideologies and required students to second-guess and reconstruct the versions of the world presented in the traditional fairy tale picture books (see Shor, 1987). Reinterpreted fairy tale picture books were then introduced. Because these books rely heavily on intermodal coupling (Exley & Cottrell, 2012; Exley & Mills, 2012) of written and visual text, time was spent building multimodal comprehension skills. These were applied to develop understanding of the ways that perspectives within the original texts had been reconstructed and reshaped in non-normative ways.

Ms. Porter elicited discussion from the students about the interests served and consequences for individuals and communities. Other lessons looked at: (1) who wrote and illustrated the texts; (2) why the author/illustrator wanted to reinterpret the original fairytale; and (3) what information remained the same or was changed (see McLaughlin & DeVoogd, 2004). The stronger framing typically involved in these types of activities has been a point of dialogue amongst critical educators of different persuasions (Martin, 1999) and taps into longstanding concerns about inadvertent imposition of textual interpretations on students.

Given the pressures on Ms. Porter and her colleagues, what we've called the "business as usual" approach represented a significant achievement. However, in planning meetings with us, Ms. Porter expressed her desire to exploit the critical potential of the new Australian Curriculum. Accordingly, Ms. Porter and her Prep class engaged in two more rounds of curriculum development, with two of us taking turns to lead the teaching through approaches two and three respectively. The next two sections document these trials.

Approach 2: Shifting the Pedagogical Strategy—Using Process Drama to Develop Critical Language Awareness

At Ms. Porter's request, one of us collaborated with her to trial five lessons employing process drama (see Exley & Dooley, in press). The aim was to explore critical language awareness activities appropriate for Prep students. The lessons were built around the postmodern picture book, *Beware of the Bears,* written by Alan MacDonald and illustrated by Gwyneth Williamson (MacDonald, 2004).

Much of the pleasure of this book arises from the way it extends Southey's (n.d.) original *Goldilocks and the Three Bears*. As is typical of postmodern picture books, the ending is left open, thereby requiring the reader to complete the story by drawing on visuals and intertextual knowledge (Anstey, 2002).

We selected process drama as a vehicle for the lessons because of its potential to redress the problems of the stronger framing, mentioned above. Process drama helps transform school from a place where teachers tell students what to think to a place where students are able to experience thinking (Heller, 1995). Furthermore, by allowing students to play out unfamiliar experiences, it enables entry into new subject positions and experiences of subtexts. The classifications between student experience and textual contents were thus once again weakened in an attempt to make textual meanings more accessible to the students. We note, however, that framing moved from relatively weak to relatively strong throughout the range of lessons.

The first two of the lessons deepened student knowledge of the traditional version of *Goldilocks*. Students completed an oral cloze by adding an adjective to a noun group (e.g., "a _____ Goldilocks") and worked in small groups to mould a peer into a Goldilocks sculpture and complete the following oral cloze: "Goldilocks is . . ." (focusing on action verbs) and "Goldilocks is saying . . ." (focusing on saying verbs). The aim was to develop an appreciation of the multiple functions of language, not to skill and drill students' knowledge of a grammatical metalanguage. Our aim was to avoid subordinating the critical to the technical—one of the limitations of the first approach. In theoretical terms, a weaker classification of knowledge and framing of pedagogy were instituted.

In the third lesson, *Beware of the Bears* (MacDonald, 2004) was then read with attention to the comprehension strategies of text-to-self connections and to concepts of viewing angle, color, and focus required for decoding textual images. This story begins with a visual of the bear family arriving home to find the carnage inflicted during Goldilocks' unauthorised visit. Deciding to seek revenge, the bears wait for Goldilocks to leave her home, enter and wreak havoc. When Goldilocks returns home, she nonchalantly exclaims that it's not her house but the site of another unauthorized visit. A double-page wordless spread is devoted to an image of the bear family exiting through the back door whilst a wolf enters through the front door. The wolf's incredulous reaction is captured in a wordless double-page spread on the last page. The researcher, in the role of teacher, set stronger boundaries around the content knowledge and the pacing and sequencing of pedagogical relations throughout the reading in an attempt to ramp up reading and viewing comprehension skills. For example, in instances of triadic dialogue, the researcher asked students to make predictions on the basis of the book's cover and as the story reached a climax. When reading the predictable refrains in the text, for example, "But these Puffo Pops were just right," the researcher deliberately stretched out the sentence beginning, then faded away to allow the students to chant the oral cloze.

The final two activities targeted speaking positions. Students formed freeze frames of scenes from the book and, when tapped on the shoulder, spoke on behalf of the character or prop they were representing. The final activity, "conscience alley," required students to take a position on the moral dilemma besetting the wolf, that of seeking revenge. A wolf puppet was introduced and students were asked to commit to a speaking position, either that of supporting the wolf in seeking revenge by standing along the left-hand side of the alley way, or talking back to the wolf's desire to seek revenge and standing along the right-hand side of the alley way.

These latter activities once again offered a weakened classification of content knowledge *vis-à-vis* outside-of-school knowledge and a stronger framing of pedagogy as the researcher qua teacher directed the students' turn of talk as a strategy to obligate all students to participate, albeit for a single turn of talk. This seemed especially important in this class, where some students were particularly enthusiastic contributors to teacher-led class discussion, whilst others used it as an opportunity to opt out of participating in oral dialogue. As it transpired, both of these activities made new instructional and regulative demands of these young students and, when Ms. Porter identified that some students were not able to "read" the weakly framed pedagogic text, she ramped up the framing by calling on each student individually and holding them accountable for making an oral contribution to each of these activities. Strengthening the control over the organization and evaluative criteria of knowledge and skill is a move sometimes made in order to complete an activity that is beyond the students (e.g., Dooley & Thangaperumal, 2011). Our reflections now raise the matter of whether this heightened level of control is counterproductive to criticality.

Approach 3: Returning to the Known to Investigate New Ways of Thinking – Using Standard Early Childhood Literacy Strategies to Get Students Thinking Differently

We continued planning with Ms. Porter and another of the researchers took the lead in teaching the sequence for approach three. The focus this time, in response to our reflections on the enablements and constraints of the process drama sequence, was to investigate the possibilities of pursuing critical ways of being and doing by adapting literacy activities with which the students and Ms. Porter were familiar.

The lesson sequence for approach three drew on strategies commonly used to teach comprehension and genres in many early-childhood classrooms. There was an oral reading of the focus text, *Into the Forest,* by Anthony Browne (2005), and then the class discussed the story and how it related to other traditional and reinterpreted fairy tales as well as other examples of children's literature. In the story, Little Red Riding Hood travels through the woods with a cake for her Grandma. Along the way she meets numerous other fairy tale characters, including Jack, who has a cow to sell, Goldilocks, and Hansel and Gretel, who are starving because they have been left to fend for themselves by the adults who were responsible for their care. Each character makes a case about why Little Red Riding Hood should give them the cake rather than proceeding to Grandma's house. The story ends with Little Red and Grandma eating the cake.

The class worked together to make decisions about the events of the story and the narrative sequence. Utilizing images from the book, students selected particular events and organized and reorganized the pictures until everyone was satisfied that the story board represented the actual story structure. The students and researcher then worked together to produce large-print captions for each of the picture displays. The students and researcher discussed the merits of each character's claim for the cake in a researcher-led class discussion. Students were asked to decide which fairy tale character deserved the cake and to justify the reason why this was as it should be.

Students offered a myriad of responses, including that Hansel and Gretel deserved the cake because they were hungry and that Grandma deserved the cake because she was old and sick. The students took the activity seriously and justified their points of view about the "worth" of particular characters over others, once it was made known that having a "who?" answer without a "why?" answer would not fulfill the evaluative criteria of the pedagogic discourse. The students were then set up in mixed-ability working groups. Instead of the stronger classification of knowledge and the stronger framing of pedagogical relations in the researcher-led group discussion, control was seemingly handed to the student groups. Each student within the group had to convince their peers to agree with them as only one answer could be forwarded from each group. The final task required the group to decide and record on large sheets of paper which fairy tale character would receive the cake and why.

During these discussions the students took turns at offering positions on who should be given the cake. Some students were adamant that Grandma should have the cake either because it was originally prepared for her, or because she was sick. Several students were excited by the word "poorly" used in the text to describe Grandma and enthusiastically used the word over and over as they made their claim for Grandma as the rightful recipient of the cake. Others argued for Hansel and Gretel given that they were starving and needed to be fed. This suggestion was rejected by some students because "Gretel was a whiner and noisy" and so didn't deserve to be fed. Counterclaims were that she had a good reason to cry so should be allowed to eat the cake. One female student argued persistently that Goldilocks should be awarded the cake because she was "pretty and nice." Others said she was also "naughty and noisy" and had no good reason for this behavior so should not be the recipient of the cake.

Finally, in one particular group, one child put forward the notion that each group member should cast a vote in order to make a decision, with the character who most people wanted to win being given the cake. With the weaker classification of knowledge and the weaker framing of pedagogy, the task was no longer about justice and deciding who most deserved the cake; it had moved instead to being about "the Grandma people should get it because there is more of them." There was some agreement with this point of view, but still others mounted a case that they should all agree before the final decision was made.

In the end a consensus was reached where Grandma would be given the cake because she was sick and poorly, but all of the group members would write their own individual votes on the sheet alongside their signatures. The task for all to agree on what was fair and equitable had proven too difficult, but the students were able to articulate their own positions, if unable to convince others to agree.

To complete the activity a representative from each group related to the rest of the class which fairy tale character would be the recipient of the cake and why. Overall the sequence seemed successful. By asking the students to consider issues of equity and power within familiar literacy activities, the students were freed up to consider the ideological base of the texts they were dealing with. In this way the known provided a fertile space for relaxing the classification of knowledge and the framing of pedagogy so that students could think critically.

One of the students, though, reminded the researcher that by embedding the critical activities back into known literacy teaching and learning approaches the "schoolness" of the activity was placed in stark relief. For at least some of the students this resulted in an awareness that the activity was not in fact about justice and equity, but rather about reading children's books and successfully "doing" school literacy. As one group reached a stalemate, the researcher started to encourage the students to think about solutions. She asked several students if they thought that cases made by others could change minds so that a single decision could be declared. One student sighed and proceeded with the following dialogue:

Student I might just go Goldilocks as this is taking too long a time. She [the student who had been demanding that Goldilocks' looks should be enough to provide her with the prized cake] will never change her mind.

Researcher That's interesting. You think we should just get it over with.

Student Yes (nods) [inaudible] it's just a book.

For this particular student the activity was first and foremost about finishing the required task rather than taking the liberty of relaxing the curriculum knowledge and pedagogical relations. There was no cake that would provide sustenance for a character, whether the character be old, poorly, hungry, or, indeed, pretty. He had an acute awareness that the task would be completed regardless of the decision made and the fairy tale unit would continue for another day.

Conclusion

Our analysis of the three approaches to the development of critical literacies in Ms. Porter's classroom supports the idea that critical literacy in the early years is not, nor should it be, a single unified method or approach. Instead, it consists of a range of approaches for teaching and learning about cultures, societies, texts, and discourses. Each of the enacted approaches demonstrated our shared commitment to the use of literacy for exploring notions of equity and social justice, yet each differed in philosophical assumptions as well as the classification of knowledge and the framing of pedagogy. All aimed for nothing less than the students being readers and viewers of a range of fairy tales who have cogent, articulated, and relevant understandings of texts, their techniques, their investments, and their consequences, and who are able to use these understandings and capacities to act mindfully and justly to impact their worlds.

The first section of the unit demonstrated some inspirational possibilities for teachers who work within narrowed curricula and under heightened back-to-basics pressure. Ms. Porter taught her students about words and sounds—the basics—at the same time as she pushed them to think about how texts represent different people through different structures and, in doing so, to different ends. She drew on text analytic traditions to teach sophisticated technical knowledge and skills for critical ends. In so resisting the narrowing of curriculum, Ms. Porter provided a comprehensive and rigorous learning experience. Her students did not stop learning literacy; rather, they learnt much more through a rich sequence of activities that weakened the classification between students' home knowledge and school knowledge and culminated in critical insights into some of the dominant texts of schooled literacy through a more robust classification of knowledge and framing of pedagogy.

The hallmark of approach two was one researcher's attempt to tackle the political aspect of critical literacies more explicitly. The process drama activities were planned to take the class out of their "normal" and familiar teaching and learning approaches. The lessons provided the students with ways to consider opinions, values, and their beliefs, and, despite some issues with the regulative discourse, the students took positions on issues related to good and bad, fair and just approaches. However the novelty of the tasks meant that a considerable amount of time, space, and classroom discourse had to be given over to regulating behaviors and routines so that the lessons could progress. This raised for us a fundamental question: at what point does regulation become counterproductive to criticality?

Returning to more familiar approaches to teaching and learning in approach three, but expecting the students to take positions on issues of some importance within these familiar sequences, was our final attempt to investigate the possibilities of critical literacies in Ms. Porter's Prep classroom. The approach provided a structure where students seemed able to consider challenging ideas and express opinions on important issues of equity and justice; criticality was clearly not subordinate to regulation. However, one student reminded us that this remained school literacy: the issues of hunger and poverty, consumerism and family were not rendered real in this teaching and learning sequence. In the end the lessons were, for at least some of the children, about "get[ting] it done so we are finished" and not about explorations of broader social issues of political or ideological importance to them. In other words, the boundary between the (text analytic) literacies of the classroom on the one side/hand and significant student experiences, lifeworlds, real speaking positions, and the power of dominant ideology on the other remained strong. This is cause for consideration about the possibilities of critical pedagogy, with its emphases on dialogic interaction, self-determination, agency, and social movements (Luke & Woods, 2009).

Our investigation provides several points of contention and possibility for introducing critical literacy in the early years. First, we conclude that critical literacy is feasible in early years classrooms, even in challenging contexts such as that presented in Ms. Porter's class. In the words of Janks (1993, p. iii), these 4.5–5.5-year-olds worked to "unmake or unpick" the ideological choices of the author and illustrator. Second, each of the three approaches provides different challenges and affordances. The challenge for teachers is to draw on diverse traditions to remake critical literacies that fit their context.

Acknowledgments

This chapter reports data collected as part of an Australian Research Council-funded project. We owe a debt of gratitude to the teachers, in particular Amber Cottrell, who has been a source of inspiration for a number of years, students and administrators at the school, and to the Queensland Teachers Union. We thank our research colleagues Vinesh Chandra, John Davis, Michael Dezuanni, Katherine Doyle, Amanda Levido, Allan Luke, Kathy Mills, and Wendy Mott of Queensland University of Technology and John McCollow and Lesley MacFarlane of the Queensland Teachers Union.

Notes

1   In this paper the term Indigenous is used to refer to students who identify as Australian Aboriginal and/or Torres Strait Islander.

References

Anstey, M. (2002). It's not all black and white: Postmodern picture books and new literacies. *Journal of Adolescent & Adult Literacy, 45* (6), 444–458.

Australian Curriculum, Assessment and Reporting Authority (2012). Australian Curriculum English. Available at: www.australiancurriculum.edu.au.

Bernstein, B. (1996). *Pedagogy, symbolic control and identity: Theory, research, critique.* Oxford, UK: Rowman & Littlefield Publishers.

Bourke, R.T. (2008). First graders and fairy tales: One teacher's action research of critical literacy. *The Reading Teacher, 62* (4), 304–312.

Browne, A. (2005). *Into the forest*. London, UK: Walker Books.

Comber, B. (2012). Mandated literacy assessment and the reorganisation of teachers' work: federal policy, local effects. *Critical Studies in Education, 53 (*2), 119–136.

Dooley, K. & Thangaperumal, P. (2011). Pedagogy and participation: Literacy education for low-literacy students of African origin in a western school context. *Language and Education, 25* (5), 385–397.

Exley, B. & Cottrell, A. (2012). Reading in the Australian curriculum English: Describing the effects of structure and organisation on multimodal text. *English in Australia, 47* (2), 91–98.

Exley, B. & Dooley, K. (in press). Critical linguistics in the early years: Exploring functions of language through sophisticated picture books and process drama strategies. In K. Winograd (Ed.) *Doing critical literacy with young children*. New York, NY: Routledge.

Exley, B. & Luke, A. (2010). Uncritical framing: Lesson & knowledge structure in school science. In D. Cole (Ed.) *Handbook of research on multiliteracies & technology enhanced education* (pp. 17–41). London, UK: Routledge.

Exley, B. & Mills, K. (2012). Parsing the Australian curriculum English: Grammar, multimodality and cross-cultural texts. *Australian Journal of Language and Literacy, 35* (2), 192–205.

Heath, S. B. (1983). *Ways with words*. Cambridge, UK: Cambridge University Press.

Heller, P. (1995). *Drama as a way of knowing*. York, ME: Stenhouse.

Janks, H. (1993). *Language and power*. Johannesburg, SA: Hodder & Stoughton and Wits University Press.

Luke, A. & Dooley, K. (2011). Critical literacy and second language acquisition. In E. Hinkel (Ed.) *Handbook on second language teaching and learning* (pp. 856–868). London, UK: Routledge.

Luke, A., Dooley, K., & Woods, A. (2011). Comprehension and content: Planning literacy curriculum in low socioeconomic and culturally diverse schools. *Australian Education Researcher, 38* (2), 149–166.

Luke, A. & Woods, A. (2009). Critical literacies in schools: A primer. *Voices from the Middle, 17* (2), 9–20.

MacDonald, A. (2004). *Beware of the bears*. London, UK: Little Tiger Press.

Martin, J. (1999). Mentoring semogenesis: "Genre-based" literacy pedagogy. In F. Christie (Ed.) *Pedagogy and the shaping of consciousness: linguistic and social processes* (pp. 123–155). London, UK: Continuum.

McLaughlin, M. & DeVoogd, G. (2004). *Good habits, great readers: Building the literacy community*. Upper Saddle River, NJ: Merrill Prentice Hall.

New London Group (1996). A pedagogy of multiliteracies: Designing social futures. *Harvard Educational Review, 66* (1), 60–93.

O'Brien, J. (1994). Show mum you love her: Taking a new look at junk mail. *Reading, 28* (1), 43–46.

Shor, I. (1987). *Critical teaching and everyday life*. Chicago, IL: University of Chicago Press.

Vasquez, V. (1994). A step in the dance of critical literacy. *Reading, 28* (1), 39–43.

Vygotsky, L. (1962). *Thought and language*. Cambridge, MA: MIT Press.

6

WHERE POEMS HIDE*

Finding Reflective, Critical Spaces Inside Writing Workshop

Amy Seely Flint and Tasha Tropp Laman

Writing holds tremendous promise as a curricular space for children to share their lives, experiences, and knowledge. Yet, this part of the curriculum is regularly shortchanged for a number of reasons. Educational policies and mandates in the past decade (e.g., No Child Left Behind and Race to the Top) have focused almost exclusively on student achievement in reading and math. Schools throughout the country shifted resources from non-tested areas, such as writing, social studies, and art, to emphasize further the importance of meeting adequate yearly progress in reading and math through high-stakes testing regimes (Au, 2007; Crocco & Costigan, 2007; Berliner, 2009). Mindful of the pressures to achieve, teachers often find themselves implementing a skills-driven curriculum that focuses on the very skills being tested. Au's (2007) metasynthesis of 49 studies about the impact of high-stakes testing on curriculum found that, as teachers navigate the high-stakes testing terrain, predominant effects of testing include the narrowing of curricular content to only tested subjects, the fragmentation of curriculum, and the increase of teacher-centered delivery.

Now as schools align curriculum with the newly adopted Common Core State Standards (CCSS) and assessments such as Partnership for Assessment of Readiness for College and Careers (PARCC), there remains little attention to writing. Key shifts in English Language Arts and Literacy include text complexity, evidence, and knowledge; the standards require students to work with complex texts, to seek evidence in the text, and to build knowledge from

* This chapter is an expanded version of: Flint, A. & Laman, T. (2012). Where poems hide: Finding reflective, critical spaces inside writing workshop. *Theory Into Practice, 51* (1), 12-19. DOI: 10.1080/00405841.2012.636328. Reprinted by permission of Taylor & Francis (http://www.tandfonline.com).

content-rich non-fiction texts. And the type of writing that is now expected is more heavily weighted towards opinion pieces, informative/expository, and some narratives. Regardless of CCSS or previously adopted state standards, there is pressure for students to achieve and be on track for postsecondary success.

Adding to the concerns around the limited time for writing instruction is the quality of writing instruction. The National Commission on Writing (2003) notes that teachers report feeling underprepared when it comes to writing instruction. They lack any real understanding of what good writing looks like and are not confident in their abilities to teach writing. Although many teachers are knowledgeable about process-oriented approaches and best practices for writing pedagogy, these practices are generally replaced with more prescriptive formats that are more closely aligned to standardized test formats. McCarthey's (2008) study of recent trends in writing instruction in elementary settings found that teachers in the same school have similar writing practices, and that teachers in low-income schools most often implement a skills-oriented program (e.g., *Writer's Advantage, Success for All),* with scripted writing exercises and a focus on mechanics and grammar. Likewise, exposure to diverse writing experiences is limited, with most writing activities falling into narrative stories at the primary grades (Cutler & Graham, 2008) and journal writing and responding to literature at the upper grades (Gilbert & Graham, 2010). Brindley & Schneider (2002) noted that the vast majority of teachers in their study relied upon district-prescribed methods to prepare students for the writing exam, including using narrative and expository prompts. Over time, students end up with a writing diet that is formulaic—one that rarely includes genres such as poetry, does not connect to their lives, and does not provide opportunities to grapple with, and think on paper about, socially significant issues and ideas.

To counter these trends in writing pedagogy and curriculum, we worked with seven elementary school teachers in two different schools as they shifted their teaching practices and professional identities. Early on in our collaborative work with the teachers, we faced many of the same challenges that other researchers and teacher educators document when making curricular and pedagogical changes. Teachers reported that scripted writing prompts and formulas constituted the majority of their writing instruction. They mentioned not feeling confident in their approach to teaching writing. They wondered about access to resources and how to meet standards in new structures.

The shifts teachers experienced in their writing instruction came about because of sustained, long-term professional development opportunities. Over a 5-year period, the teachers joined teacher study groups, read professional books about writing instruction, and participated in collaborative planning. Through these engagements, teachers began to revise their teaching. They implemented a writer's workshop approach—encouraging students to choose their own topics, teaching mini-lessons, conferring with students, and publishing student work. Teachers noticed a change in classroom dynamics as well as children's literacy learning. Not only were children more engaged in writing, the teachers commented that they knew their students better than ever before. Personally significant topics were common, but so too were important social issues such as divorce, bullying, homelessness, war, and natural disasters.

To complement these new directions in the teachers' writing instruction, we initiated conversations with them about critical literacy practices. At the core, critical literacy invites teachers and students to consider the varied ways literacy practices matter to the participants and their places in the world (Bomer & Bomer, 2001; Vasquez, 2004; Heffernan & Lewison, 2005; Laman, 2006). We continued to meet monthly with teachers, where we discussed professional readings about critical literacy such as *For a Better World* (Bomer & Bomer, 2001), *Creating Welcoming Schools* (Allen, 2007) and *Creating Critical Classrooms* (Lewison, Leland, & Harste, 2008).

In this chapter, we examine students' writing and shifts in teachers' practices when a teacher-developed unit of study that integrated poetry with issues related to social justice was offered. Through this poetry study, the teachers began to reposition children and curriculum, and in the process, built interest in navigating the terrain of more critical approaches to literacy instruction.

Two Schools, Many Opportunities

Our work took place in two elementary schools in the Southeastern region of the United States. This region has experienced a tremendous increase in students labeled English Language learners. In fact, the Southeast now has one of the largest populations of minority students attending public schools in the nation (Suitts, 2010); both school sites reflect these demographic trends.

Baylor Elementary (all names are pseudonyms) is a neighborhood school located in a mid-sized city. This school includes 350 students with over 14 languages represented in the school and with 55% of students receiving free and reduced lunch. Data were collected over a 9-month school year with students in five first-, second-, and fifth-grade classrooms. The five teachers at Baylor have each taught more than 10 years. They ranged in their experiences with a writing workshop approach from 1 year to 4 years.

Richardson Elementary is a school located off what is affectionately termed International Highway in a large, urban Southeast city. The neighborhood, comprised mostly of older apartment buildings and small single-family homes, is transitory in nature with many children moving in and out of the school on a regular basis. The school has approximately 750 students, with over 98% receiving free and reduced lunch and 57% receiving pull-out English Language services. The data collected from students and teachers in two third-grade classrooms at Richardson are part of a larger on-going study that focuses on teachers' overall changing beliefs about writing, English Language learners, and professional identity.

Within the unit of study on poetry and social justice, the teachers compiled text sets that contained a wide array of free-verse poetry for children to read and draw upon as mentor texts, texts that children could use as models for studying poetry and crafting their own, including a number of poetry books related to important social issues, such as *My Name is Jorge: On Both Sides of the River* (Medina, 2004), a collection of bilingual poems about a young immigrant's experiences in America; *Love to Langston* (Medina, 2006), a biographical text chronicling Langston Hughes' life, including the writer's experiences with prejudice; and *Been to Yesterdays: Poems of a life* (Hopkins, 1999), a memoir that captures the young author's experiences with race, class, and divorce.

Additionally, the teachers in both schools read a number of critical literacy texts to their students that invite readers to problematize and make visible socially significant issues in communities and the world. According to Leland, Harste, Ociepka, Lewison, and Vasquez (1999), critical literacy texts do not make difference invisible, but rather explore which differences make a difference; they enrich our understanding of history and life by giving voice to those who traditionally have been silenced or marginalized; they show how people can begin to take action on important social issues; they explore dominant systems of meaning that operate in our society to position people and groups of people; and they do not provide happily-ever-after endings for complex social problems. Examples of such texts include *A Day's Work* (Bunting, 2004), about a young boy and his grandfather from Mexico who seek work as day laborers; *Freedom Summer* (Wiles, 2005), which chronicles the bittersweet aftermath of the Civil Rights Act on a small Mississippi town; and *Coolies* (Soentpiet & Soentpiet, 2003), a story of Chinese immigrants working on the transcontinental railroad.

To understand the critical literacy practices enacted within these elementary settings, we visited classrooms 1–4 mornings per week. During writing workshop, we audio- and videotaped poetry mini-lessons, writing conferences, and share times. We collected students' writing samples from writer's notebooks as well as published poems. At the end of the year, we each conducted focus group and individual interviews with children and their teachers regarding what they learned about poetry in general and critical literacy in particular.

The teachers began the study by immersing children in the genre, first reading and noticing key features of poetry. They implemented mini-lessons with key goals being to notice the world as poets do and to collect ideas for poetry while also engaging in a recursive cycle of drafting, revising, editing, and publishing poetry.

Linking Poetry and Critical Literacy

Since the 1980s, literacy educators have recognized the benefits of a process-oriented approach to writing that frees teachers and students from a rigid, product-oriented writing pedagogy (Graves, 1983; Calkins, 1986). A writer's workshop focuses on writers and how to do the things that writers really do—research, explore, collect, interview, talk, read, and write. Students learn to look at texts the way mechanics look at cars or musicians listen to music, and to use the particular knowledge system of a writer (Harste, 1992). Over time, they build the habits of mind of writers and develop a strategic vision for the writing they will do.

Alongside the call for a more authentic approach to teaching writing, poetry advocates urge educators to teach poetry and argue for its relevance and place in the literacy curriculum (Enochs, 2010). Poetry can be a powerful medium for students to reflect on language, culture, experiences, and memories (Espinosa & Moore, 1999; McKenna, 2010; Schlessman, 2010). Poetry is ideal for developing language and literacy skills because of the unique qualities of the genre: brevity, rhythm, focused content, strong emotional connection, and powerful imagery (Hadaway, Vardell, & Young, 2001). Further, poetry offers a setting where children can be themselves and embrace their own experiences. Certo (2004) concluded that "teaching great poetry to students enhances their perceptions, improves their writing, challenges their minds, and enriches their lives" (p. 266). And yet, poetry is often overlooked in the context of elementary schools.

If writing workshops in general, and teaching poetry in particular, are still not widely enacted in elementary classroom settings, critical literacy practices are frequently non-existent. Critical literacy feels big and not possible for many teachers. Teachers wonder how to begin, what materials to use, what conversations to have (Lewison, Flint, & Van Sluys, 2002; Lewison, Leland, & Harste, 2007; Marshall & Sensoy, 2011).

In a review of the literature on critical literacy, Lewison, Flint, and Van Sluys (2002) identified four social practices that reflect a critical literacy curriculum: (1) disrupting the commonplace; (2) interrogating multiple perspectives; (3) focusing on socio-political issues; and (4) taking action to promote social justice. In conceptualizing critical literacy within these four dimensions, language and literacy are not neutral acts, but rather are situated in personal, social, historical, and political relationships. Our analyses of students' poems and participants' interviews show that their compositions and ideas reflected these four dimensions and evoked what McCormick (2000) called "aesthetic safe zones." Children wrote about their personal lives, incorporated their primary language, used poetry to speak out against injustices, and represented curricular understandings through transmediation by responding to texts using a range of sign systems (e.g., texts, images, songs) to deepen their understandings and create new forms, in this case, poetry (Siegel, 1995).

Disrupting the Commonplace: Students Put Words to their Worlds

In building a critical literacy curriculum, it is essential to begin with the personal so that learners can reflect on issues that play out in their everyday lives, such as gender, race, and class, and to consider ways of disrupting commonplace practices that often go unnoticed, such as the movies they watch, playground games they play, and gendered stereotypes. Poetry invited students to address the personal in ways that that the teachers had not seen in earlier narrative writing samples. Students revealed more about their feelings, fears, and lived experiences than they had previously shared with peers and teachers. Jeffrey, a third-grade teacher, noted how some of the more reticent or shy students were sharing their written work with others: "I was surprised when Salina [student] wanted to read her work today. She never shares her writing." This kind of sharing created curricular openings for the teachers as they supported students in writing about the issues that mattered to them. After introducing Georgia Heard's (1998) strategy of poetry doors—heart, observation, concerns about the world, wonder, and worry—a number of children thought about their own topics related to these doors of poetry. Chunhua wrote a poem entitled "Worries" which served as a catalyst to talk with her teacher about bullying she was experiencing.

Worries
I was sad.
Some people were mean to me.
My feelings hurt.
Because some friends are mean.
It was the first day of school.
                    (Chunhua, grade 2)

The children's poetry itself reminded us "how dense with seriousness" (Bomer & Bomer, 2001, p. 23) students' writing and their lives can be. For many of the children, poetry provided an unobstructed view of their concerns, thereby opening doors for critical classroom conversations and potential future inquiries.

Interrogating Multiple Perspectives: Incorporating Cultural and Linguistic Resources

Within the life of the classroom, the subtle and not-so-subtle literacy practices conveyed through social practices include, but are not limited to, the languages educators use and permit students to use, as well as the kinds of texts they select and share with students. These choices affect what children come to see as valued literacy practices, and in short, determine what they choose to write. In selecting texts to include in the critical literacy and poetry text set, teachers, many for the first time, chose texts that reflected multiple perspectives and languages, including Spanish and African-American language. As students noted linguistic features in the selected poems and participated in conversations that addressed social issues, they appropriated and experimented with language forms and structures in their own writing. The opportunity for students to read and write texts that exemplified other languages and familiar dialects enabled them to see that linguistic diversity offers an avenue for taking on and conveying multiple perspectives.

Additionally, students wrote their own poems containing Spanish and features of African-American language. During a writing conference, Donna, a second-grade teacher, asked Sonia, a bilingual student, what her mother said to her when she was crying. Sonia told Donna, "No llores, está bien." Donna encouraged Sonia to write the phrase in Spanish and also to translate it for her readers.

Tears
When I am sad I cry
Tears roll away and never come back
Sometimes they slide down my cheeks
And my mom tells me
"No llores está bien"
Don't cry it's okay
And it's true

(Sonia, grade 2)

Providing an array of diverse and critical mentor texts and encouraging children to draw on their linguistic resources situated students' cultural and linguistic repertoires within an additive perspective (Nieto, 2009), one that values children's home language(s) while fostering the development of English. Poetry broadened teachers' perspectives regarding how children can learn academic and conversational English by building on their linguistic resources. The teachers noted that English Language students were drawn to the books that incorporated Spanish. Two first-grade teachers, Theresa and Sarah, shared bilingual poems with the children even though they (the teachers) did not speak Spanish. Theresa said, "Hector was writing something about rain. I knew the words in Spanish and when I said them, Hector beamed. When I asked him, 'How do you say this in Spanish?' he thought that was something." The teachers noticed that children were excited to teach their classmates and them how to say words in Spanish, and that multilingual writing brought a level of authenticity to the children's poems. This new perspective encouraged students to take risks with their language resources and in their writing.

Focusing on Socio-political Issues: Taking on Critical Issues in New Ways

A third dimension of critical literacy addresses socio-political issues. Other educators document how poetry facilitates students' exploration of socio-political issues such as Hurricane Katrina and the 2010 earthquake in Haiti (Watson, 2010), immigration (Schlessman, 2010), and race (Damico, 2005).

Integrating critical literacy texts within the poetry study provided students with opportunities to *transmediate*, or work across, texts. In this case, students moved from picture book and textbook formats to poetry. For example, Susan and Jeffrey, third-grade teachers, introduced the students to different texts on immigration. The teachers and students read and discussed these texts, and created multiple responses, including drawings. These engagements invited students to begin putting their ideas on paper about the Civil Rights era and current immigration issues. Some students moved from these initial ideas to drafts of poems reflecting their understandings of the time period. After listening to the story *Coolies* (Soentpiet & Soentpiet, 2003), Kyleigh focused on the plight of the Chinese immigrants working on the transcontinental railroad.

Chinese

Chinese, Chinese, they knew few English.
Chinese, Chinese they wanted equal payment.
Chinese, Chinese they were treated badly.
Chinese, Chinese almost every day is tragic
Chinese, Chinese they cherish their ancestors.
Chinese, Chinese why can't everyone just get along?
(Kyleigh, grade 3)

Engaging with critical literacy means asking questions about "language and power, people and lifestyles, morality and ethics, and who is advantaged by the way things are and who is disadvantaged" (Comber, 2001, p. 271). Poetry was an avenue for students to explore historical concepts in new ways. Children's poems also moved teachers to consider how children's poetry went beyond rote memorization and instead demonstrated children's indepth engagement with important social issues. Donna shared that, "This poetry unit emerged into more than discussions of what poets do, but also discussions of the issues that poets write about." Similarly, Susan, a third-grade teacher, commented: "The students are using what they know about Cesar Chavez in their writing." The integration of poetry into other disciplines provided further evidence for the teachers and students that writing about socially significant topics can, and does, happen in a variety of contexts.

Taking Social Action: Children Speak Back to their World

The most challenging dimension to actualize in classroom practice is taking social action to promote social justice. The teachers in this study had varying experiences regarding critical literacy practices and levels of intentionality in incorporating more critical practices into the classroom curriculum. The teachers were continually surprised by how much the students recalled when reading critical literacy texts. Susan said, "They [the students] remember so much about the book. It really is quite amazing."

In this study, teachers did not engage in social action projects that went beyond their classroom; yet by incorporating critical literacy text sets and a wide range of poetry into the study they facilitated critical reflection, which, is a form of social action (Freire, 2003). Poetry is a genre that invites resistance. Poets and poetry have been integral to social movements. Although students did not engage in social action projects, we see their poetry as a form of social action—a speaking out. Students used poetry as a way to write about their concerns about their worlds, including topics such as homelessness, war, and bullying.

Lilly, a third-grader from Vietnam, contemplated the concept of culture and why it was necessary for people to have culture. She framed her thinking in an *I Wonder* poem, a structure introduced to her from Georgia Heard's (1999) poetry. Heard suggests that young writers consider their questions and demonstrates how a writer's questions can fuel a poem. Lilly used the stem, *I wonder*, as an inspiration for her own poem and as a way to speak back to a rather abstract but pervasive construct—culture. Lilly problematized what it means to have a culture, if all people have culture, and what in fact culture means. Ciardiello (2010) reminded educators that, "Social justice issues inspire poetry" (p. 468). And so it did with these students.

Discussion and Implications

Research and teaching resources are replete with ideas for creating a more culturally responsive and critical curriculum (Bomer & Bomer, 2001; Lewison, Leland, & Harste, 2008; Allen, 2010). Many suggest that by offering a curriculum that is authentic and meaningful to children, real differences will be made in teaching and learning. Although these strategies and implications are important to making change, it seems that for many teachers there continues to be a gap between what is understood as best practice and what is actually implemented in the classroom. Studies such as Brindley & Schneider's (2002) work remind us that teachers' beliefs about writing development may not be congruent with actual classroom practice. The prevalence of state- and district-mandated tests might be the culprit. It may also be that the suggested critical curricular moves feel too distant to implement. The poetry units were a possible entrée into offering a curriculum that honors the life experiences of the students and became a segue to more critical work. Just as critical literacy must build from students' lived experiences rather than from a teacher-directed plan regarding a social issue they deem worthy of study, so it may be for educators new to critical literacy practices. Building critical curricula from a familiar classroom structure such as implementing a poetry study in a writing workshop may be the necessary step to a critical curriculum—one that not only embraces the personal, but also positions students to be advocates for themselves and the world in which they live.

The familiarity of the writing workshop allowed teachers to see children's writing in new ways because students' work was vastly different from their previous writing. Introducing poetry into this structure offered teachers and students opportunities to engage in new practices that could be considered critical. By including multilingual texts within the classroom poetry text sets, teachers began to reposition language and language learners in the classroom. Teachers facilitated multilingual students' first-language use by encouraging them to include first languages in their poetry. These small steps were significant as teachers took reflective stances about the integral role of students' first languages in their classrooms and in students' literacy development.

Reading and writing poetry that focused on a myriad of topics, from life experiences to immigration and the Harlem Renaissance, created space for teachers to imagine even greater possibilities about how a critical literacy curriculum might be enacted. Students' own poems were seeds of larger social issues, which are fodder for critical curricular inquiries.

As we continue this work with our teacher colleagues, we are committed to building literacy curricula that link children's personal experiences to larger social issues. Because these topics are on children's minds, teachers can use social justice texts and poetry to help children make sense of their worlds. Poetry also has the potential to raise teachers' expectations for children. Teachers saw that their students were thoughtful and concerned about their lives and their worlds. This, in turn, helped teachers see the need for students to explore important issues within their classroom communities and to create a generative critical curriculum grown from the places where their poems hide.

References

Allen, J. (2007). *Creating welcoming schools: A practical guide to home-school partnerships. with diverse families.* Newark, DE: International Reading Association.

Allen, J. (2010). *Literacy in the welcoming classroom: Creating family–school partnerships that support student learning.* New York, NY: Teachers College Press.

Au, W. (2007). High-stakes testing and curricular control: A qualitative metasynthesis. *Educational Researcher, 36* (5), 258–267.

Berliner, D. (2009). MCLB (much curriculum left behind): A US calamity in the making. *The Educational Forum, 73,* 284–296.

Bomer, R. & Bomer, K. (2001). *For a better world: Reading and writing for social action.* Portsmouth, NH: Heinemann.

Brindley, R. & Schneider, J. J. (2002). Writing instruction or destruction: Lessons to be learned from fourth-grade teachers' perspectives on teaching writing. *Journal of Teacher Education, 53,* 328–341.

Bunting, E. (2004). *A day's work.* New York, NY: Clarion Books.

Calkins, L. (1986). *The art of teaching writing.* Portsmouth, NH: Heinemann.

Certo, J. (2004) Cold plums and the old men in the water: Let children read and write "great" poetry. *The Reading Teacher, 58 (3),* 266–271.

Ciardiello, A.V. (2010). "Talking walls": Presenting a case of social justice poetry in literacy education. *The Reading Teacher, 63,* 464–473.

Comber, B. (2001). Critical literacies and local action: teacher knowledge and a "new" research agenda. In B. Comber & A. Simpson (Eds.) *Negotiating critical literacies in classrooms* (pp. 271–282). Mahwah, NJ: Lawrence Erlbaum.

Crocco, M. & Costigan, A. (2007). The narrowing of curriculum and pedagogy in the age of accountability: Urban educators speak out. *Urban Education, 42,* 512–537.

Cutler, L. & Graham, S. (2008). Primary grade writing instruction: A national survey. *Journal of Educational Psychology, 100,* 907–919.

Damico, J. (2005). Evoking hearts and heads: Exploring issues of social justice through poetry. *Reading Teacher, 83,* 127–146.

Enochs, E. (2010). Pedagogy in perspective: The historical case for teaching poetry. *Journal of Children's Literature, 36,* 27–43.

Espinosa, C. & Moore, K. (1999). Understanding and transforming the meaning of our lives through poetry, biography, and songs. In C. Edelsky (Ed.) *Making justice our project: teachers working toward critical whole language practice* (pp. 37–55). Urbana, IL: National Council Teachers of English.

Freire, P. (2003). *Pedagogy of the oppressed: 30th anniversary edition.* New York, NY: Continuum.

Gilbert, J. & Graham, S. (2010). Teaching writing to elementary students in grades 4–6: A national survey. *Elementary School Journal, 110,* 494–518.

Graves, D. H. (1983). *Writing: Teachers and children at work.* Portsmouth, NH: Heinemann.

Hadaway, N., Vardell, S., & Young, T. (2001). Scaffolding oral language development through poetry for students learning English. *The Reading Teacher, 54,* 796–807.

Harste, J. C. (1992). Inquiry-based instruction. *Primary Voice, 1,* 3–8.

Heard, G. (1998). *Awakening the heart: Exploring poetry in elementary and middle school.* Portsmouth, NH: Heinemann.

Heffernan, L. & Lewison, M. (2005). What's lunch got to do with it? Critical literacy and the discourse of the lunchroom. *Language Arts, 83,* 107–117.

Hopkins, L. (1999). *Been to yesterdays: Poems of a life.* New York, NY: Boyd Mills Press.

Laman, T. T. (2006). Changing our minds/changing the world: The power of a question. *Language Arts, 83,* 203–214.

Leland, C., Harste, J., Ociepka, A., Lewison, M., & Vasquez, V. (1999). Talking about books: Exploring critical literacy: You can hear a pin drop. *Language Arts, 77 (1),* 70–77.

Lewison, M., Flint, A. S., & Van Sluys, K. (2002). Taking on critical literacy: The journey of newcomers and novices. *Language Arts, 79,* 382–392.

Lewison, M., Leland, C., & Harste, J. C. (2007). *Creating critical classrooms; K-8 reading and writing with an edge.* London, UK: Routledge.

Marshall, E. & Sensoy, O. (Eds.) (2011). *Rethinking popular culture and media.* Milwaukee, WI: Rethinking Schools.

McCarthey, S. (2008). *Current trends in writing instruction.* Paper presented at the annual conference of the National Reading Conference, Orlando, FL.

McCormick, J. (2000). Aesthetic safety zones: Surveillance and sanctuary in poetry by young women. In L. Weis & M. Fine (Eds.) *Construction sites: Excavating race, class, and gender among urban youth* (pp. 180–195). New York, NY: Teachers College Press.

McKenna, T. (2010). Pain and poetry: Facing our fears. *Rethinking Schools, 24,* 12–17.

Medina, J. (2004). *My name is Jorge: On both sides of the river.* New York, NY: Boyd Mill Press.

Medina, T. (2006). *Love to Langston.* New York, NY: Lee and Low Books.

National Commission on Writing (2003). *The neglected R: A need for a writing revolution.* Chicago, IL: National Commission on Writing in America's Schools and Colleges.

Nieto, S. (2009). *Language, culture, and teaching: Critical perspectives,* 2nd edn. London, UK: Routledge.

Schlessman, E. (2010). Aqui y alla: Exploring our lives through poetry—here and there. *Rethinking Schools, 24,* 24–29.

Siegel, M. (1995). More than words: The generative power of transmediation for learning. *Canadian Journal of Education, 20,* 455–475.

Soentpiet, Y. & Soentpiet, C. (2003). *Coolies.* New York, NY: Philomel Books.

Suitts, S. (2010). A new diverse majority: Students of color in the South's public schools. Retrieved from: www.southerneducation.org.

Vasquez, V. (2004). *Negotiating critical literacies with young children.* Mahwah, NJ: Erlbaum.

Watson, R. (2010). Five years after the levees broke: Bearing witness through poetry. *Rethinking Schools, 24 (4),* 18–23.

Wiles, D. (2005). *Freedom summer.* New York, NY: Aladin.

7

CRITICAL LITERACY ACROSS THE CURRICULUM

Learning to Read, Question, and Rewrite Designs

Barbara Comber and Helen Nixon

Early versions of critical literacy in elementary classrooms emphasized the deconstruction of texts in order to interrogate specific representations of groups of people, ideologies, and power relations. In other words, teachers encouraged children to question the versions of reality about women and men, about young and old, about people of different ethnicity and class that were presented to them in texts (e.g., O'Brien, 2001). Informed by both feminist poststructuralist theory (Mellor, Patterson, & O'Neill, 1987; Gilbert, 1989) and critical discourse analysis (Fairclough, 1995), this work problematized the status quo as it was portrayed in the media and everyday texts (Janks, 1993) and books for children (Baker & Freebody, 1989; Luke, 1991). More recently, attention has been paid to the importance of children's agency through text production and related social action (Janks, 2010; Janks & Vasquez, 2011). Since the publication of the New London Group's (1996) seminal paper on multiliteracies and the work of Kress and colleagues (Kress & van Leeuwen, 2006; Mavers, 2011; Bezemer, Diamantopoulou, Jewitt, Kress, & Mavers, 2012), the idea of *design* as a key element of print and multimodal text production has circulated more widely in literacy studies. Recognizing that digital literacies allow young people to produce a range of multimedia texts, including visual designs, researchers from the New Literacy Studies have written about the affordances of multimodality for developing students' literacy repertoires (Rowsell & Pahl, 2007; Street, Pahl, & Rowsell, 2011). In this body of work "literacy" is understood not as a one-dimensional skill, but as repertoires of practices that change according to the demands of different sociocultural contexts and the affordances of different modes and media (Luke & Freebody, 1997; Gutierrez & Rogoff, 2003).

Kress and van Leeuwen (2006, p. 50) argue that "the task of a designer is seen as 'architectural': the shaping of available resources into a framework which can act as a 'blueprint' for the production of the object, entity or event." Recent, accessible digital technologies (such as mobile phones, iPods and iPads) allow individuals, including children, to coordinate and manage multiple modes in any one interaction or production, using photographs, tables, drawings, and prose, for example. Janks (2010) also incorporates *design* into her synthesis model of critical literacy, using it as a catch-all word to describe "critical text production" (p. 155). Through analyzing the production of several multimodal and multimedia texts produced in South African classrooms, Janks demonstrates that it is in the process of *designing* and *redesigning* texts that students learn how they can have agency through producing and sharing texts, learning how texts actually work, and learning the affordances of different modes and options for meaning making. As Janks and Vasquez (2011) note, there have been historical trends in critical literacy: initially focusing on critical reading, moving to the teaching of writing from a critical perspective, to multimodal design, analysis and redesign. However, they emphasize that:

> the project remains the same—understanding the relationship between texts, meaning-making and power in order to undertake transformative social action that contributes to the achievement of a more equitable social order (p. 1).

While multiliteracies researchers have given new prominence to children making meaning *across* modes, early childhood sociocultural researchers have emphasized its importance for some decades. Researchers focusing on children's drawing as part of their text production consider the wide range of semiotic resources that children employ in order to make meanings (Dyson, 1989; Genishi & Dyson, 2009; Christianakis, 2011). Genishi & Dyson (2009) point out that teachers can learn more about young children's meaning making interests and intentions for their writing when children talk about their drawings. However, in the contemporary era, with an increasing emphasis on high-stakes assessment, there may be less time for exploring expanded views of literacy (Pandya, this volume), including multimodality, in elementary classrooms. Christianakis (2011, p. 25) points out that it is ironic that literacy policy and research ignore "pictorials" given their importance in "highly regarded fields like science and architecture." She notes that multimedia modes are seen as threats to the so-called basics, such as writing.

Ironically, new spaces for "marginalized" pedagogies, such as environmental education, place-based pedagogy and Indigenous studies, may have been created through disasters associated with the degradation of environments, climate change, pandemics, and the unpredictable violence associated with terrorism. Studying global change and specific risks, and representing and communicating the subsequent learning, can be accomplished most successfully through a multiliteracies approach. When children are growing up in rapidly changing environments it is important that they are able to represent their understandings of social and material change and also their hopes and desires for ways in which their places might be improved. In this context, content area curriculum can be seen as a generative site for work in critical literacy for several reasons. In many countries where literacy curriculum and pedagogy are increasingly prescribed, and teachers are required to follow mandated approaches, creative spaces may no longer exist within the official English or literacy curriculum per se. In such contexts, other subject areas, such as Social Studies or Science or Design and Technology, provide alternative spaces for teachers to design creative and critical curricula. In these school subjects learners are inducted into the discursive practices associated with particular ways of knowing the world (Lee, 1996). Hence, pursuing critical literacy across the curriculum is both *strategic*, in the sense that it creates extra time for this pursuit, and *necessary*, in the sense that it demonstrates to young learners that all texts can be interrogated, even those that appear to claim most authority. In this chapter we argue that critical engagements with *place* offer one way forward in contemporary policy conditions for the provision of rich material for critical discourse analysis, multimodal design, and agency across the curriculum.

The potential of working with young children to consider the *design of environments* in particular places has been recognized by architects, geographers, youth researchers, and social scientists (Clark, 2010; Dudek, 2011; Morrow, 2011) and research in literacy studies has begun to make connections with spatial theory and the social production of space (Leander & Sheehy, 2004). However, until recently very little critical literacy work in schools explicitly addressed the politics and materiality of place in terms of access, condition, use, design, and ownership of space and place (Comber, Thomson, & Wells, 2001; Vasquez, 2004; Comber, Nixon, Ashmore, Loo, & Cook, 2006; Janks & Comber, 2006; Comber & Nixon, 2008; Sánchez, 2011; Vander Zanden & Wohlwend, 2011). There are three main ways in which we, as university researchers, have explored *design* as an integral part of place-based critical literacy pedagogy with teachers in classrooms. First, the notion of *spatial literacy* has informed collaborative projects conducted with teachers located in an area of urban change, especially as this concept has been conceptualized in architecture (Comber et al., 2006). Second, we have explored *place-based pedagogies* with teachers in both urban and rural communities (Gruenewald, 2003; Comber, Nixon, & Reid, 2007; Smith & Sobel, 2010). Third, we have worked with teachers investigating the potential of *design*, conceptualized as a key element of multiliteracies (New London Group, 1996), in film-making projects focusing on students' "placed" identities in urban settings (Comber & Nixon, 2004, 2011).

In one region, for over a decade, we have worked with elementary-school teachers who have been developing a critical literacy curriculum infused with a focus on place and concepts of design and "belonging." Their curriculum has been informed by the changing material conditions of the students' neighborhoods, associated with a program of urban renewal, and ultimately by the demolition and reconstruction of their school buildings. Working across different curriculum subject areas, teachers have built young people's knowledge of design, ecologies, and local histories at the same time as they have introduced them to complex repertoires of literate practices.

Below we introduce the concept of place-based pedagogy, explain how and why it might connect to an expanded notion of critical literacy, and then illustrate ways in which one teacher implemented a curriculum around the key idea of belonging. Our aim is to demonstrate the potential of across-curricula place-based pedagogy, to illustrate how it allows young people to connect with their places, environments, and each other, and explore how it provides powerful motivation to participate in complex meaning making, design, and communication practices.

Place-based Pedagogy and Critical Literacy

Since Gruenewald (2003) identified synergies between *critical* pedagogy with its emphasis on social justice, and *place*-and *community-based* pedagogies with their emphasis on local citizens' rights, some literacy researchers have explored how place-based pedagogies and critical literacy might inform each other in practice (Comber, Nixon, & Reid, 2007; Comber & Nixon, 2008; Comber, 2010). Both place-based pedagogies and critical literacy are underpinned by the shared assumptions that young people need to develop a sense of agency. That is, students need to develop the belief that they can make a significant positive difference in the world and they need to develop the literate repertoires required to take action. In addition, both approaches assume that:

- places and texts are constructed, and they could be made differently to suit the interests of different groups of people;
- the ways in which people and places are represented are open to questioning;
- communication, social and spatial relationships involve power relations.

Place-based pedagogy (Gruenewald, 2003; Gruenewald & Smith, 2008; Smith & Sobel, 2010) has gained attention in the last decade as the effects of globalized economies, climate change, and dwindling renewable resources are better understood by scientists and the general public. There is some (if, as yet, insufficient) recognition by educational policy makers of the need to develop broad understandings about environmental literacy and ethical citizenship as part of young people's educational entitlement. Place-based pedagogy conceptualizes learning and curriculum in ways that emphasize people's relationships to their place, their environments and habitats. Such approaches typically stress people's responsibilities as producers of waste and consumers of products and resources.

While place-based pedagogies are equally appropriate, and necessary, in rural, regional, remote, and urban contexts, the physical and social contexts in which schools are situated mean that different possibilities and limits for inquiry and action are available. For example, students and teachers who are located in the bioregion of the Murray-Darling Basin and river system in Australia have more opportunities than their urban counterparts to engage in hands-on field research about habitats and indigenous plants and animals. Those living close to the actual rivers could also become involved in continuous projects on water quality (Comber, Nixon, & Reid, 2007). Smith (2011) reports on an ongoing project conducted in Oregon where students are involved in long-term forestry planning, monitoring of wetlands, removing invasive species, and so on. Sánchez (2011) recounts how elementary-school children investigated the history of the Harlem Renaissance as part of a broader place-making project to be shared with their parent community. School communities located in areas of urban renewal have opportunities to become involved in the consultation processes at various levels (Comber et al., 2006; Thomson, 2008). However, all schools are situated in material and social communities and are themselves built environments, and as such can become the focus of shared inquiries (see Johnson, 2008). Teachers might take a sociological, historical, anthropological, environmental, or geographical perspective (amongst others) with the class as they make "place" the object of study and induct students into different ways of knowing about it.

Opportunities for place-based pedagogy in school curricula are yet to be fully developed, perhaps because they require multidisciplinary approaches. Distilling key principles of critical pedagogies of place could lead teachers to investigate questions about people and places in different ways in subjects such as science, history, or art. In this chapter we illustrate how one teacher made space for critical literacy across a range of elementary-school subjects.

Locating Schools and Teachers in Time and Place

Marg Wells is the teacher whose work we describe in this chapter. Wells has a long history of place-based pedagogy and critical literacy (see Comber et al., 2001; Comber & Nixon, with Grant & Wells, 2012), having taught for 30 years, mostly in poor neighborhoods. She works in an elementary school located in the western suburbs of Adelaide in an area formerly known as "The Parks." Now referred to as Westwood, the area is the site of Australia's largest urban renewal project. Post World War II semidetached publicly subsidized housing is being demolished and replaced by new housing designed for first-home buyers. Many families who were attracted to the area by cheap rental accommodation are no longer able to afford to live there. Along with these wider developments, a decision was also made to close two nearby elementary schools and to build a new "superschool" on the grounds of the school where Wells teaches; hence three small neighborhood schools were combined into one large new school. The relevance of place-based pedagogy is clear in this context.

The western suburbs are home to an extremely culturally diverse community, including Aboriginal families, recently arrived immigrants and refugees, and first- and second-generation immigrant families. For example, the school includes Aboriginal, Sudanese, Chinese, Macedonian, Vietnamese, Cambodian, and Anglo-Australian students. In 2008 65% of students were classified as speaking English as an additional language and 68% of students qualified for School Card, an indicator of poverty.

Wells developed her knowledge of critical literacy, place-based pedagogy, and culturally inclusive teaching over many years. Below we firstly discuss her typical practice, which focuses on young people's feelings of belonging in the spaces of the school and its surrounds, before illustrating how she made space for critical literacy across the curriculum and explicitly built students' knowledge of the design of built environments.

Belonging—The School as a Meeting Place

As described in her diary record below, Wells spends the first term of each year working with her class on a school-based program she called *Setting the Scene*, where the classroom ethos and appropriate ways of acting and interacting in the classroom are explicitly negotiated. Concepts such as bullying, justice, well-being, respect, goal setting, and friendship are explored through a range of activities. As she explains it, Wells does this "all under the umbrella of belonging." She emphasizes to students the importance of a classroom culture and building and maintaining spaces that make them feel good and as though they "belong." She explains that for the first weeks of the year:

> Setting up the room, labeling drawers, displaying artwork and presented work, playing get-to-know-you games, establishing routines and procedures, working together and making the room/space "ours" is the main focus. Feeling like students "belong" in the classroom is fundamental to being successful—to feel valued, accepted, part of a group (and yet an individual as well), comfortable, safe and able to take risks is necessary for learning to flourish.

Literacy theorists have noted that this concept of "belonging" is an integral part of building positive student identities:

> Belonging occurs in an educational setting when formal learning engages with the learner's lifeworld experience, when their learning interacts with the learner's identity. Such learning builds on their knowledge, interests and motivations.
>
> *(Kalantzis & Cope, 2008, p. 233)*

While Wells' curriculum and pedagogy are underpinned by her firm understanding of the importance of belonging, at the same time she is also subject to the usual non-negotiable demands of the school, district, and education system. Her grade 3/4 class discussed here, for example, participated in the whole school's "literacy block" program for three days a week between 8:50 a.m. and 10:50 a.m. Here students were grouped for activities including guided reading and various reading, grammar and punctuation, and writing activities (e.g., writing narratives to practice for national testing). Students also read for about 20 minutes at the start of every day and recorded their progress using Lexile Levels, a commercially produced reading scheme designed to improve students' comprehension when they read self-selected books (scholastic.com.au/schools/education/lexile/).

Each year, one of the key ways in which Wells helps young people to engage with concepts about place, space, and belonging is through a series of *neighborhood walks* where class members together walk the nearby streets in which many of them live. On these walks Wells has a number of specific goals for students' learning and their sense of well-being. Students take photographs of significant buildings and various architectural design features, such as pillars, verandahs, windows, and so on. They also photograph key signage in the local area: street names, public notices and warnings, and business names in various languages. These images contribute to individual work and class products, such as a class photo-story entitled *The Walk* in which their collective images and accounts of their journeys through the neighborhood are assembled in one text. Wells introduces similar processes to each new class and invests significant time in establishing young people's relationships with each other, within their classroom, school, and neighborhood spaces. This work involves "critical literacy" as young people are positioned as *researchers* who investigate the relationships between people, place, and representation and are encouraged to discuss and share their diverse knowledges and experiences of, and views about, these matters.

In reviewing the key pedagogical principles of Wells' approach we have found the work of feminist geographer Doreen Massey extremely generative. Space and place have often been ignored in considerations of pedagogy. Indeed, research on literacy pedagogy tends to highlight the linguistic, cultural, social, and sometimes political elements of practice whilst consigning the temporal and spatial elements to *context*. However, Wells' pedagogy continuously foregrounds both place (the neighborhood, the library, the playground climbing frame) *and* social spaces (the school canteen, the sport courts). Massey (2005, p. 151) argues that "place as an ever-shifting constellation of trajectories poses the question of our throwntogetherness." Further, she states that "there can be no assumption of pre-given coherence, or a community or collective identity," and that "place demands negotiation" and "invention" (Massey, 2005, p. 141). This theorization of place allowed us to understand Wells' pedagogy as positively exploiting the affordances of cultural diversity and change in the built environment as motivational resources for learning. In her focus on "belonging spaces" and neighborhood communities and dwellings, this teacher draws young people's attention to the ways in which places are put together and to the realization that collectively they can develop new understandings about people's involvements with those places.

Seeing Design Features in Built Environments

In the year before the new school was to be built, Wells reported that she wanted her students to "become architects" in the sense that they would orient to spaces *like* architects do. Having worked previously with an architect in a collaborative landscape design project (Comber & Nixon, 2008), she realized her students would need new knowledge and information in order to learn to look differently at the designs of the built environment. Guided by her earlier work, she began by having students think about *eggs* (as a home or "belonging space" and as a shape) and invited them to collect egg shapes in everyday life (see Comber et al., 2006 for Wells' earlier work around this shape). She thus began with a concept that students knew about from their own experience then designed simple science experiments so that students could test the weight-bearing strength of eggshells. For example, students tested how many layers of books and papers it took to break empty shells. Wells moved on from there to introduce the architectural terms "dome" and "arch" that relate to the egg shape. She printed and laminated colored images of various items that incorporate a dome shape into their design (for example, army helmet, igloo, chair, lantern, toilet bowl) as well as images of domes and arches in the design of various parts of different buildings. The purpose was to demonstrate their characteristics and to enable students to study examples of domes and arches as *design features* of buildings. At the same time, in Art they explored egg designs and built collages, so they were considering the "egg" from multiple design perspectives.

As part of the curriculum area of Design and Technology, students built cardboard domes and tested their strength in comparison to other shapes. They planned and carried out experiments (using cardboard and toy cars) to check how much weight an arch could carry before it would collapse. In a characteristic pedagogical move, Wells began with conversations about what children already knew about the designs of specific buildings and their functions, before moving to more abstract concepts about spaces and structures, to studying representations of them, to making models, to reading other more complex textual representations (including texts that incorporated architectural terms, design concepts, drawings, and plans). For example, in relation to the egg, Wells gradually moved from students' concrete understanding of an egg as a particular kind of space, place, and shape that has a specific function to consideration of how it might be reimagined and *redesigned*. She then helped students to expand and connect these understandings with more abstract concepts such as arches and domes and their design functions in adding height, strength, and beauty to building constructions.

Near the end of the first school term of that year Wells began to relate the concept of "belonging" to the actual physical spaces of the school–"where they feel good, what they enjoy doing, and [they] begin to see that different activities in different spaces impact on this . . . and that they are different for everyone." Activities included taking photos, making a photo-story (*My Belonging Spaces*) and writing (personal school history and recounts of students' first day at school). After a range of work exploring school memories, belonging, directions, and structures, the students focused on the spaces inside the school buildings and conducted inquiries amongst their peers on questions such as:

- Where do we feel safe and happy in our school?
- How are the learning areas of our school used?
- What do we want in our new school?

The Media Studies teacher assisted Wells' students to prepare films focusing on what happens at school "inside the buildings," literally offering students a different lens for representing people in places. Wells designed many subinquiries and tasks to explore the relationships between people and place in the school that also helped students to assemble new and expanded literacy repertoires. In planning this work Wells was explicitly informed by the state curriculum framework in terms of the so-called cross-curricular "essential learnings" (futures, identity, interdependence, and thinking) and the curriculum learning areas (i.e., Design and Technology, English, Health and Physical Development, Science, Society and Environment, and Maths). For instance, to meet the designated outcomes for English and Drama that term, students organized to present their research at the school assembly. They also worked on improving their abilities to give peers and others oral directions to find their way around the school, in the classroom, and from home to school. They wrote a descriptive paper about the design of their house, noting key architectural features, such as verandahs, roofs, eaves, fences, and so on. In terms of resource based-learning, they searched books and internet sites for information on buildings, building features, and materials. In Maths they learned to draw to-scale floor plans of their own houses. This is not simply working on a theme, but rather systematically building young people's knowledge of the ways in which places are designed and built through different disciplines and by developing discipline-specific literacies. By explicitly working *across* the curriculum, Wells supported her students to develop understandings of complex concepts at the same time as they acquired the *linguistic and semiotic resources* required to represent what they were learning and to share this knowledge with others. Building field knowledge through complex inquiries is fundamental to developing critical literacy repertoires; without these understandings, text analysis and the capacity for agency will remain limited (Comber & Nixon, 2011; Luke, Woods, & Dooley, 2011; Luke, 2013).

Reading and Rewriting the School as a Built Environment

Meanwhile, Wells decided to focus students' attention on the physical changes that were happening as the new "superschool" was being planned and erected. She explained that "With the old buildings earmarked for demolition, and a totally new school planned to be built, I wanted my students to be involved in thinking and planning what the new school should look like."

In practice, over the 2-year period when the new school was designed and built, this resulted in a range of different tasks, including reading the architects' plans for the new school; designing their preferred plans for the new school; regularly interviewing the project manager about design features, spaces, and progress of the building; photographing the new building at each stage, and producing successive PowerPoint presentations about building progress; photographing, researching, and drawing the building equipment; interviewing students and staff about their memories of their experiences at the school, and reporting on these things to the wider school community.

The year that the new building was constructed, Wells explicitly positioned her students as journalists who were investigating the changes which were occurring around them and the perspectives of different stakeholders about those changes: former and current teachers, parents, school workers (volunteers, janitors, cafeteria staff), students, the school principal, the project manager, and so on. Students were taught to interview peers and adults and to participate in progress meetings with the project manager of the new school construction. For many of Wells' students who were learning English as a second or third language, asking questions confidently and audibly in public was a significant challenge. Wells ensured students were well rehearsed by practicing with each other, and well prepared by taking along written protocols or lists of questions and audio-recording devices. Students were being inducted into research and investigative journalism repertoires of practices. But these are not simply generic practices. For example, because Wells' students had studied the different materials that could be used in buildings, they were able to ask informed questions about these matters. They became interested in the different machines brought to the school to assist with various stages of preparing the ground, laying the foundations, and constructing the building. They also became interested in how the building would be heated and cooled. All of this was taken seriously and Wells brought in experts associated with the build who would be able to address such questions.

It is important to note that these children were witnessing outside of the school grounds the demolition of buildings and construction of new housing, and/or renovations of old housing, as part of the wider urban renewal project in the area. However, for many of these children the opportunity to live in a new or improved house was unlikely. Hence their access to in-depth learning about the construction and improvement of built environments could not be taken for granted in the out-of-school world. By making it the object of study within the classroom, Wells invites these children to engage at a deep level with material change and to develop the skills to communicate knowledgeably about it.

Within the teacher's broader critical literacy project, in which children were positioned as co-researchers of places and the politics of places and not as passive victims or observers of change, the teacher's systematic attention to expanding children's knowledge about building design helped them to become critical readers of, and respondents to, official planning documents. As Luke, Dooley, and Woods (2011, p. 150) argue, reading comprehension is "a cognitive *and* social *and* intellectual phenomenon," and thus, "substantive knowledge content and visible connections to material, phenomenal, cultural and intellectual worlds are keys to sustainable achievement gains." Guided by Wells, these students realized during the process of careful examination of the plans that the design for their new school did not include a space for Drama, something that they currently enjoyed in the old school's layout. Working collaboratively with her, they then wrote a submission to the newly appointed principal to request that the new school design be altered to include a drama/performance space. Their collective rationale for why this space was so important to their learning was positively received, and the school plans were altered accordingly, making this a powerful example to the children of their potential agency as critical readers and communicators.

Conclusions

In this chapter we have drawn on the work of one teacher whose practice demonstrates the affordances of place-based pedagogy and critical approaches to pedagogy for students' literacy learning in the middle years of elementary schooling. For instance, across the archive of student work samples produced in her classroom over time, we can see instances of young people conducting surveys, writing recounts (of their first day at school), descriptions (of a house design), and directions (for getting to school), producing photo-stories (of the neighborhood walk and "my belonging space"), undertaking and documenting experiments (about the strength of dome structures), learning how to produce storyboards (for films about their preferred places in the school), planning a whole-school assembly to report on their work, and so on. Learning about new genres and media of communication is thus accomplished in the context of students representing and sharing their experiences of places, including the "changing places" of the school and neighborhood. Because they slowly and systematically build up their knowledge and information before designing their texts and writing, students have readily available to them the vocabulary and conceptual resources required to design and to create their productions. This results in more detail and accuracy, but also helps to develop the resources required to successfully *redesign* their own and others' texts for their own purposes.

In order to produce complex and thoughtful products with impact in the world, it is necessary for students first to build up their conceptual knowledge and linguistic and semiotic resources. Rushing to prepare products, even with the incentive of new media and software, can result in poor outcomes. Building up students' field knowledge through practice and successive iterations, and mobilizing their understandings developed from their experiences, places them in a powerful position to design texts that represent their learning in its depth and complexity. Multiple opportunities to share their learning and their productions, and to discuss related concepts and questions, also allows students to consider different angles and perspectives on issues and problems and to become better informed about them.

Ambitious projects such as these take time and persistence; hence the full story and analysis of such pedagogy and its impact on focal students are beyond what can be reported here. However, some common themes and principles can be described. First, such projects are relevant to students' concerns and situated in the everyday but dynamic worlds of schools and their surroundings. Second, students are explicitly encouraged and assisted to connect their prior everyday knowledge with new and academic forms of knowing across the learning areas. Third, such projects include creative and challenging language and literacy events that assist students to learn the discourses (vocabulary, genres, media) associated with formal knowledge in subject disciplines and beyond. Students are given multiple opportunities to test out and practice their developing expertise with different modes of meaning making. High standards are set for learners and the goals are ambitious in terms of the production and sharing of knowledge in complex multimedia texts. Finally, wherever possible, social and public outcomes for the work are planned (e.g., publications in school newsletters, formal presentations at school assemblies, books produced for class and school libraries) and students are encouraged and enabled to assume responsibility and exercise agency about issues that matter to them and their communities.

References

Baker, C. & Freebody, P. (1989). *Children's first school books: Introductions to the culture of literacy*. Oxford, UK: Basil Blackwell.

Bezemer, J., Diamantopoulou, S., Jewitt, C., Kress, G., & Mavers, D. (2012). *Using a social semiotic approach to multimodality: Researching learning in schools, museums and hospitals*. NCRM Working Paper 1/12: Centre for Multimodal Research, Institute of Education: London. Retrieved from: http://mode.ioe.ac.uk/2012/02/16/using-a-social-semiotic-approach-to-multimodality-researching-learning-in-schools-museums-and-hospitals/.

Christianakis, M. (2011). Children's text development: Drawing, pictures, and writing. *Research in the Teaching of English, 46* (1), 22–54.

Clark, A. (2010). *Transforming children's spaces: Children's and adults' participation in designing learning environments*. New York, NY: Routledge.

Comber, B. (2010). Critical literacies in place: teachers who work for just and sustainable communities. In J. Lavia & M. Moore (Eds.) *Cross-cultural perspectives on policy and practice: Decolonizing community contexts* (pp. 43–57). New York, NY: Routledge.

Comber, B. & Nixon, H. (2004). Children re-read and re-write their neighborhoods: critical literacies and identity work. In J. Evans (Ed.) *Literacy moves on: popular culture, new technologies and critical literacy in the elementary classroom* (pp. 127–148). Portsmouth, UK: Heinemann.

Comber, B. & Nixon, H. (2008). Spatial literacies: emergent pedagogies. *Pedagogies, 3* (2), 221–240.

Comber, H. & Nixon, H. (2011). Critical reading comprehension in an era of accountability. *Australian Educational Researcher, 38* (2), 167–179.

Comber, B., Nixon, H., Ashmore, L., Loo, S., & Cook, J. (2006). Urban renewal from the inside out: spatial and critical literacies in a low socio-economic school community. *Mind, Culture and Activity, 13* (3), 226–243.

Comber, B. & Nixon, H., with H. Grant & M. Wells (2012). Collaborative inquiries into literacy, place and identity in changing policy contexts: implications for teacher development. In C. Day (Ed.) *International handbook on teacher and school development* (pp. 175–184). London, UK: Routledge.

Comber, B., Nixon, H., & Reid, J. (Eds.) (2007). *Literacies in place: Teaching environmental communication.* Newtown, Sydney, NSW, Australia: Primary English Teaching Association.

Comber, B., Thomson, P., & Wells, M. (2001). Critical literacy finds a "place": writing and social action in a neighborhood school. *Elementary School Journal, 101* (4), 451–464.

Dudek, M. (2011). Play in an adult world: designing spaces with children. In P. Foley & S. Leverett (Eds.) *Children and young people's spaces: Developing practice* (pp. 73–88). Milton Keynes, UK: Palgrave Macmillan & Open University.

Dyson, A. (1989). *Multiple worlds of child writers: Friends learning to write.* New York, NY: Teachers College Press.

Fairclough, N. (1995). *Critical discourse analysis: A critical study of language.* London, UK: Longman.

Genishi, C. & Dyson, A. H. (2009). *Children, language and literacy: Diverse learners in diverse times.* New York, NY: Teachers College Press: & Washington, DC: National Association for the Education of Young Children.

Gilbert, P. (1989). Student text as pedagogical text. In S. De Castell, A. Luke, & C. Luke (Eds.) *Language, authority and criticism: Readings on the school textbook* (pp. 195–202). London, UK: The Falmer Press.

Gruenewald, D. (2003). The best of both worlds: A critical pedagogy of place. *Educational Researcher, 32* (4), 3–12.

Gruenewald, D. & Smith, G. (Eds.) (2008). *Place-based education in the global age: Local diversity.* New York, NY: Lawrence Erlbaum Associates.

Gutierrez, K. & Rogoff, B. (2003). Cultural ways of learning: individual traits or repertoires of practice. *Educational Researcher, 32* (5), 19–25.

Janks, H. (Ed.) (1993). *Critical language awareness series.* Johannesburg, SA: Witwatersrand University Press and Hodder & Stoughton Educational.

Janks, H. (2010). *Literacy and power.* New York, NY: Routledge.

Janks, H. & Comber, B. (2006). Critical literacy across continents. In K. Pahl and J. Rowsell (Eds) *Travel notes from the new literacy studies: Instances of practice* (pp. 95–117). Clevedon, UK: Multilingual Matters.

Janks, H. & Vasquez, V. (2011). Critical literacy revisited: writing as critique. *English Teaching: Practice & Critique, 10* (1), 1–6.

Johnson, K. (2008). Teaching children to use visual research methods. In P. Thomson (Ed.). *Doing visual research with young people* (pp. 77–94). London, UK: Routledge.

Kalantzis, M. & Cope, B. (2008). *New learning: Elements of a science of learning.* Cambridge, UK: Cambridge University Press.

Kress, G. & van Leeuwen, T. (2006). *Reading images: The grammar of visual design*. London, UK: Routledge.

Leander, K. & Sheehy, M. (Eds.) (2004). *Spatializing literacy research and practice*. New York, NY: Peter Lang.

Lee, A. (1996). *Gender, literacy, curriculum: Re-writing school geography*. London, UK: Taylor & Francis.

Luke, A. (1991). The political economy of reading instruction. In C. Baker & A. Luke (Eds.) *Towards a critical sociology of reading pedagogy: Papers of the XII World Congress on Reading* (pp. 3–26). Amsterdam, Netherlands: John Benjamins.

Luke, A. (2013). Regrounding critical literacy: representation, facts and reality. In M. Hawkins (Ed.). *Framing languages and literacies: Socially situated views and perspectives*. New York, NY: Routledge.

Luke, A., Dooley, K., & Woods, A. (2011). Comprehension and content: planning literacy in low socioeconomic and culturally diverse schools. *Australian Educational Researcher*, *38* (2), 149–166.

Luke, A. & Freebody, P. (1997). Shaping the social practices of reading. In S. Muspratt, A. Luke, & P. Freebody (Eds.) *Constructing critical literacies: Teaching and learning textual practice* (pp. 185–225). Cresskill, NJ: Hampton Press.

Luke, A., Woods, A., & Dooley, K. (2011). Comprehension as social and intellectual practice: rebuilding curriculum in low socioeconomic and cultural minority schools. *Theory into Practice*, *50* (2), 150–164.

Massey, D. B. (2005). *For space*. London, UK: Sage.

Mavers, D. (2011). Image in the multimodal ensemble: children's drawing. In C. Jewitt (Ed.). *The Routledge handbook of multimodal analysis* (pp. 263–271). London, UK: Routledge.

Mellor, B., Patterson, A., & O'Neill, M. (1987). *Reading stories*. Perth, WA, Australia: Chalkface Press.

Morrow, V. (2011). Researching children and young people's perspectives on place and belonging. In P. Foley & S. Leverett (Eds.) *Children and young people's spaces: Developing practice* (pp. 58–72). Milton Keynes, UK: Palgrave Macmillan & Open University.

New London Group (1996). A pedagogy of multiliteracies: designing social futures. *Harvard Education Review*, *66* (1), 60–92.

O'Brien, J. (2001). Children reading critically: a local history. In B. Comber & A. Simpson (Eds.) *Negotiating critical literacies in classrooms* (pp. 37–54). Mahwah, NJ: Lawrence Erlbaum Associates.

Rowsell, J. & Pahl, K. (2007). Sedimented identities in texts: instances of practice. *Reading Research Quarterly*, *42* (3), 388–404.

Sánchez, L. (20011). Building on young children's cultural histories through placemaking in the classroom. *Contemporary Issues in Early Childhood*, *12* (4), 332–342.

Smith, G. (2011). Linking place-Based and sustainability education at Al Kennedy High School. *Children, Youth and Environments*, *21* (1), 59–78.

Smith, G. A. & Sobel, D. (2010). *Place- and community-based education in schools*. London, UK: Routledge.

Street, B., Pahl, K., & Rowsell, J. (2011). Multimodality and new literacy studies. In C. Jewitt (Ed.) *The Routledge handbook of multimodal analysis* (pp. 191–212). London, UK: Routledge.

Thomson, P. (2008). Schools and urban regeneration: challenges and possibilities. In B. Lingard, J. Nixon, & S. Ranson (Eds.) *Transforming learning in schools and communities: The remaking of education for a cosmopolitan society* (pp. 302–319). London, UK: Continuum.

Vander Zanden, S. & Wohlwend, K. (2011). Paying attention to procedural texts: critically reading school routines as embodied achievement. *Language Arts, 88* (5), 337–345.

Vasquez, V.M. (2004). *Negotiating critical literacies with young children*. Mahwah, NJ: Lawrence Erlbaum Associates.

8

LOOKING AND LISTENING FOR CRITICAL LITERACY*

Recognizing Ways Youth Perform Critical Literacy in School

Elisabeth Johnson and Lalitha Vasudevan

There is a movement in critical literacy curriculum and pedagogy to study "everyday texts," i.e., the texts we encounter daily on billboards, in mailboxes, on TV, school cafeteria menus, and clothing labels (Vasquez, 2004). This move recognizes how young people analyze "literary" texts as well as texts that have personal meaning and broad social implications in worlds beyond school. In noting this, we do not mean to dichotomize school and everyday texts, but to emphasize rich opportunities available through integrating young people's "out of school" textual engagements into schoolwork.

Centering everyday texts is crucial to enacting responsive, relevant critical curricula. But everyday texts invite affective responses that exceed logical, rational, verbal, and written responses within a framework of critical analysis techniques (Alvermann, Moon, & Hagood, 1999; Janks, 2002; Vasquez, 2004). For example, deconstructing a beloved cartoon or remaking an ad campaign might spark resistance, laughter, or a carnivalesque moment when norms for classroom power relations and comportment are temporarily upended (Grace & Tobin, 1999). What else might such reactions signify? In this article, we regard these responses, similar to Sipe's (2007) reading of young children's performative responses, as critical literacy performances—moments when students use their bodies to communicate their critical perspectives that, in turn, are positioned and interpreted by teachers and peers. However, critical literacy performances may be less recognizable given the verbo- and logo-centricity (a tendency to privilege spoken and written

* This chapter is an expanded version of: Johnson, E. & Vasudevan, L. (2012). Seeing and hearing students' lived and embodied critical literacy practices. *Theory Into Practice, 51* (1), 34-41. DOI: 10.1080/00405841.2012.636333. Reprinted by permission of Taylor & Francis (http://www.tandfonline.com).

language over other communicative modes like silence, visual image, laughter, gesture, music) of critical curriculum and pedagogy.

We make the case, in this chapter, that teachers must expand current definitions of critical *literacy* practices to include a performance lens that recognizes embodied texts and responses. Following a working definition of "critical literacy," we include three vignettes focusing on tenth-graders who help us put these theories into practice: first Rukiya's,[1] then Santo and Jessica's, and finally Lucretia's performances illustrate the silent, invisible, taboo, and politically incorrect ways youth embody and perform critical literacy daily. We conclude with implications critical literacy performances have for teachers and researchers. Ultimately, we argue that students use their bodies to perform critical literacy—that is, to respond to and convey their critical engagements with myriad texts—in ways that are underrecognized, may defy rationality, or transgress teacher expectations for the politically correct or what teachers deem to be classroom-appropriate (Janks, 2002).

Critical Literacy: A Contingent Definition

Critical literacy has taken many shapes on a not-so-linear trajectory. It is a term with distinct meanings "in particular places at particular times . . . informed by our personal and professional histories" (Comber, 2006, p. 53). Certainly definitions are in constant, contextual negotiation as curriculum is enacted between students and teachers. However, context-specific definitions often foreground classroom teachers' experiences, charging them with scaffolding and recognizing particular critical literacy practices that largely depend on deconstructing texts. Moreover, many deconstructive activities fail to account for differential frames of reference, cultural histories, and personal experiences that make students' textual understandings distinct from those assumed by progressive pedagogues (Enciso, 2007). For example, identifying and deconstructing the media's manipulative machinations are commonplace critical literacy practices (Lewis, Doerr-Stevens, Tierney, & Scharber, 2013). Rather than positioning youth as duped by a capitalistic, consumer-driven economy, educators might begin asking about students' life experiences with money, family values about consumption, and what texts mean to them. Therefore, in the interest of recognizing contingent relationships with texts and capital, we turn to the body, a site where these complicated relationships play out across the human lifespan.

The body is a text produced by socially circulating norms for gender, race, sexuality, class, age, and ability (Kamler, 1997). Through daily, bodily repetitions (i.e., speech, gesture, and dress), we reproduce and reinscribe these meanings (Butler, 1999; Bettie, 2003; Youdell, 2006). For instance, people frequently position (i.e., assign seemingly fixed roles to) babies dressed in blue as boys, teen girls as boy-crazy, and Latino youth as native Spanish speakers. But if we watch longer, listen differently, engage with, or suspend these readings, every person might be understood otherwise (Gustavson, 2007), with greater variation accorded to combinations of phenotype, dress, and actions over time (Wortham, 2005).

Likewise, what critical literacy means in school can differ from the ways people read, write, speak, listen, and gesture critically beyond teacher radars. This leads us to conceptualize critical literacy as performed (Blackburn, 2003), positioned (Bomer & Laman, 2004), and produced (Youdell, 2006). In other words, what it means to be critically literate is produced by widely circulating social norms for critical literacy. Yet, youth and teachers not only mirror but also disrupt these norms every day, as they perform and position each other. Practices that might count (or be recognized) as critical literacy include speaking, dressing, or gesturing to express particular ways of being that belie, subvert, and expose social norms and power imbalances. Such performances are *critical* because they allow youth to explore and expose ways power circulates. In this sense, power is not a static force or entity to be exchanged, but rather is made and remade through interactions and people's recognition of, and reactions to, one another.

Teaching and research in the areas of critical media literacy and multimodality have expanded verbo- and logo-centric definitions of literacy to include a focus on ways media texts work in multiple modes (e.g., the ways sound, image, and text work in tandem to position and produce messages [Siegel, 2006; Vasquez, 2007; Jewitt, 2008]). We encourage a turn to the local, daily texts inscribed on to and expressed by the body to disrupt reductive interpretations of young people's classroom performances and expand meanings of text and literacy. Embodied texts like clothing, hair, and accessories are those most frequently used to position students (Forman, 2005) *and* fundamental to the identity work in which we all engage (Pomerantz, 2008). Moreover, affective relationships to embodied texts take complicated, conflicted forms absent in many logical, rational rubrics for critical literacy practice (Janks, 2002[2]).

Critical Literacy Performances in an English Classroom

During 2006–2007, Liz Johnson, the lead author of this article, conducted a year-long ethnographic study that focused on teacher and student negotiations surrounding pop culture text meanings on which the following vignettes are based.[3] She did not set out to study critical literacy with this project. Instead, she wondered what pop culture texts were important to young people and how those texts were used when participants performed themselves and positioned one another in school. Through observational fieldnotes, ethnographic interviews, and photo-ethnographies,[4] Liz identified a range of popular texts in this classroom (e.g., gestures, clothing, and accessories, including personal tech like iPods, cell phones, PlayStation Portables).

As Liz examined the ways young people identified themselves using these texts, she frequently saw and heard students question the ways power circulated in school, media, and social texts. But instead of labeling these ways of reading the word and the world "critical," focal youth used different terms for these perform-ances, for example, "speaking loud enough to be heard," "speaking open-mind-edly," having "swag," "speaking the 100% truth," and "talking about life in the community." Although some critical literacy performances took center stage,[5] most of them occurred backstage in interviews with Liz, or during class for Liz and smaller peer audiences.

Ms. Phagan, the tenth-grade English teacher in Room 323, encouraged stu-dents to "go deeper" and "get political" by analyzing the subtexts of what they read and wrote. Even though she invited critical perspectives, they were paired with opposing perspectives, which often mirrored the views of adults responsible for student discipline and control (Foucault, 1979). We argue that such practices produced a classroom space that privileged multiple, instead of critical, perspec-tives and positioned literacy as a neutral practice.

The classroom and individual interview contexts for the three vignettes we explore in this chapter included audiences that both recognized and failed to recognize these youths' performances as critical literacy performances. In saying so, we wish to illustrate the ways critical literacy is an embodied performance that is always and already occurring, regardless of whether or not it is recognized as such. We hope these illustrations provoke new ways to see, hear, and foster students' critical literacy performances in school. It should be noted that the fol-lowing vignettes are written in the first person as a means of retaining the lead author/researcher's positionality in this study.

Looks Can Be Deceiving: Critical Literacy Performances in Less Likely Places

Peers and teachers alike thought 16-year-old Rukiya was popular, or "down," as she put it. She hung out with a school crowd reputed for frequent spending on new clothes and kept up with the latest fashion trends, i.e., wearing fresh Uptowns and Jordans almost weekly, matching clothing colors to sneaker details, weaving hot orange streaks into silky black tresses, and dressing in what peers dubbed the "gangsta preppy" look. This meant she juxtaposed "gangsta" brands like Rocawear with "preppy" brands like Aeropostale. Her style attracted my attention. Many classmates admired her flair, and others, like Jessica, disclosed dressing's importance for Rukiya: "She's [Rukiya's] motivated to come [to school] when she has new clothes to wear" (fieldnotes, May 5, 2007).

I also assumed Rukiya was really into spending on clothing, shoes, jewelry, and hairstyles since it frequently came up in her peer conversations. For example, during a project when students created life-sized diagrams of Shakespeare char-acters from *Othello*, Rukiya called friends' attention to the "Rodrigo" group that had drawn sneakers on the character's feet. And when students strutted down Room 323's aisles, catwalk chatter fluttered between Rukiya and her tablemates. Sometimes she identified shifts in students' style choices, noting, for example,

"She's here with the earrings thuggin' big." Other times she questioned her own looks, "Do I got too much curls?" And Rukiya always had something to say about the rules of style in practice, such as: "Everybody who wears Converse everyday wears Converse everyday. It's like an everyday thing. Not no Uptowns... You can't wear white Uptowns everyday."

Along these lines, I initially noted that Rukiya seemed to perform the clothes-minded teen in the photoethnography she composed for this research project (a series of photos individual participants took to document and discuss pop culture texts important in their lives in and beyond school). Specifically, Rukiya took many pictures of clothing and shoes. When I asked her to talk about the snapshots, Rukiya positioned clothing as a text, critical to performing and positioning identities, geographic and ethnic locations, and socioeconomic status: "I feel like clothes make a person. They describe basically you, your background, where you come from, what's in your house . . ." She went on to describe how "everything is connected: TV, music, friends, dressing, phones. Everything is like all connected, like everything. It starts from TV. We see the girls modeling, being in the videos . . . we want to look like them. We want to be like them." With "we see" and "we want" Rukiya positioned herself and her peers as duped teenagers who fall victim to the forces of targeted marketing, while aspiring to mimic the lifestyles promoted by fashion models, television shows, and popular music.

As our conversation unfurled, Rukiya explained that clothing and accessories were important texts in her identity performances, and were also texts she relied upon with which to read others. However, she didn't consider it "wise" to pay a lot of money for consumables like food and lip gloss even though peers and Lil Mama, the rap artist, made claims to the contrary. She explained:

Rukiya: A new song came out called "Lip Gloss" by Lil Mama. I don't know if you ever heard of it.

Liz: No. You have it? We'll hear it.

Rukiya: It talks about lip-glossness [sic].

Liz: How so?

Rukiya: And now you hear everybody. She talks about her lip gloss how when she put it on how she do it. When she walks down the hall everybody looks at it. And now, to be honest, you hear a lot of girls now they wanna go get Mac lip gloss. Before they used to go to beauty supply for 99-cent lip gloss. Now they wanna buy fifteen dollar lip gloss from Mac, Victoria Secret. And I'm like, "Are you serious?" Like they now wanna do that just because the video came out. That shows how much of an influence videos and songs have on us.

Liz: But it doesn't. Tell me *your* reaction to something like that.

Rukiya: Me? Stuff like that, it doesn't bother me because I feel like just with food, for example, my friend Daniel, my mother, when she goes food shopping, she buys name brands of Western Beef. She'll buy a can of

> corn. It won't be Del, Dole, whatever. It'll be the Western Beef and
> he [Daniel] feels like he's so [pause] For his mother, everything she
> buys is, everything she buys is like name brand. And when he comes
> to my house he'll be like, "Ewww, I can tell a difference. Ewww," this
> and that. To me there's no difference. And the reason I'm bringing
> that up is because Mac lip gloss and 99-cent lip gloss look the same on
> your lips. There's no difference for me to spend fifteen dollars when I
> could spend a dollar and save money. So for me, I think of it more [sic]
> wiser.

Rukiya started positioning herself with duped teens, but later positioned herself
apart from this trope by stating her preference for cheaper consumables, e.g., 99-
cent lip gloss and Western Beef brand foods. Even though Rukiya initially noted
an early desire to look and be like a model, that desire faded when wearable items
lacked performative valence or tangible difference. Items worth money improved
social positioning, feeling, and being. Items not worth the price looked or tasted
the same, but cost more. Notably, Rukiya never hid her lip gloss tubes from view
when she refreshed her shine at the table before dismissal. With each lip gloss
application, Rukiya performed a wise spender: wiser to her, frugal to some, and
cheap to others.

From Political to Satirical: Recognizing a Range of Critical Responses

During English class, Santo, a 15-year-old Dominican-Ecuadorian youth, was
usually playful. He sang things like, "When you loop de loop you poop," jokingly
called his teacher Ms. Phagan "the Phagster," and blurted "shiitake mushrooms"
when he blundered. Santo frequently volunteered to talk in center-stage, teacher-
facilitated discussions, sharing elaborate personal and political opinions.

Santo sometimes sat with Jessica, a 16-year-old Chinese-American who usually
wore white t-shirts and skinny jeans atop black Converse Allstars. She was into
Velcro wallets, sometimes painted her nails black, and loved the band AC/DC.
Jessica's attendance in this first-period class was fairly sporadic and she left school
unexpectedly around the middle of the second semester. When she was in class,
Jessica actively participated in teacher-facilitated discussions and spent a good deal
of small-group work time chatting with peers in side conversations about life
outside of school, e.g., her job at the kosher Chinese restaurant, cute boys she was
hanging out with, and the latest fights and make-ups between friends.

I witnessed several of Santo's critical literacy performances across the year,
including his center-stage efforts to counter the Iraq war, critique George W.
Bush, and position teacher edits as censorship. I also recorded Santo's numerous
critical performances centering race. These took place *backstage* for classmates and
me. The following events offer some insight into a few ways Santo used backstage

spaces for playful, critical literacy performances in interviews with me and classroom exchanges with tablemates like Jessica.

Early in data collection, I sat with Santo, who was working on a small-group skit for history class the following day. Out of teacher earshot, Jessica, one of his group members, asked, eyeing Santo, if anyone had seen *The Amazing Racist*[6] on Youtube[7] (Shaffir, 2006, 2008). With that, the young Chinese-American launched into a scene about the racist [portrayed by Ari Shaffir] in a sushi bar, transitioning to Shaffir in a Mexican restaurant, urging store employees not to throw tomatoes at him because "your cousin picked that!" She closed by describing Shaffir confronting a Chinese guy with a leashed dog, asking if "he will make fried dog." Jessica and Santo were rolling with laughter. She pointed at him as he laughed, doubled over. Santo one-upped the story, remembering that Shaffir had said, "Mexicans can only do two things: work and have babies." With this, he and Jessica erupted with laughter, Santo almost falling off of his chair.

Their conversation transitioned to talk beyond the scope of assigned classwork, transgressed their peers' comfort levels, and seemed to subvert their teacher's classroom norms and attention. To illustrate, Santo and Jessica discussed *Jackass Number Two's*[8] fart mask scene, a "butt beer tube" (for ingesting alcohol anally), *Saw III*,[9] dancing in iPod commercials, X-rated iPods, and scenes of the elderly in *Jackass: The Movie*. After a few exchanges, their tablemate Corey reminded them of my presence, and, presumably, of classroom norms for adult-sanctioned topics, warning, "Stay on topic guys. She's [Liz] writing everything you say" (fieldnotes, October 26, 2006), but Jessica and Santo continued. When Ms. Phagan checked in, Santo mentioned that the film *The Alamo* would fit with their project. When she exited, Santo and Jessica turned to discuss Harold and Kumar,[10] Hilary Duff,[11] and *Spaceballs*.[12]

Beyond teacher purview, but in front of me, Santo and Jessica discussed a variety of topics typically taboo in classrooms. Rather than belabor race with serious concern, or ignore it—two possible responses in race talk—they played with race and racism just like they played with topics like old age, farting, and pornography. Even though being serious about or ignoring racial issues was not the *only* approach for race work in school, race was rarely centered in official classroom work, and playing with racial issues was certainly not the norm.

To some, Santo and Jessica's banter and giggling might seem "off task." To my eyes and ears, their rambunctious physicality, continued performance despite adult presence, and willingness to joke freely and politically incorrectly about race disrupted norms for race talk and democratic dialogue in the classroom. Who decides when, why, and how we have critical conversations about race? And who says these interactions have to be serious? In their conversations, Santo and Jessica demonstrated how embodied responses and critical readings can expose unequal power relations without sounding like the nightly news.

Here Santo and Jessica performed and positioned one another as White, non-White, and Chinese in words and gestures surrounding the *Amazing Racist* video.

Their critical literacy performances underscore the affective dimensions of pop culture texts and the affordances of playful backstage conversations about race and racism. They also expose the limitations of representing critical literacy curriculum in the classroom as a serious, center-stage endeavor. Santo and Jessica's backstage talk illustrated how young people negotiate textual meanings for contingent media texts in ways that are more creative and complicated than often planned for by teachers. Santo and Jessica used pop culture texts to make a space where they could broach race talk, joking about race and its role in their lives. The students' use of "politically incorrect" humor to joke about race and racism counters dominant discourses of democratic dialogue, race talk, and antiracist curriculum in school that portray appropriate class talk as teacher-mediated exchanges filled with silences, conflicts, and outbursts (Boler, 2004).

The Sounds of Silence: The Critical Valence of the Quiet, Adorned Body

Lucretia was perceived as a good student by many and a little naïve by others. She was also positioned as a loner—someone who most fellow students didn't think they could get close to. Cursorily grouped with "the Black girls" by peers, none of "the Black girls" considered her someone they would hang out with outside of school. Performing and positioned as the loner, Lucretia cultivated an image of difference through style choices that did not conform to norms that teachers and students produced for Black girls in her school. According to Lucretia, this meant crafting her own style, sometimes making clothes her own by cutting them up, or mixing colors without matching, but "mixin' it right." Such mixes and cuts rarely mimicked the branded trends or match-heavy clothing she saw on most people in her historically Black neighborhood or school. She wore these styles with gusto, in spite of, surrounded by, and at times buoyed by, peer reactions.

Dressing "differently" and choosing to move through school alone sometimes came at a price for Lucretia, as people actively worked to interpret her embodied silence. Peers would classify her clothing choices or her individual presence as weird, antisocial, shy, or lonely. This did not often prompt Lucretia to speak, but she was also not always silent. Over the course of a year talking, sitting, and working with Lucretia in school, I witnessed her critical literacy performances in multiple modes. For instance, during a whole-class writing assignment, Lucretia challenged peers about their views on the school's cell phone ban in writing and speech. On several other occasions, Lucretia vocally questioned Santo (her tablemate) about his perspectives on race relations and ways he positioned her, racially, i.e., when he accused her of trying to accessorize and talk like a White person. However, in the case of the following event and others in and beyond the classroom, Lucretia's critical literacy performance occurred through her silence. Sometimes she appeared to go about her business, without flinching—appearing to ignore direct comments, questions, or requests. In the following vignette, I depict and discuss one such occurrence when Lucretia performed critical literacy through a silent response to both her teacher and a fellow student in English class.

One morning in Room 323, Lucretia slid into class while independent reading was coming to a close and the whole-class lesson was beginning. As she walked from the door to her seat, I noticed she was wearing a pair of big, dark designer sunglasses along with an oversized green pearl necklace and matching bracelet. Ms. Phagan wanted the class to chart the differences between two versions of *The Three Little Pigs*. After students charted independently, she invited individuals to approach the chalkboard and record their findings. Lucretia was one of the first to go up voluntarily. When she approached the board, sunglasses in place, her classmate Katarina called out, "It's sunny, huh?" Lucretia smirked a little and mumbled to herself (loud enough for me to hear), "Ha! She's trying to be sarcastic." Lucretia scrawled her point on the board and made it back to her seat just in time for the school announcements to come over the public address system. Students were chit-chatting across the room as the student emcee recited the day's events. Lucretia studied her scrawl on the board while the announcements closed and then started to trek back to the board. As she passed through the dead zone between student tables and the blackboard, Ms. Phagan leaned over and whispered a request for Lucretia to "take her sunglasses off, please." Unflinching, Lucretia continued to the board, revised her writing, and returned to her seat. She eased into her chair, leaned over to me, and explained that she had had an allergic reaction. "I'm not taking my glasses off," she said. "I'm not wearing them for fashion." Neither she nor Ms. Phagan brought them up again that day, and at the close of the period, Lucretia exited the room, sunglasses still on.

Multiple researchers have drawn attention to the affordances adornments provide young people to perform identities and counter subject positions (Moje, 2000; Swain, 2002; Bettie, 2003; McCormick, 2003; Hagood, 2004; Forman, 2005; Knight, Dixon, Norton, & Bentley, 2006; Youdell, 2006; Pomerantz, 2008). More recently, researchers have been teasing out the powerful messages behind silent actions that are typically less considered in verbo-centric classrooms (Schultz, 2009; Johnson, 2011). In her explanation to me, Lucretia was very clear about the time and place for fashion, drawing a distinction between her decision to wear sunglasses that day to cover up an allergic reaction, and the fashion statement they might signify on other days. However, her teacher was not privy to this verbal explanation for both her wearing of the sunglasses and refusal to remove them. For Ms. Phagan and her classmates, Lucretia performed the silent, possibly ignoring student whose behavior could be overtly defiant as she failed to acknowledge or comply with a teacher's direct request that she remove a clothing item or accessory.

Broader discourses produce subjectivities for youth, subjectivities that populate their dress and style with an overwhelming amount of personal significance. Discourses of youth surveillance also filtered into the school's policies, policing and prohibiting particular clothing items and technological devices. Such practices are commonplace in this and other urban schools with questionable test scores and/ or increased incidents of violence. Signs prohibiting headgear and technological devices plastered doors and hallways, and during the year, I witnessed school adults confiscate student devices, ask for the removal of headgear, command that shirts be turned inside out, or on some quiet occasions, ignore the presence of "banned" clothing and accessories altogether (Figure 8.1).

If we consider the many meanings that wearing sunglasses inside might carry, aside from style and sun protection, the list could include attempts to obscure shyness, intoxication, medically dilated pupils, blindness, wounds or deformities, eye contact, or identity. Even with a litany of possible meanings for the wearing of sunglasses indoors, discourses about youth and their preoccupation with fashion and evasion in school overwhelmed this event.

What made Lucretia's performance critical? Lucretia's silent refusal to comply and remove her sunglasses coupled with a refusal to explain her lack of compliance with the adult classroom authority underscored and disrupted classroom power imbalances. She could have easily turned to Ms. Phagan and shared that she'd had

FIGURE 8.1

an allergic reaction. Lucretia had decent grades, good attendance, and a generally positive relationship with her English teacher. But an explanation would have implied a request for permission to don sunglasses inside. Instead, Lucretia refused to explain the shades and remained unflinchingly silent, acting as though she hadn't even heard the request whispered directly into her ear. Lucretia's comment to me evidenced her personal understanding that sunglasses might be prohibited if motivated by style, but her silent accessorizing left her motivation for wearing the sunglasses unknowable, uncolonizable (Li Li, 2004), and illuminated the arbitrary nature of power some school adults leverage over student bodies. Consequently, Lucretia's performed unhearing provided Ms. Phagan an opportunity to rethink her request—a request she did not reiterate. Sunglasses weren't banned in school, didn't detract from the day's lesson, and Lucretia was "not wearing them for fashion." She did wear them, nonetheless.

Recognizing the Unseen in Adolescents' Critical Literacy Performances: Implications for Practice

How we engage with an artifact, context, or text changes our relationship to it. Similarly, our modes of response and ways of reading expressions and performances change how we make sense of one another. Thus, we situate our understandings about critical literacy within the discursive practices of youth themselves, which are not limited to prevailing definitions and images articulated by distant others, e.g., researchers, educators, curriculum writers, educational policymakers. In doing so, we shifted our research stance to consider how young people like Rukiya, Santo, Jessica, and Lucretia were embodying critical literacy as they performed themselves in various contexts, through interactions with the material, cultural, and discursive texts around them. Such a stance has implications for classroom practice.

For instance, we attended to the ways critical literacy was evident in unexpected postures and practices that might otherwise be dismissed as "off task" or "duped" (e.g., laughter, humor, and modes of dress). Young people engage with texts in and out of school-sanctioned instructional time. Their critical literacy is "packaged" multimodally, embodied and expressed across space and time. Considering the embodied dimensions of critical literacy not only increases curricular relevance for students as it centers texts circulating in their lives, but it is a pedagogical posture that also assumes students perform critical literacy in ways we might not be positioned to see, hear, or acknowledge.

Educators will inevitably encounter unplanned moments that challenge classroom norms or teacher comfort—moments when critical literacy is possibly being performed differently. In such instances we all might ask one another and ourselves: Why are particular ways of speaking, moving, and dressing disallowed? Who is invested in such rules? Where or when are taboos lifted? Why? How might this moment mean otherwise? But the question remains, if teachers don't see or hear many of the moments students perform critical literacy, what should they do? If we assume critical literacy to be at once performed, positioned, and produced in classroom contexts, educators become integral to both the positioning of these performances in curriculum, and the classroom production of critical literacy. This means creating curricular conditions which position students' visible and invisible critical literacy performances at the center of classroom inquiry, and that position students as critically literate in a range of modes and genres. When teachers provide such curricular conditions, they are effectively producing critical literacies that look and sound different, that surprise students and teachers, and provoke questions about the ways we define, identify, and even assess what it means to be critically literate in school.

We invite teachers to assume a stance that dances on the edge of cooptation and dismissal of students' texts, and to design projects that ask students to describe and document issues and concepts on their own terms, with texts that might surprise or disrupt what projects and content are about. For example, teachers interested in tapping into students' already wise, but possibly invisible, critical consumption practices, might initiate critical projects with inquiries into how and why we (and other people) do and do not spend money. Juxtaposing value systems with context-specific, contingent data would surely yield surprising information for students and teachers while compiling a broad spectrum of situated experiences to question, discuss, and wonder beyond. Moreover, students' local inquiries could be pushed and framed by contemporary documentaries or internet exploration about life and spending in other countries. But to encourage students to push boundaries, to surprise us and their peers, teachers will likely need to acknowledge and even break classroom norms and taboos—modeling their own critical literacy performances that, like the politically incorrect jokes between Jessica and Santo, might not fall under the readily recognizable rubric of critical literacy. By leaning pedagogically into the critical literacy performances of students, teachers can unpack and build on literate practices in seemingly taboo classroom acts.

Notes

1 All participant names are pseudonyms.
2 Janks illustrates the limits of critical media analysis given affective responses to media.
3 To retain the lead author/researcher's positionality in this study, these vignettes are written in the first person. For more about this study, see Johnson (2011) or Johnson (2012).
4 Photoethnography is a method used in participatory action research to provide participants the opportunity to document and describe their perceptions on the topic of inquiry (Farough, 2006). Even though this was not a participatory action project, Liz sought insights into participant understandings and negotiations of popular culture texts. According to Pink (2001), conversations around photos may challenge researcher understandings of how participants position themselves in relationship to other people, social phenomena, and the conducted inquiry.
5 In the 1950s, Erving Goffman, a prominent Canadian social psychologist, utilized dramaturgical concepts to theorize distinctions between the performed and private self. His front and backstage assume that there are not audiences for backstage

performances. Poststructural performance theory conceptualizes people in perpetual performance (Butler, 1999; Bettie, 2003; Youdell, 2006). Here, center and backstage distinguishes performances loud enough to garner whole-class attention from backstage performances for far fewer, imagined, or absent audience members.

6 A series of videotaped comedy works by Ari Shaffir, a Los Angeles stand-up comedian, which features him acting in an overtly racist manner.

7 A video-sharing website where users can upload, view, share, and respond to video clips.

8 A 2006 comedy film based on the MTV series Jackass compiling stunts, pranks, and skits.

9 The third installment in the horror film series, released in 2006.

10 Characters in a comedy film series.

11 American actress, singer, songwriter, and entrepreneur born in 1987 and famous for starring on the TV show Lizzie McGuire.

12 A science fiction parody film directed by and starring Mel Brooks, released in 1987.

References

Alvermann, D. E., Moon, J. S., & Hagood, M. C. (1999). *Popular culture in the classroom: Teaching and researching critical media literacy.* Newark, DE: International Reading Association.

Bettie, J. (2003). *Women without class: Girls, race, and identity.* Berkeley, CA: University of California Press.

Blackburn, M. (2003). Exploring literacy performances and power dynamics at the loft: Queer youth reading the world and the word. *Research in the Teaching of English, 37,* 467–490.

Boler, M. (2004). *Democratic dialogue in education: Troubling speech, disturbing silence.* New York, NY: Peter Lang.

Bomer, R. & Laman, T. (2004). Positioning in a primary writing workshop: Joint action in the discursive production of writing subjects. *Research in the Teaching of English, 38,* 420–465.

Brooks, M. (Producer), & Brooks, M. (Director). (1987). *Spaceballs* [motion picture]. United States: Metro-Goldwyn-Mayer.

Burg, M., Hoffman, G., Koules, O. (Producers), & Bousman, D. L. (Director). (2006). *Saw III* [motion picture]. United States: Lionsgate.

Butler, J. (1999). *Gender trouble.* New York, NY: Routledge.

Comber, B. (2006). Critical literacy educators at work: Examining dispositions, discursive resources, and repertoires of practice. In K. Cooper and R. E. White (Eds.) *The practical critical educator: Critical inquiry and educational practice* (pp. 51–65). The Netherlands: Springer.

Enciso, P. (2007). Reframing history in sociocultural theories: Toward and expansive vision. In C. Lewis, P. Enciso, & E. B. Moje (Eds.) *Reframing sociocultural research on literacy: Identity, agency, and power* (pp. 49–74). Mahwah, NJ: Erlbaum.

Farough, S. (2006). Believing is seeing: The matrix of vision and White masculinities. *Journal of Contemporary Ethnography, 35,* 51–83.

Forman, M. (2005). Straight outta Mogadishu: Prescribed identities and performative practices among Somali youth in North American high schools. In S. Maira & E. Soep (Eds.) *Youthscapes: The popular, the national, the global* (pp. 1–22). Philadelphia, PA: University of Pennsylvania Press.

Foucault, M. (1979). *Discipline and punish: The birth of the prison*. Trans. A. Sheridan. New York, NY: Vintage.

Grace, D. J. & Tobin, J. (1998). Butt jokes and mean-teacher parodies: Video production in the elementary classroom. In D. Buckingham (Ed.) *Teaching popular culture: Beyond radical pedagogy* (pp. 42–62). London, UK: Routledge.

Gustavson, L. (2007). *Youth learning on their own terms: Creative practices and classroom teaching*. New York, NY: Routledge.

Hagood, M. (2004). A rhizomatic cartography of adolescents, popular culture, and constructions of self. In K. L. M. Sheehy (Ed.) *Spatializing literacy research and practice*. New York, NY: Peter Lang.

Howard, R., Johnson, M. (Producers), & Hancock, J. L. (Director). (2004). *The Alamo* [motion picture]. United States: Imagine Entertainment.

Janks, H. (2002). Critical literacy: Beyond reason. *Australian Educational Researcher, 29,* 7–27.

Jewitt, C. (2008). Multimodality and literacy in school classrooms. *Review of Research in Education, 32,* 241–267.

Johnson, E. (2011). "I've got swag": Simone performs critical literacy in a high school English classroom. *English Teaching Practice and Critique, 10* (3), 26–44.

Johnson, E. (2012). Performative politics and radical possibilities: Reframing pop culture text work in schools. *Journal of Curriculum Theorizing, 28* (1), 158–172.

Jonze, S., Knoxville, J., Tremaine, J. (Producers), & Tremaine, J. (Director). (2002). *Jackass: The movie* [motion picture]. United States: Paramount Pictures.

Kamler, B. (1997). Text as body, body as text. *Discourse: Studies in the Cultural Politics of Education, 18,* 369–387.

Knight, M. G., Dixon, I. R., Norton, N. E. L., & Bentley, C. C. (2006). Critical literacies as feminist affirmations and interventions: Contextualizing Latina youth's constructions of their college-bound identities. In D. D. Bernal, C. A. Elenes, F. E. Gonzalez, & S. Villenas (Eds.) *Chicana/Latina education in everyday life: Feminista perspectives on pedagogy and epistemology*. Albany, NY: SUNY Press.

Lewis, C., Doerr-Stevens, C., Tierney, J. D., & Scharber, C. (2013). Relocalization in the market economy: Critical literacies and media production in an urban English classroom. In J. Avila & J. Z. Pandya (Eds.) *Critical digital literacies as social praxis: Intersections and challenges* (pp. 179–196). New York, NY: Peter Lang.

Li Li, H. (2004). Rethinking silencing the silences. In M. Boler (Ed.) *Democratic dialogue in education: Troubling speech, disturbing silence* (pp. 69–88). New York: Peter Lang.

Lil Mama (2007). Lip gloss. On *VYP: Voice of the young people* [CD]. New York: Jive.

McCormick, J. (2003). "Drag me to the asylum": Disguising and asserting identities in an urban school. *The Urban Review, 35* (2), 111–127.

Moje, E. B. (2000). "To be part of the story": The literacy practices of gangsta adolescents. *Teachers College Record, 102* (3), 651–690.

Pink, S. (2001). *Doing visual ethnography: Images, media, and representation in research*. London, UK: Sage.

Pomerantz, S. (2008). Style and girl culture. In C. A. Mitchell & J. Reid-Walsh (Eds.) *Girl culture: An encyclopedia* (pp. 64–72). Westport, CT: Greenwood.

Schultz, K. (2009). *Rethinking classroom participation: Listening to silent voices*. New York, NY: Teachers College Press.

Shaffir, A. (2006, December 28). Amazing racist: Mexicans again! [video file]. Retrieved from http://www.liveleak.com/view?i=c6292e272d.

Shaffir, A. (2008, April 22). The amazing racist—Asians [video file]. Retrieved from http://www.youtube.com/watch?v=2RoNemjcjGE.

Siegel, M. (2006). Rereading the signs: Multimodal transformations in the field of literacy education. *Language Arts, 84,* 65–77.

Sipe, L. (2007). *Storytime: Young children's literary understanding in the classroom.* New York, NY: Teachers College Press.

Swain, J. (2002). The right stuff: Fashioning an identity through clothing in a junior school. *Gender and Education, 14* (1), 53–69.

Tremaine, J., Knoxville, J., Jonze, S. (Producers), & Tremaine, J. (Director). (2006). *Jackass number two* [motion picture]. United States: Paramount Pictures.

Vasquez, V. (2004). *Negotiating critical literacies with young children.* Mahwah, NJ: Lawrence Erlbaum Associates.

Vasquez, V. (2007). Using the everyday to engage in critical literacy with young children. *New England Reading Association Journal, 43,* 6–11.

Wortham, S. (2005). *Learning identity: The joint emergence of social identification and academic learning.* New York, NY: Cambridge University Press.

Youdell, D. (2006). *Impossible bodies, impossible selves: Exclusions and student subjectivities.* The Netherlands: Springer.

9

COMMUNITIES AS COUNTER-STORYTELLING (CON)TEXTS*

The Role of Community-Based Educational Institutions in the Development of Critical Literacy and Transformative Action

Enid M. Rosario-Ramos and Laura Ruth Johnson

Solórzano and Yosso (2002) define counter-storytelling as "a method of telling the stories of those people whose experiences are not often told (i.e., those on the margins of society). The counter-story is also a tool for exposing, analyzing, and challenging the majoritarian stories of racial privilege" (p. 32). In this chapter we argue that community-based institutions may use counter-storytelling practices as a way of challenging inequalities in their social worlds and of enacting social change.

Background Literature

Counter-storytelling educational institutions are characterized by a merging of community spaces and educational spaces, as community issues become central to the academic and intellectual development of young people. In activist communities, learning is connected to social change. In that sense, teaching and learning are processes through which community members—including adults and the youth they work with—reconstruct and reclaim their positions within society. Educational institutions within counter-storytelling communities actively participate in social change by doing more than teaching young people academic skills for adult life. They embody the practices of counter-storytelling and transformative action and allow young people to participate in the here and now as they develop into more sophisticated and central participants in their communities.

* This chapter is an expanded version of: Johnson, L. R. & Rosario-Ramos, E. M. (2012). The role of educational institutions in the development of critical literacy and transformative action. *Theory Into Practice*, *51* (1), 49-56. DOI: 10.1080/00405841.2012.636337. Reprinted by permission of Taylor & Francis (http://www.tandfonline.com).

Literacy is central to these processes. The ability to read the world and the word (Freire, 1970) as a collective process allows communities to challenge historical narratives that devalue their experiences, but also to support the development of such skills in and by young members. Intergenerational relationships are crucial in these processes as young people develop literacy skills and practices through their participation in discursive communities. On the other hand, as youth become more active participants in community struggle, their voices become part of the legacy of resistance and social change of the communities they inhabit.

Critical literacy involves the analysis and critique of the social structures that create inequality and the texts that embed these unequal relations, as well as the active engagement in the reconstruction of these social structures and their corresponding textual representations. Schools have traditionally offered few opportunities for students to critically analyze the socio-political histories and cultural lives and practices of their communities and to actively participate in the process of reading, and rewriting, their worlds (Freire, 1970). Worse yet, many schools have viewed low-income communities of color as hindrances to the academic success of students from those communities, rather than as resources and sites for the development of skills and knowledge (Briggs, 2002; Lewis, 1961; Moynihan, 1965).

Given the above concerns, we seek to explore how communities and community-based institutions can serve as contexts for not just the acquisition of knowledge but also the development of critical literacy frameworks among youth. Using examples from qualitative research projects conducted separately by the authors in a low-income, ethnically Puerto Rican community, we elaborate ways that schools can promote critical literacy, function as counter-storytelling institutions in which students are encouraged to critically examine society, and offer students opportunities to enact change within their communities. These ways include implementing curricula that challenge master narratives embedded in disciplinary knowledge, discursive practices that encourage and support reflection, and the utilization of the community as a textual resource.

Our views of critical literacy are informed by social justice-oriented theories in the field of education, most namely Freirian perspectives (1970) of education as a liberatory process that can lead to transformation and action. We are also inspired by participatory and popular education theories and approaches that advocate for social change and civic engagement as not only consequences of education but also as critical components of the educational process (Horton & Freire, 1990; Ginwright & Cammarota, 2007; Morrell, 2009). In our view, the types of community institutions that have the potential to address and promote critical literacy in authentic ways are situated within communities that have had to face marginalization and discrimination based on ethnicity, language, and socioeconomic class. However, it is not enough for community institutions just to be located within these communities to enable critical perspectives and bring about transformative action. They also need to have been founded upon principles of social justice with the intent of offering educational alternatives to residents and providing services and programs within a collective framework (Antrop-González & DeJesús, 2006).

Communities that provide rich opportunities for counter-storytelling are those that have historically had to contend with being defined by master narratives and dominant discourses about success and achievement. They have often been vilified and demonized in the public media for being infested with all sorts of "social ills", such as poverty, gang violence, undereducation, drug use, and teen pregnancy. Although residents in these communities would certainly admit to harsh realities and conditions, the ways that their lives and realities are constructed and portrayed by others as problematic and deficient ignore each community's cultural resources and social capital (Bourdieu, 1977).

These counter-storytelling contexts are often urban environments which were divested of institutionalized social and educational resources when White residents fled in the 1960s; during this time many served as sites of riots and rebellions, as community residents responded to national and local crises and challenged oppressive conditions. Many of these areas remained blighted and underresourced throughout the 1970s and '80s, as well as became hubs of political activism, giving birth to local grassroots community organizations offering educational, cultural, economic, and health services to residents. Because many of their community's resources and institutions have historically been taken away or destroyed, residents are acutely aware of the precarious position of their community relative to the larger society; thus, they are skilled at identifying and critically analyzing the sources of such injustice.

Programmatic Context

The educational programs used here as examples are all part of the Cultural Center,[1] a larger community-based organization that has been at the forefront of the community activism in the neighborhood where both authors did their research. This community-based organization and its affiliated institutions are located in an ethnically Puerto Rican neighborhood that has historically struggled with poverty, violence, displacement, and discrimination. However, despite—and perhaps as a result of—the difficult social conditions that residents were often forced to endure, local institutions have, for over three decades, been committed to the struggle for justice. The organization's community-building efforts have addressed a wide range of social issues, including education, health, violence, and affordable housing, among others. As part of this organization's educational agenda, various programs have been developed to address the needs of neighborhood residents. These include three separate but interconnected programs: an alternative high-school program, a General Educational Development (GED) program, and an educational program for young mothers that provides educational services for students' children. We will refer to these as the High School, the GED Program, and the Family Educational Center, respectively.

In addition to these three structured educational programs, the Youth Space stood as evidence of the role of youth in local activism. This arts-based youth-led space provided young people with a venue to discuss and address relevant issues such as neighborhood violence, educational disparities, and discrimination, among others.

The educational programs were central to the community organization's mission and its efforts towards social change. The staff and students of these programs were routinely seen contributing to community events and projects developed to address the needs of people in the neighborhood. Thus, the educational programs were, at the same time, the result of the community's commitment to transformative action and a central part of its sustainability.

The interconnections between the different community organizations in the neighborhood allow for permeability of information, people, and efforts across institutions, at the same time creating a sense of alignment and common purpose among the people and organizations involved. Furthermore, as these educational programs continue to be a close partner to community-based activist institutions, the boundaries between the school and community are blurred. In that sense, being positioned inside this larger group of institutions, and actively participating in the social change efforts within the neighborhood, allows these programs to create educational spaces where learning and active participation in transformative action are intertwined.

Findings

Three themes have emerged from our understanding of counter-storytelling communities. We will use the educational programs and the youth-led space mentioned above and their surrounding community as a case to illustrate: (1) how counter-storytelling institutions engage in the reconstruction of master narratives; (2) how the community becomes a classroom in these spaces; and (3) the role of intergenerational relationships in critical literacy learning and in reclaiming dignity.

Narratives that Humanize: Community Counter-Storytelling

Critical race theory provides a theoretical and methodological tool to examine the role of racial discrimination—and its intersections with other forms of oppression—in the organization of U.S. society (Ladson-Billings & Tate, 1995; Delgado Bernal, 1998; Solórzano & Yosso, 2002). Critical race theory and methods emphasize the need to challenge dominant ideologies and discourses as part of commitment to social justice. We argue that community institutions with a history of commitment to transformative action can and should join in the tradition of counter-storytelling because their practices often challenge mainstream discourses and social practices that marginalize people from non-dominant backgrounds (Freire, 1970; McLaren; 1989; Hooks, 1994). Ideally, these institutions are staffed by individuals who share and understand the experiences of students and community residents. Educational institutions can serve as production spaces for counter-narratives about communities, pedagogy, and student experiences, particularly if shared cultural-historical repertoires of practice (Gutiérrez & Rogoff, 2003)—or "ways of engaging in activities stemming from observing and otherwise participating in cultural practices" (p. 22)—help teachers and staff design and implement instructional activities that not only build upon students' backgrounds but are deeply rooted in their lived realities. Institutions that embody critical literacy frameworks—through their discursive, instructional, and institutional practices—are better positioned to provide students with models and strategies for engaging in this form of social analysis and to support their development of critical literacy frameworks.

For example, in an interview conducted for the first author's research project, the principal of the High School echoes views espoused by critical educators about the importance of challenging persisting ideas about success that privilege individualistic and meritocratic views of society and human experience. These deficit-oriented ways of explaining underachievement tend to blame inequality on presumed intellectual and character flaws of minoritized[2] communities by often perpetuating images of their children as uncommitted, unruly, and incapable of academic success. As this principal explained below, challenging these narratives requires a counter-narrative that redefines academic success by tying individual success to collective engagement:

> Those conditions, those situations that our students are going through are a manifestation of, not just the wrong individual experiences but their experiences as people . . . Successful, to the majority of high schools with these young students who are going through these problems, is getting them out of those problems, is having them go live in the suburbs, or having them go into a college that's far away so that they don't have to deal with what they dealt with their whole lives, right? ⠂. . Instead what we tell them is that they have the capacity to be successful, which means that they become leaders in their community.

Counter-storytelling communities have the potential of providing young people with structured opportunities to redefine their experiences and their relationships with their communities. These institutions focus their attention on emphasizing and capitalizing on the community resources available, rather than contributing to traditional narratives that view their community members as dangerous, careless, and irresponsible. In the educational programs we studied, young people were conceptualized as important assets for social change. Also, as the principal explained, success in this community referred to young people's ability to develop and use their skills to contribute to the community's efforts towards social justice. Educational institutions' commitment to transformative action involves the deconstruction and reconstruction of traditional narratives about students' abilities and experiences, about the role and purpose of education and achievement, and the nature and location of knowledge.

Yet, such commitment does not end with the discursive practices of the staff of these educational programs. The organizations' commitment to counter-storytelling also involved the creation of spaces where young people themselves could rewrite their own narratives. For example, the counter-storytelling tradition of this community included the use of spoken-word poetry as a tool for rewriting narratives and contributing to change. The Youth Space, as explained earlier in this chapter, is evidence of the relationship between literacy, counter-storytelling, and community activism. At this space, young people from the neighborhood organized events where poetry, hip-hop, and theater become tools for challenging injustice and redefining unequal social structures.

For example, in the poem *Why I Don't Cry Blood,* Jordan, a graduate of the High School and leader of the Youth Space, described the violence of her life experiences. She discussed her family's struggles with drug addiction and violence, as well as her own involvement with gangs. She discussed these experiences as the result of having to "deal with this white privilege, colonialism, colored people oppressed bullshit." Thus, she explained her family's experiences as the result of larger social systems of inequality rather than stemming from character flaws of her family members. She also alluded to being "born into a family that has no knowledge [of] it," referring to the understanding of the structural nature of inequality as an impediment to their ability to enact change. Yet, literacy appears in her poem as a tool for negotiating and reconstructing these inequalities and the narratives that sustain them. As Jordan explained; "all my struggles and heartaches is in the color of my ink." And her "ink" did not remain in paper. Jordan often read her poetry at community events and presented her work at her college, where she was also a student leader.

At the Family Educational Center's literacy program for mothers, local authors led writing and poetry workshops that facilitated students' creative expression. One student, a mother in her 20s who had become pregnant as an adolescent, wrote a poem about her father's hometown of Ponce, Puerto Rico, and the carnival masks for which they were famous. Another poem she was especially known for is entitled *Powerful Woman*, in which she deployed her own experiences to celebrate woman of all "races and colors" and "shapes and sizes," repeating the refrain "Powerful Woman, that's me," finally ending more collectively with a strong "Powerful Woman, that's *we*." Within this piece, she tackled stereotypes about low-income women of color by projecting her own vision of what it means to be "powerful": "a woman that thinks about her kids . . . intelligent, self-confident, independent . . . a woman with a mind of her own." When discussing her poetry, she acknowledged the program, and the larger work of the community-spaced organization, as a "space" where she was able to gain "dignity" and "pride in [her] culture" and learn about the "importance of community." She described her overall experience in the program thusly: "it helped me discover the special person inside of me." Through this writing, she was able to use writing to celebrate aspects of her background, most namely her familial heritage and role as a woman. These writings, and her numerous performances of them at local events (and she also performed them at a conference in New York City), served to affirm her own background and identity, as well as destabilize and challenge majoritarian narratives about women and mothers in her community and their opportunities to be independent and successful.

Community as Classroom: The Use of Community Spaces as Instructional Contexts

A primary way that institutions can serve as sites of counter-storytelling is by utilizing students' own lives and communities as contexts for the development of critical literacy skills. Relevant social and political issues and concepts such as the democratic process, housing, underage drinking, immigration, obesity, and gentrification can be discussed in connection with current community struggles, and employed as textual resources, often engendering the creation of new texts.

For example, young Latina mothers attending the Family Educational Center's literacy program that was studied by the second author participated in demonstrations to save a community mural from being covered by a condominium. The mural, entitled "The Crucifixion of Don Pedro," was the oldest Puerto Rican mural in the city and depicted historical figures significant to the island's independence movement. There exist numerous photographs documenting the standoff between community members and the construction crew, where program women are pictured among community leaders and activists holding placards containing slogans such as "Stop Gentrification Now." In another photograph, which appeared in a local university Latino student publication, one student's son was perched on scaffolding, with the mural serving as a backdrop.

The mural event gave rise to numerous discussions and activities within classes at the program: a group of women wrote a collaborative story centering on the mural, classes reviewed the mural's historical content, and groups discussed the related issues of gentrification and the displacement of Puerto Ricans at the root of the mural's uncertain future. The creation of the collaborative story involved students in the tasks of discussing, drafting, composing, and revising, all traditionally important oral and written communication skills. In addition, as they were creating this written text, they were engaging in dialogue around the content of the mural, as well as providing a critique of the social and economic forces that threatened it, and, more broadly, also jeopardized the vitality and stability of their community. As they were deliberating about how to begin their story one student asked, "Why now they want to come into our community and make gentrification?" Another student described how they should begin: "Start talking about the mural and what it means to be Puerto Rican." As another student began to draft the story, she stated: "We feel that they can't destroy our memories . . . something that they didn't create."

Another afterschool multimedia project, that has been observed by both authors as a part of their research and their involvement with the community referenced throughout the article, involved youth in using literacy to address the issue of underage drinking. Students participated in discussion groups to identify an important social issue around which to design an educational campaign. They conducted research on the topic and designed a survey to collect data from community members. They then used this data to produce posters and a book aimed at disseminating this information and raising community awareness about the issue. Large, colorfully designed posters were featured prominently in storefront windows along the main community strip, proclaiming "Teach me how to live responsibly" or "This is the real me," with accompanying statistics culled from the surveys about underage drinking in the community: "93% of community teens surveyed say their parents do not serve them alcohol" and "3 out of 4 community teens don't think drinking makes them look cool." Students also planned and implemented a series of the events, designing eye-catching postcards to publicize each activity, which promoted cultural and creative expression over less productive pursuits such as drinking. Each card featured a close-up photograph of a community youth involved in the project and slogans such as "Drop the bottle, Pick up the mic" and "Drop the bottle, Let the pen flow." All of the cards also included the following verbiage: "Facing our issues isn't easy. Alcohol doesn't make them easier."

The above examples demonstrate how significant community events and issues can serve as springboards for a variety of educational and literacy activities, and facilitate critical dialogue around topics meaningful to students' lives. In these ways, the community becomes a classroom that fosters knowledge and skills, as well as enables critiques of, and action against, unequal and oppressive social and economic conditions. This type of promotion and engagement on the part of schools and educational institutions entails more than merely addressing community issues within the classroom setting. Rather, students must be engaged as active participants in activities and projects and their involvement must be linked with instructional content, both in and out of the traditional classroom.

In both of the above cases, students became dynamic participants in issues that directly, and sometimes deeply, affected their lives, such as gentrification and alcohol use/alcoholism. At the same time that they were involved in these efforts, they were creating texts that allowed for critical reflection on their import and significance and the transmission of these experiences to others within the community and beyond. By providing such opportunities for engagement, students insert themselves, their communities, and their families into the educational process and work towards positive change and transformation of their communities (Horton & Freire, 1990). In the process, they are challenging discourses that position youth as either perpetrators of social ills, or merely complacent bystanders of community problems. Furthermore, this approach acknowledges students' families and communities not only as "funds of knowledge" (Gonzalez, Moll, & Amanti, 2005), or sources of knowledge, skills, and experiences that can be integrated into the classroom, but as contexts containing vast storehouses of experiences and skills that can themselves serve as instructional settings. What differentiates the approaches described in our research is that they are not merely concerned with validating and integrating existing familial and community knowledge into the classroom, but also with building new knowledge and experiential frameworks.

Intergenerational Learning and Reclaiming History and Dignity

In counter-storytelling communities, the histories and experiences of multiple generations often interact. In their work as active agents of change, young people are given the opportunity to learn alongside and about previous generations. This is supported by their interactions with members of older generations who not only are willing to share the lessons learned through the communities' histories of struggle, but also allow young people to actively contribute to and shape the direction of new efforts for social change. Furthermore, histories of struggle interact as multiple generations come together to derive meaning from their different experiences and to create alignment in their goals.

In communities struggling for justice, youths' pathways towards central participation are supported by adults who are committed to collective struggle, recognize the value of youth voices in resistance, and are willing to engage in transformative action with them (Antrop-González & De Jesús, 2006). Through the development of interpersonal relationships with caring adults who model critical literacy and counter-storytelling, students learn to take ownership and responsibility for the future of their communities. Students recognize and appreciate these opportunities. In the words of a young man who described his engagement in community-building efforts:

> Well it gives you—it shows a sense of responsibility. It also shows . . . that you should be aware because you know these things are happening in the community. Or, you know we're trying to change things in the community and it's—it's a sort of a preparation to transcend into adult life. Because a lot of these issues surround adults and they are the one who really deal with it but then again it's like we got our voice too.

These opportunities for intent participation (Rogoff, Paradise, Mejía Arauz, Correa-Chávez, & Angellilo, 2003)—or learning through intentional observation of informal community activities—serve as authentic contexts for developing important literacy skills. As they participate in community-building efforts, students learn the power of language as a tool to challenge inequality. Writing poetry, creating art, and producing multimedia texts are just a few examples of the literacy skills young people employ as they engage in authentic processes of social change. This learning is not decontextualized and alienated from students' community lives, but is deeply embedded in their experiences as community members and supported by their relationships with caring adults. Furthermore, these skills are acquired in contexts where learning is not merely an individual intellectual process but is a social practice embedded in real-life situations that can have significant consequences for the lives of students and their families. A female high-school student explained the kinds of texts she liked to produce:

> Love, hate, struggle, same things I like reading about actually . . . I've started actually writing a lot about our political prisoners, about [the neighborhood], and my ethnic, my Puerto Ricanness.

The issues mentioned by this student are constantly debated and discussed within her community. In that sense, her participation as a student in the high school and a leader of the Youth Space, mentioned earlier, has given her access to critical discourses about issues relevant to the community while supporting the development of critical literacy frameworks and skills that allow her to be actively engaged in counter-storytelling.

One example of a project where intergenerational exchanges provided opportunities for youths to work alongside community adults in the struggle for justice was the campaign for the release of Puerto Rican political prisoners. Many community resources were used to advocate for the release of Puerto Rican political prisoners, two of whom had been community organizers in the neighborhood studied. These two men were also involved in the creation of the educational programs discussed here. Young people, through their participation in educational programs and other community projects, had the opportunity to learn about the community's fight for the liberation of their prisoners. Furthermore, they had the opportunity to work with adults in the community to bring awareness to the campaign for the liberation of these men. One way young people were involved was through the development and presentation of a play about the lives of Puerto Rican political prisoners while incarcerated. This project was done in collaboration with present and former political prisoners who offered their stories to the young people. Naturally, literacy played a central role in crafting this theater piece. The young people involved listened to interviews with the prisoners and other community members, developed scripts for the play, built the stage scene, worked on promoting the play, and even participated in a tour that included stops in various cities in the United States and Puerto Rico.

A key outgrowth of this approach to critical literacy is the way it enables students to reclaim their dignity in the face of deficit perspectives about minoritized communities. For example, at the aforementioned program for young parents studied by the second author, young Latina mothers were trained to conduct oral history interviews with older generations of women in their family—mothers, aunts, and grandmothers in a class entitled "Women, Oral History, and Community Memory." They designed an interview guide, practiced interviewing, wrote reflective papers on the interviews, and presented their findings to their peers. In interviews with their female forebears, students gained knowledge about their family and local history and the struggles incurred by many women in their families. These narratives offered them valuable lessons about resilience and fortitude, and highlighted the commonality of experiences across generations of women.

The process of conducting and discussing the interviews also led them to make connections between the preservation of their familial stories and histories and the survival of the community. One student, a 28-year-old mother of three, expressed her belief that "when you interview someone you get educated," and another mother thought it was important to gather the history of one's family and community "so we can pass [it] on to our kids." Another student mentioned the community mural that had recently been the focus of protests, to emphasize the importance of preserving culture. In her words: "interviews are history." Other students spoke to the overall significance of sharing stories to cultural survival, as evidenced in the cautionary words of one student: "If you don't tell stories they get destroyed." The earlier example of the young mother writing poetry about her father's hometown also illustrates how learning about one's history can help fortify connections with the past. The genesis of this poem, entitled *Me Recuerdo*, was a mask-making activity, where students were involved in making *papier mâché* masks, which had their origins in her father's birthplace.

Through these projects and endeavors, students were able to rediscover and reclaim family and community narratives and celebrate them as worthy of examination. Such a perspective provides a rejoinder to the "breaking cycles" rhetoric used in many educational programs that urge residents in low-income communities to sever ties with previous generations and their communities in order to get ahead and be successful. As we have described earlier, the discourse in this community promoted returning to the *barrio*, or neighborhood, as a critical metric of one's success. The organization facilitated this interchange between older generations of graduates from the high school and literacy program and current students by hiring these individuals to work for their programs and providing opportunities for them to "give back." For example, graduates were regularly invited to serve as panelists for an annual portfolio evaluation required of graduates from the High School and Family Educational Center's literacy program. The director of the Cultural Center's childcare and the director of their AIDS/health education program were both graduates of the organization's educational programs. And, as this piece was being written, the Family Educational Center's literacy program was creating and beginning to implement a series of presentations that would feature mothers who had graduated from the program since its inception in 1993 to share their experiences with adolescent mothers who were currently enrolled.

Such exchanges and events help promote intergenerational dialogue and mentorship, as well as foster understandings of common struggles as they forge new paths for their futures.

Concluding Remarks and Implications for Practice

We have argued that communities where the struggle against oppression is a constant battle are uniquely positioned to provide critical education that allows young people to develop critical literacy skills and frameworks as they participate in transformative action. This education requires community members and caring adults who actively engage in challenging deficit-oriented master narratives about oppressed communities, who are capable of feeling *critical hope* (Duncan-Andrade, 2009) for and with their communities, and who engage in resistance and transformative action as a way of reclaiming their community's dignity and humanity.

In order to contribute to communities' struggles for justice and to their commitment to supporting young people's development of critical literacy frameworks, we offer some ideas for organizing teaching and learning:

- Develop learning activities around community issues relevant to the lives of students and their families.
- Identify local organizations committed to social change and capitalize on their efforts and resources to engage students in community-building processes.
- Create learning activities that enable opportunities for students to learn from and with adult members of their communities.
- Facilitate and promote students' access to a variety of texts that reflect their realities, and foster students' own production of texts—broadly defined to include print, film, and other media—describing and depicting their lived experiences.
- Provide mentorship opportunities that connect previous generations of participants of the educational programs to current enrollees as a way of encouraging and supporting intergenerational exchange of resources and dialogue about the community's experiences.

Although other researchers have documented and described the ways that community contexts and students' lived realities serve as resources in the development of critical literacy, our work is unique in the way that it explores how specific institutions can function as sites for counter-storytelling and provide settings for interconnected processes of reflection and action. In this process, critical literacy is not merely the goal or outcome of literacy instruction, but offers a means of becoming more actively involved in the community—what we refer to as literacy for action—and further developing one's capacities to engage in critique, or action for, literacy.

Notes

1 All names of people and places are pseudonyms.
2 We use the word *minoritized* to highlight the socially constructed nature of minority status, which responds to unequal power relationships and social dynamics, rather than mere demographic data.

References

Antrop-González, R. & DeJesús, A. (2006). Toward a theory of *critical care* in urban small school reform: Examining structures and pedagogies of caring in two Latino community-based schools. *International Journal of Qualitative Studies in Education, 19,* 409–433.

Bourdieu, P. (1977). *Outline of a theory of practice.* Cambridge, UK: Cambridge University Press.

Briggs, L. (2002). La Vida, Moynihan, and other libels: Migration, social science, and the making of the Puerto Rican welfare queen. *CENTRO: Journal of Center for Puerto Rican Studies, 14,* 75–101.

Delgado Bernal, D. (1998). Using a Chicana feminist epistemology in educational research. *Harvard Educational Review, 68,* 555–582.

Duncan-Andrade, J. M. R. (2009). Note to educators: Hope required when growing roses in concrete. *Harvard Educational Review, 79,* 181–194.

Freire, P. (1970). *Pedagogy of the oppressed.* New York, NY: Seabury Press.

Ginwright, S. & Cammarota, J. (2007). Youth activism in the urban community: Learning critical civic praxis within community organizations. *International Journal of Qualitative Studies in Education, 20,* 693–710.

Gonzalez, N., Moll, L., & Amanti, C. (Eds.) (2005). *Funds of knowledge: Theorizing practices in households and classrooms.* Mahwah, NJ: Lawrence Erlbaum.

Gutiérrez, K. D. & Rogoff, B. (2003). Cultural ways of learning: Individual traits or repertoires of practice. *Educational Researcher, 32,* 19–25.

Horton, M. & Freire, P. (1990). *We make the road by walking: Conversations on education and social change.* Philadelphia, PA: Temple University Press.

Hooks, B. (1994). *Teaching to transgress: Education as the practice of freedom.* New York, NY: Routledge.

Ladson-Billings, G. & Tate, W. (1995). Toward a critical race theory of education. *Teachers College Record, 97,* 47–68.

Lewis, O. (1961). *La Vida: A Puerto Rican family in the culture of poverty—San Juan and New York.* New York, NY: Random House.

McLaren, P. (1989). *Life in schools: An introduction to critical pedagogy in the foundations of education.* New York, NY: Longman.

Morrell, E. (2009). Critical research and the future of literacy education. *Journal of Adolescent & Adult Literacy, 53,* 96–104.

Moynihan, D. P. (1965). *The Negro family: The case for national action.* Washington, DC: U.S. Government Printing Office.

Rogoff, B., Paradise, R., Mejía Arauz, R., Correa-Chávez, M., & Angelillo, C. (2003). Firsthand learning through intent participation. *Annual Review of Psychology, 54,* 175–203.

Solórzano, D. & Yosso, T. (2002). Critical race methodology: Counter-storytelling as an analytical framework for education research. *Qualitative Inquiry, 8,* 23–44.

SECTION III

Revisions of Critical Literacy

10

TEXT COMPLEXITY

The Battle for Critical Literacy in the Common Core State Standards

Michael Moore, Don Zancanella, and JuliAnna Ávila

Introduction: A Plethora of Terms

When a new education policy is imposed from above it often takes control of whatever aspects of schooling it targets as well as the language and concepts connected to those aspects of schooling. For example, when No Child Left Behind (NCLB) was instituted, terms such as "highly qualified" (i.e., "highly qualified teacher") and "scientific" (i.e., "scientifically based research") quickly came to mean, at least within the boundaries of NCLB, what the authors of the policy wanted them to mean. A teacher was qualified to teach a particular subject in accordance with the definition in the policy, and other definitions related to teacher qualifications, as well as various levels of teacher qualifications, were, for all intents and purposes, irrelevant.

Related to this is the way in which particular policies may avoid the use of particular terms. To use NCLB again as an example, the use of the term "qualitative research" was avoided in official materials related to NCLB. This caused research from qualitative perspectives to be devalued or even disregarded in discussions about NCLB, despite the fact that the research landscape of education immediately prior to NCLB featured a rich mix of various research methodologies and many prominent researchers had argued that thoughtful policy making should take research from a range of perspectives into consideration.

Now a new policy, the Common Core State Standards (CCSS), has been imposed on schools and teachers across most of America. Although the political process used to create and adopt the policy is somewhat different from NCLB (as we will explain later in the chapter), what is not different is the way in which particular terms and concepts are being aggressively shaped or, in some cases, avoided.

In this chapter, we examine how both the term and concept of reading/literacy, which has a complex history and a rich body of research, is made to mean what the authors of the CCSS want it to mean. To do this, they rely on two naïve notions of reading/literacy, one of which suggests that simply reading difficult texts makes one a better reader, and the other, which suggests that meaning lies in the text and only in the text. Just as importantly, CCSS authors ignore another notion of reading/literacy, known as "critical literacy." By examining the particular view of literacy taken up by the CCSS, we expose some of the assumptions on which they are based. In addition, we step outside the CCSS and apply a critical literacy lens—drawing on Luke (2012) and others—to the Standards themselves.

Reading Between the Lines, a 2006 ACT study, played a significant role in shaping the CCSS and in shaping the new terms of how we think about reading. This study compared high-school instruction with the expectations of college course work. According to *Reading Between the Lines*,

> The most important implication of this study was that a pedagogy focused only on "higher order" or "critical thinking" was insufficient to ensure that students were ready for college and careers: what students could read, in the terms of its complexity, was at least as important as what they could do with what they read.
>
> *(This passage is directly quoted in the CCSS; p. 2.)*

Although neither "higher order thinking" nor "critical thinking" is subsequently defined in the ACT report (or used in the CCSS English Language Arts Standards), it is clear that the authors intended to diminish the importance of instruction that focused on such thinking or at least to suggest that such thinking is a by-product of the reading of complex texts. This diminishing of critical thinking as an instructional concept implies that the act of reading of complex texts *in and of itself* should be the primary driver of learning to read.

If *Reading Between the Lines* or the CCSS had defined "critical thinking" or its attendant pedagogies, they might have pointed out that approaches to instruction that value higher-order thinking typically draw on Bloom's taxonomy and involve synthesizing information to inform comprehension. Such teaching encourages students to seek connections between experiences, other readings, texts, and media to apply to the comprehension of a text; it may also encourage students to challenge basic assumptions of a text and question its intent and inferences. The outcome of such pedagogy is often described as "critical thinking" and represents a disciplined thinking process that may challenge aspects of any given text. These challenges may include questions about a text's situation in a political, cultural, economic, or social context. As a whole, this view of higher-order thinking/critical thinking could well be described as a socio-cultural view (Vygotsky, 1978; Bruner, 1990; Wertsch, 1991). It also overlaps with what has come to be known as *critical literacy* (Freire, 1970; Aukerman, 2012; Avila & Moore, 2012; Luke, 2012). It is the absence of "the critical" in the CCSS that we find problematic.

By making "text complexity" the primary focus of the CCSS and by implying that critical thought is at best a side-effect of reading complex texts (and even that instruction focusing on critical thought is detrimental), the CCSS authors provide a vision of schooling that overvalues texts and undervalues readers, teachers, and sociocultural contexts. Furthermore, by failing to show how concepts such as high-order thinking, critical thinking, and critical literacy are related to text complexity in a clear and explicit fashion, the authors of the CCSS essentially dumb down the Standards, suggesting that reading well is just a matter of figuring out what the author says. In the following, we argue drawing on critical literacy would have been a better approach for the CCSS authors to take.

Text Complexity and Critical Literacy

In the CCSS, the concept of text complexity is put forth as a universal means of improving the ability of students to read. We can say this because Reading and Literature Standard Ten, which is the standard that focuses on text complexity, appears at all grade levels and in both the Reading Literature and Reading Informational Text strands. In every instance the wording is virtually the same: "By the end of the year, read and comprehend [literary or informational texts] at the high end of the [specific grade level] text complexity band independently and proficiently."

In Appendix A (http://www.corestandards.org/), we learn what the term text complexity means. Put simply, text complexity is the idea that students are now reading less complex (i.e., difficult) material in school than in past years; that if we return to having them read more complex material, their reading ability will improve; and that judging the relative complexity of a text involves the application of basic readability formulas plus expert judgment of the qualitative feature of a given text plus teacher judgment related to who will be doing the reading and what task(s) they will be asked to perform. Adams (2009) is cited as supporting the CCSS approach: "To grow, our students must read lots, and more specifically they must read lots of 'complex' texts—texts that offer them new language, new knowledge, and new modes of thought" (p. 182). To put it more bluntly, if kids are required to read harder books, kids will become better readers.

However, if one returns to *Reading Between the Lines*, one finds a slightly more nuanced explanation of what makes a text complex. It states that complex text is complex in relationships, richness, structure, style, vocabulary, and purpose (p. 17). These words imply that a complex text may be complex because of how it is used ("purpose"), its meaning in a particular setting or context ("relationships"), and its subjective qualities ("richness"). While the CCSS definition of text complexity does include some attention to these elements (mostly through the "Reader and Task" part of the model), the text complexity model is so rudimentary that questions such as where does the concept of "purpose" fit in and could engaging in self-reflection qualify as a "task" are impossible to answer. Again, one is tempted to return to our slightly sarcastic way of defining the CCSS approach: If kids read harder books, they'll become better readers.

An alternative perspective is one supplied by critical literacy, a well-researched way of explaining the nature of literacy as well as to approaching instruction, which the CCSS nonetheless ignore. Critical literacy focuses on how discourses interact with culture, power systems, economics, and social systems. According to Luke (2012),"The term *critical literacy* refers to the use of the technologies of print and other media of communication to analyze, critique, and transform the norms, rule systems and practices governing the social fields of everyday life" (p. 5). This is a quite different perspective on literacy from that found in the CCSS. Instead of assuming that a high level of literacy is the product of reading complex texts, critical literacy assumes that a high level of literacy is the product of working with texts of all kinds *in complex and authentic contexts*.Critical literacy certainly includes analyzing and parsing discourses for relationships, richness, structure, style, vocabulary, and purpose, as the ACT report recommends. But in the view of critical literacy, all of these elements are embedded in and even created by the "social fields of everyday life" (Luke, 2012).

So why didn't the authors of the CCSS draw upon the rich literature of critical literacy? Why did they choose to describe literacy in what, to many literacy scholars in the twenty-first century, would seem to be an almost willfully naïve manner, more reminiscent of the New Critics from the 1930s (Ransom, 1979)? To answer this question, we first need to step back and provide an ecology of the education reform movement. This is necessary because the CCSS as well as the concept of text complexity are products of this movement.

An Ecology of the Common Core State Standards

It is not possible to name a specific moment when the current era of education reform began, but one oft-cited starting point is the 1989 Charlottesville, Virginia Summit hosted by then President George H.W. Bush and led by Arkansas Governor Bill Clinton. Summit participants were characterized in the *New York Times* as "scared to death about the quality of the schools" (Fisk, 1989). Embedded in the discussions that took place at Charlottesville were the seeds of what would later become the core tenets of education reform: accountability, goals, competition, and teacher quality (Zancanella & Moore, in press). Helping to fuel the reform fires were emerging and proliferating public policy organizations that developed a keen interest in education and kept reform at the forefront of state and national politics with a barrage of shocking statistics, especially regarding test scores on the National Assessment of Educational Progress.

These organizations were so effective that, by the year 2000, a Brookings Institute paper noted that "standards-based reform" was the most prominent and widely accepted strategy to come out of the still-young reform movement:

> Although enormous variation is evident in the quality of state standards and assessments and in the sophistication of state thinking about implementation, we believe that a broad enough consensus exists across the states on the core elements of this strategy to warrant our characterization of standards based reform as America's *de facto* national education policy.
>
> *(Schwartz & Robinson, 2000, p. 173)*

This approach would be the ruling one for over another decade.

In 2001 the rewrite of the Elementary and Secondary Education Act became known as "No Child Left Behind" (NCLB). All 50 states complied with the act for fear of losing federal monies, which would not be forthcoming otherwise. The literacy arm of NCLB was the Reading First Act, which poured a billion dollars a year into elementary schools with low scores. NCLB and Reading First opened the door to standards and standards-based assessments connected to a national infrastructure. NCLB was also pivotal because state control of schools merged with private commercial enterprises for control of curricula. Reading First designated only a certain handful of commercial programs as purchasable with federal dollars, thereby closing the door on a number of publishers and opening the door of a large bonanza for others. Further, only certain types of research (primarily quantitative psychometric research) were used to justify the approaches teachers were to use in Reading First classrooms. This is the research that would be funded for the next 10 years, until Reading First began to lose favor, partly because of studies by the National Center for Education Evaluation and Regional Assistance (2009) showing the program had little positive impact.

Of course even schools not touched by Reading First had to comply with the NCLB testing requirements. Smagorinsky (2012) estimated that state testing alone generated 20–50 billion dollars a year in lucrative state contracts. Sanctioned publishing companies of literacy materials also made state tests. Thus, over time, both financial links between curricula and testing began to become more pronounced.

Also during the NCLB era, entrepreneurs and non-profit enterprises began to play a larger role in educational policy making. Prominent groups included The Education Trust, Achieve, Inc., The Fordham Foundation, America's Choice, The Walton Family, and the Broad Foundation. Each took a different approach, but in general, their method was to use their funds (which came from a wide range of public and private sources) to push the "reform" agenda. As previously stated, this included more focus on test-based accountability, teacher quality/accountability, and competition. However, all of them combined could not match the influence of the Bill and Melinda Gates Foundation (Barkan, 2012).

To date, the Bill and Melinda Gates Foundation has awarded $208,525,418 in grant money for elementary and secondary education (Ash, 2012). Because these organizations had been quite successful (in fund raising and impacting policy), when one critique of NCLB was that state standards (and therefore state tests) were too diverse, it was not surprising to see them support the idea of a common set of standards across states. In fact, they were so supportive of the idea that it actually emerged from within these organizations, especially Achieve. In a rather short period from 2010 and 2011, the notion that states would sign on to using a set of standards produced by a non-profit think tank (again, Achieve, in partnership with the National Governors Association and the Council of Chief State School Officers) went from being an improbability to a certainty.

One of the main reasons the concept gained such rapid acceptance was because The Gates Foundation funded a wide range of public and private organizations to assure the approval of CCSS (Zancanella & Moore, in press). Gifts included $35 million to the National Governors Association and the Council of Chief State School Officers to direct The Common Core Standards as well as $6.3 million to the American Federation of Teachers and The National Education Association to ensure that the teachers' unions were receptive.

What is perhaps most notable about this entire process, from the emergence of the think tanks and non-governmental or quasigovernmental education reform entities, through the growth of the reform movement, up to the current implementation of the CCSS, is the way in which independent actors such as Achieve and the Gates Foundation began to reshape the entire educational landscape of the United States. This both empowered the reform movement and insulated it. Barkan (2012) noted,

> Moreover, the large private foundations that fund the ed[ucation] reformers are accountable to no one—not to voters, not to parents, not to the children whose lives they affect. The beefed-up political strategy extends the damage: the ed[ucation] reformers (most of whom take advantage of tax-exempt status) are immersing themselves in the dollars-mean-votes world of lobbying and campaigning (p. 50).

Ball (2008) refers to the new social education order as the "power elite" that brings members into newly articulated relationships with state education and education policy. In order to understand the CCSS and the key concepts of text complexity, it is important to understand the newly reformed education state that allowed for the development of national standards with virtually no input from traditional state stakeholders.

This new state, which Ball (2009) defines as one of "network governance," changes the ways schools are organized and promotes the privatization of education reform. Not only can this "power elite" shape policy, it can create opportunities for private-sector services (Burch, 2006). These services include: test development and the attendant preparation (including information and communication technologies (ICTs), data analysis and management, content materials and ultimately remedial services. Ball (2012) contends that, "policy networks do constitute a new form of government, albeit not in a single and coherent form, and bring into play in the policy process new sources of authority" (p. 9).

This history of education reform and the structures that have emerged from it (such as those Ball describes) are important to understand because the CCSS and the concept of text complexity were written/designed by actors who emerged from this history and these structures and take their legitimacy almost entirely from them. A key example is David Coleman who, with Sue Pimental, is typically credited as being one of the "lead authors" of Common Core English Language Arts Standards. In keeping with the pattern of influence coming from outside traditional education institutions and structures, Coleman came to the CCSS project not from a school or university or state department of education but from the world of business consulting and entrepreneurship. Thus, one can learn a good deal about Coleman and, by extension, the CCSS, by studying the role of the Coleman's former employer, consulting firm McKinsey and Company, in education reform.

McKinsey and Company is an example of a multinational consulting agency that first noted the financial ripeness of education reform. Beginning in the 1990s, it became a conduit for social, political, and economic relationships with reformers. Former McKinsey employees such as Sir Michael Barber and Coleman entered the reform area and bartered these connections on both sides of the ocean into lucrative and influential education positions. Barber, who was head of U.K. Prime Minister Tony Blair's Deliverology Unit (Barber, 2011) from 1997 to 2007, is now Chief Education Advisor for Pearson, the publishing giant, and a major player in the CCSS curriculum models and assessments. Coleman, self-described chief writer of the English Language Arts CCSS, was a McKinsey consultant. He is now President of the College Board. In describing "policy networks," Ball (2009) uses the term "market of authorities" (p. 9). Actors such as Barber and Coleman use their access to money and power as a way to build profitable businesses related to education or gain profitable positions within existing education-related businesses (profit or non-profit) and to influence public education policy. (And lest one assume non-profits such as the College Board do not lead to riches, Gaston Caperton, its previous president, was paid $1.3 million dollars per years and 19 other College Board employees make over $300,000 per year [Lorin, 2011].)

Pedagogy of the Newly Oppressed

New players such as Barber and Coleman are in positions that allow them to shape public education while also remaining connected to an array of think tanks and businesses that are quite different from the groups that have been involved in the making of education policy in the past. This matters because these new actors bring to policy making a different and, we would argue, underinformed view of teaching, learning, and schooling. Indeed, David Coleman has never been a classroom teacher, teacher educator, school administrator, or state education official. Yet he helped lead the development of the CCSS for English Language Arts. This occurred because he is an active participant in the new policy networks Ball describes. Here we can begin to see the linkage between the new landscape of education policy making and implementation (i.e., Ball's networks) and the CCSS. We can also begin to understand how this new landscape impacted the view of literacy embedded in the CCSS.

In an interview published in the *The Atlantic* (Goldstein, 2012), Coleman remarked, "I'm scared of rewarding bullshit." According to Goldstein's article, "By bullshit, Coleman means the sort of watered down curriculum that has become the norm in many American classrooms." To understand Coleman's thinking better, one can go to a video from a gathering of educators at the New York Department of Education in 2011. There, he said, "[A]s you grow up in this world you realize people really don't give a shit about what you feel or what you think." According to Coleman (Tyre, 2012), "a pedagogical pendulum has swung too far, favoring self-expression and emotion over lucid communication." Remarks such as these suggest two things: (1) that Coleman's understanding of what happens in contemporary classrooms is a caricature of what actually happens. Informed researchers would be unlikely to make such broad-brush generalizations about the "pedagogical pendulum," especially when being interviewed about an extremely important policy initiative; and (2) Coleman views texts as objects people produce to meet the needs of employers and other superiors ("people really don't give a shit") and that the work of readers and writers is to produce what those superiors require. Even to put the issue in these terms, however, is to take the view that acknowledges context and how it shapes literacy events.

The regrettable thing about Coleman's view is in what he *does not* say: Students need to be able to read and write in a range of contexts and to analyze the way literacy functions in those contexts. Such contexts include school, the workplace, and the civic square. We suggest that he doesn't say that because his view of literacy is a naïve one, in which readers and writers in school and the workplace are given tasks to perform and they perform those tasks *without* analyzing the context—or at least only analyzing the features of the context the teacher or employer asks them to analyze.

There are certainly traditional stakeholders such as boards of education, administrators, and teachers who would feel comfortable with this view of literacy. However, there is a significant, well-researched alternative view of literacy in the works of scholars ranging from John Dewey to Paulo Freire to Lisa Delpit to Allan Luke that would, and this alternative is known as critical literacy. Luke (1995), whose is among the most widely cited authorities of critical literacy argues that

Texts are moments when language connected to other semiotic systems is used for symbolic exchange. All texts are located in key social institutions: families, schools, churches, workplaces, mass media, government, and so on. Human subjects use texts to make sense of their world and to construct social actions and relations required in the labor of everyday life. At the same time, texts position and construct individuals, making available various meanings, ideas, and versions of the world (p. 13).

Unfortunately, when the CCSS were crafted, the literature on critical literacy was ignored. This is not a trivial oversight. Among the key aspects of critical literacy is the idea that literacy must be relevant to students and that the best way for it to become relevant, especially among the increasing numbers of marginalized students, is to encourage students to find points of relevance between literacy and their own lives. Freire (1998), in a frequently cited statement, argues that the purpose of literacy is:

> more than to psychologically and mechanically dominate reading and writing techniques. It is to dominate those techniques in terms of consciousness; to understand what one reads and to write what one understands: it is to *communicate* graphically. Acquiring literacy does not involve memorizing sentences, words or syllables—lifeless objects unconnected to an existential universe—but rather an attitude of creation and re-creation, a self-transformation producing a stance of intervention in one's context (p. 86).

Similarly, Bartholomae and Petrosky (2011), in their collection called *Ways of Reading*, warn us that, "A danger arises in assuming that reading is only a search for information or main ideas" (p. 6). The authors point out that such reading places a premium on memorizing and not on students' abilities to solve the problems that an essay proposes. Because the perspectives embodied in critical literacy are absent from the CCSS, curricula based on the standards may well suggest that literacy is *not* a give and take of ideas; that literacy is *not* about multiple perspectives; that literacy is *not* about using reading to create new knowledge; that although all texts exist in a social and cultural context, the reading of them *does not*.

The absence of an understanding of how literacy is embedded in and produced by social and cultural contexts is already being seen in how the CCSS are being interpreted. If we acknowledge that, in the end, standards "mean" largely what the test based on them indicate they mean, then an important interpreter of the CCSS is the Partnership for Assessment of Readiness for College and Careers (PARCC) (one of two assessment consortiums funded by the new entrepreneurs and federal Race to the Top monies to provide assessments for CCSS). PARCC has published several guides showing how, based on the CCSS, texts should be read and taught. For example, one focuses on reading Lincoln's Gettysburg Address (http://www.parcconline.org/sites/parcc/files/High-School-

Exemplar-Lincoln-Gettysburg-Address.pdf). These guides appear to be modeled on presentations made by David Coleman and Susan Pimental (http://www. teachersdomain.org/special/ccvid11/ccvid11.ela/). According to the guide, "A text dependent question specifically asks a question that can only be answered by referring explicitly back to the text being read."

Like Coleman's "don't give a shit" remark, this perspective on literacy suggests that the meaning of text is in the text itself without regard to who is reading it or the context in which it's being read. The meaning is determined by the teacher, and the student's job is to extract the teacher's meaning from the text. We say "the teacher's meaning" rather than "the meaning" because 40 years of research on reading comprehension and the reading of literature has shown that meaning is not a changeless, static feature of the text but rather something constructed by readers in contexts (see Rosenblatt, 1978; Valencia & Pearson, 1987; RAND Reading Study Group, 2002). In addition to PARCC, Student Achievement Partners (http://www.achievethecore.org/steal-these-tools/close-reading-exemplars), a group founded by Coleman, has also produced guides to using the CCSS. There, Coleman states that,

> Rather than asking students questions about their prior knowledge or experience, the standards expect students to wrestle with text dependent questions: questions that can only be answered by referring explicitly back to the text in front of them. In a shift away from today's emphasis on narrative writing in response to decontextualized prompts, students are expected to speak and write to sources—to use evidence from texts to present careful analysis, well-defended claims, and clear information.
>
> *(http://www.achievethecore.org/steal-these-tools/text-dependent-questions)*

Once again, for Coleman the meaning of the text is all that matters. Even though he uses the term "decontextualized" in a negative way, he is implying that context is only supplied by texts (and those texts are supplied only by the teacher). Yet, background and prior knowledge are indispensable tools for any teacher trying to make a connection between what a student knows and what a student needs to know. To make a workplace analogy, in Coleman's world, one would be welcomed to a new job by being told, "Look only at the company sales manual for your guidance. If there's something you don't understand, do not talk to your co-workers or attempt to draw upon your experience in previous jobs or draw upon your prior reading." Compare Coleman's meaning with the widely accepted meaning of what a reader does from the RAND Reading Study Group's (2002) *Reading for Understanding*:

> In considering the reader we include all the capacities, abilities, knowledge, and experiences that a person brings to the act of reading. Text is broadly construed to include any printed text or electronic text. In considering

activity, we include the purposes, processes, and consequences associated with the act of reading.

(http://www.rand.org/pubs/monograph_reports/MR1465.html)

A closer look at the specifics of the CCSS bears this out. Under the heading "Key ideas and details," students are to "cite strong and thorough textual evidence" (p. 38: "Cite strong and thorough textual evidence to support analysis of what the text says explicitly") to show they understand the explicit meaning of the text. Next students must identify the central theme or idea of the text by using evidence from the text ("provide an objective summary of the text") and third, students must know how complex characters develop motivations ("how the characters are introduced and developed") yet again, but using evidence from the text. One might say, "Well, the intention is for students to draw from the text to support their arguments but that doesn't mean they can't also draw on their prior knowledge or explore when texts might have multiple meanings." But unfortunately, based on how the CCSS is being interpreted by both the tester makers (PARCC) and the authors of the standards themselves, that is exactly what it does mean.

While we have thus far set Coleman's view of literacy against the critical literacy view of literacy (partly because Coleman's view is rather extreme), it is more accurate to say that approaches to reading and interpreting texts in school can be said to exist along a continuum. On one end is a strict interpretation of the words of the text without regard to the social, political, and cultural contexts related to the text and the reading event. What goes on in classrooms can fall anywhere along this continuum. In a teacher-centered classroom, where textual interpretation is tied to the teacher's authority, this particular act of reading is easily assessable and has the benefit of occurring in much the same way in multiple classrooms across time and space. Long before the new entrepreneurs arrived and even before Bill Gates was counting his first billion dollars (we're betting Gates had a billion by 1993), Fairclough (1993) argued that the appropriateness of a text and who gets to decide its meaning is a question of power. Critical literacy, on the other hand, interprets and critiques texts by viewing them as thoroughly contextualized and therefore as products of the same social structures and power relationships that shape daily life. At the other end is a critical literacy perspective, any text, from an ad for detergent to a classic novel, derives its meaning and the importance of its meaning from who produced, the social and historical circumstances of its production, the social and historical circumstances under which is read and used. "Reader, text and activity are also interrelated in dynamic ways that vary across pre-reading, reading, and post reading" (RAND Reading Study Group, 2002, p. 11.) The authors go on to say that, "the sociocultural context mediates students' experiences, just as students' experiences influence the context" (p. 12).

The previously mentioned materials for teaching the Gettysburg Address are described by PARCC as

a carefully developed set of steps that assist students in increasing their familiarity and understanding of Lincoln's Gettysburg Address through a series
of text dependent tasks and questions that ultimately develop college and
career readiness skills identified in the Common Core State Standards.

(http://www.parcconline.org/sites/parcc/files/
High-School-Exemplar-Lincoln-Gettysburg-Address.pdf)

The implication is that if the teacher and student do as the materials suggest, the
student will comprehend the Gettysburg Address.

But which Gettysburg Address are we going to privilege in a classroom? There
are five known versions and these differ in detail; published newspaper versions
also differ. Authorship can be challenging. Conventions, grammar, genres, and
semiotic forms are all in a state of flux and the boundaries between information
and knowledge, fact and fiction are fluid (Janks, 2011). Each version of the address
exists in its own social context. Two versions were given as gifts to two of Lincoln's secretaries. One version, which appears to be the standard, was written well
after the speech and is known as the Bliss version (Boritt, 2006). The speech was
largely forgotten until the 1880s, when Gettysburg became the focus of a reunion
between the North and the South. Coleman might well say, "All that's irrelevant.
All you should do is read the text in front of you." On the other hand, a critical
literacy perspective would acknowledge that, as twenty-first-century students in
this classroom, we are bringing our own backgrounds and experience to making
sense of this text and the text is bringing its historical and political context to the
experience, and to ignore either is to "misread" the Gettysburg Address. In the
world of the CCSS, the Gettysburg Address isn't really a historical document—it
is a text to be read in school to demonstrate the act of reading. Viewed in that
way, it's easy to see why context doesn't matter. (This is ironic given that the
CCSS include reading that's done within the teaching of history/social studies.)

Related to Coleman's view of text is his view of writing. He encourages moving students writing away from narrative and towards using writing to convey
complex information, to inform and to argue. Overall, he calls his approach
"reading like a detective and writing like an investigative reporter" (Goldstein,
2012, p. 1). It's a strange quote in that detective work and investigative reporting situate their practitioners in messy cultural, historical, social, and economic
contexts. Perhaps he would have been better off quoting Sergeant Friday from
Dragnet: "Just the facts, ma'am."

Coleman and Pimental (2011) have also produced *Publishers' Criteria for the
Common Core State Standards in English Language Arts and Literacy, Grades 3–12*.
These are especially noteworthy because they are a product of two actors in what
might be called the CCSS policy network, were produced under contract with
the Gates Foundation, and are intended to influence commercial publishers, the
largest of which is Pearson, whose executives include former McKinsey consultant Michael Barber. Thus one can understand how the various "nodes" of the

network are linked. What the guidelines argue is, given what we've seen from Coleman so far, not surprising: "The criteria make plain that developing students' prowess at drawing knowledge from the text itself is the point of reading" (p. 1). This is an even starker formulation of the context-free view of literacy than the "don't give a shit" formulation. At least in the "don't give a shit" formulation there is a boss (and hence a context) waiting for one's report. In the publisher's criteria view, the job of the student is to summarize and recite back to the teacher whatever "knowledge" is in the text (or, we would again argue, whatever knowledge the teacher or test maker thinks is in the text). Coleman and Pimental note that the link between comprehension and knowledge is obvious in science and history, but the same principle exists in all reading. Other tasks included in such readings about such texts are that students are able to spot and identify the main idea of a paragraph, section, or text.

Applying Critical Literacy to the Common Core State Standards

Like the Gettysburg Address, the CCSS can be read strictly as a decontextualized text, but, like the Gettysburg Address, they are not unconnected to the wider world. For example, we might ask, who owns the CCSS? The answer to this question might help us understand the political orientation of the CCSS. However, the answer to this question is elusive. The standards are not necessarily national standards (which would be unconstitutional), and states had the option—at least the putative option—of adopting them or not. Once adopted, does this mean the states own the standards? Some states, like Georgia, have gone as far as renaming the standards as the Common Core Georgia Performance Standards. If they do own the standards, can they opt out of them? Change them? Opting out of the standards might be very costly to budget-strapped states because the federal government, through the U.S. Department of Education, has funneled millions of dollars to many states in the form of Race to the Top grants, with very particular strings attached to the grants. Additionally, Race to the Top monies are funding the two assessment consortia.

Does the Bill and Melinda Gates Foundation own the CCSS? This Foundation clearly funded their development and publication. However, the Foundation funded the CCSS through the National Governors Association and the Council of Chief State School Officers. These groups commissioned the standards. But the need for the standards grew from a complex policy milieu involving philanthropists, think tanks, testing corporations, and the Federal Government (Zancanella & Moore, in press).

Do the writers of the English Language Arts standards, led by David Coleman, own the CCSS? Coleman and Susan Pimental have already issued publishing guidelines. Since many of the writers of the CCSS came from testing companies (ACT, SAT, Achieve), will the testing companies own the CCSS? This question comes with the knowledge that testing under NCLB had an immense influence on curriculum and how state standards were interpreted.

Similarly, one could ask: who benefits from the CCSS? Achieve? Pearson? David Coleman? Questions such as "who does this text belong to?" and "who benefits from its production" are precisely the kinds of questions central to critical literacy. As one can see, reading the CCSS critically widens our view to include intentions, motives, and the questions of power and authority. Read in this way, the CCSS begin to seem less like a set of benign academic goals and more like a means of reordering

> pedagogical and scholarly activities towards those which are likely to have a positive impact on measurable performance outcomes for the group, the institution, and increasingly the nation and as such is a deflection of attention away from aspects of social, emotional or moral development that have no immediate measurable performative value.
>
> *(Ball, 2012, p. 32)*

Perhaps most importantly, critical literacy requires that readers ask, "who or what is *left out* of this text or reading event?" Ironically, nowhere in any of the burgeoning literature on the standards is there a mention of the key issue that largely determines success in schools, which is our nation's growing problem: poverty. We have long known from research (Herbers et al., 2012) that kids who come to school suffering from the ravages of poverty tend to do poorly in school, and this gap grows rather than diminishes (Sirin, 2005; Obradovic et al., 2009; Robbins, Stagman, & Smith, 2012). The standards do not address poverty. Also, the standards do not address the varying levels of ability that teachers encounter within their classrooms that have their root causes in social, cultural, and economic reasons; these questions are rooted in critical literacy approaches.

How will the CCSS orient the way students learn? Fundamental to a critical literacy view of the document is first and foremost the notion that readers bring their knowledge of the world to every text. In writing about Foucault, Ball (2013) acknowledges that Foucault can be "difficult," but adds,

> Nonetheless his texts are also "writerly" texts, that is they include an invitation to participate in the thinking about a problem, to engage in the co-production of ideas. He leaves open points of entry for the reader to bring meaning to bear but never makes things easy (p. 12).

As readers read they constantly build theories about what they are reading and either elaborate these or tear them apart and build new ones that allow all aspects of their world to change these theories. We as teachers shape and allow these theories to grow or not to grow. If this transactive notion is acceptable then we have to acknowledge that in any group of students there will be multiple theories and interpretations. Teachers can create an environment where "students are encouraged to make connections and respond to text in a variety of ways such as dialog, personal writing, drama, and visual arts" (Creighton, 1997, p. 3). The CCSS discourage these strategies because of the time spent raising and discussing largely "irrelevant" questions that are not tied to or specifically answered by the text.

Conclusion

A curriculum built around force-feeding students difficult texts and asking them answer only "text-dependent" questions is a curriculum *built* to "reward[...] bullshit." Critical literacy is the opposite of such an approach. Critical literacy *critiques* bullshit.

There is, however, a deeper, more profound way in which the CCSS violate what critical literacy teaches us. That is, that at the heart of critical literacy practice is the ability of the individual educator to define what any given set of curricular standards will look like once enacted in their particular classroom. The "network" of governmental, non-profit, and for-profit entities that collaborated to create the CCSS and are now collaborating to ensure that they are implemented is anathema to the spirit and methods of critical literacy. To put it another way, the CCSS say: "This is what literacy is. Use it this way." Critical literacy asks, "What *is* literacy for me, for us, for this community, at this time, in this place, and how can it be used by all of us to reach our goals?"

References

ACT, Inc. (2006). *Reading between the lines: What the ACT reveals about college readiness in reading*. Iowa City, IA: Author.

Adams, M. J. (2009). The challenge of advanced texts: The interdependence of reading and learning. In E. H. Hiebert (Ed.) *Reading more, reading better: Are American students reading enough of the right stuff?* (pp. 163–189). New York, NY: Guilford.

Ash, K. (2012, November 14). Top U.S. foundations awarding grants for elementary and secondary education, *Education Week*, Retrieved from http://www.edweek.org/ew/articles/2012/11/14/12starwars.h32.html.

Aukerman, M. (2012). "Why do you say yes to Pedro, but no to me?" Toward a critical literacy of dialogic engagement. *Theory Into Practice, 51* (1), 42–48.

Avila, J. & Moore, M. T. (2012). Critical literacy, digital literacies, and Common Core State Standards: A workable union? *Theory Into Practice, 51* (1), 27–33.

Ball, S. J. (2008). New philanthropy, new networks and new governance in education. *Political Studies, 56*, 747–765.

Ball, S. J. (2009). Privatising education, privatizing education policy, privatizing educational research: Network governance and the 'competition state'. *Journal of Education Policy, 24* (1), 83–99.

Ball, S. J. (2012). *Global education inc.* New York, NY: Routledge.

Ball, S. J. (2013). *Foucault, power and education*. New York, NY: Routledge.

Barber, M. (2011). *Deliverology 101*. Thousand Oaks, CA: Corwin.

Barkan, J. (2012). Hired guns on astroturf: How to buy and sell school reform. *Dissent*, 49–57.

Bartholomae, D. & Petrosky, A. (2011). *Ways of reading*. Boston, MA: St. Martins Press.

Bloom, B.S., Engelhart, M.D., Furst, E.J., Hill, W.H., & Krathwohl, D.R. (1956). *Taxonomy of educational objectives: The classification of educational goals; Handbook 1: Cognitive domaine*. New York, NY: Longmans, Green.

Boritt, G. (2006). *The Gettysburg gospel: The Lincoln speech that nobody knows*. New York, NY: Simon & Schuster.

Bruner, J. (1990). *Acts of meaning*. Cambridge, MA: Harvard University Press.

Burch, P.E. (2006). The new education privatization: Educational contracting and high stakes accountability. *Teachers College Record*, *108*, 582–610.

Coleman, D. & Pimental, S. (2011) Publishers' criteria for the Common Core State Standards in English Language arts and Literacy, Grades 3–12. Retrieved from http://www.corestandards.org/assets/Publishers_Criteria_for_3-12.pdf.

Creighton, D.C. (1997). Critical literacy in the elementary classroom, *Language Arts*, *74* (6), 3–8.

Elementary and Secondary Education (2001). Retrieved from http://www2.ed.gov/policy/elsec/leg/esea02/index.html

Fairclough, N. (1993). The appropriacy of appropriateness. In Fairclough, N. (Ed). *Critical language awareness*. London, UK: Longman.

Fisk, E. B. (1989). Education; Lessons. *New York Times*, December 13.

Freire, P. (1970). *Pedagogy of the oppressed*. New York, NY: Seabury Press.

Freire, P. (1998). *Education for critical consciousness*. New York: The Continuum.

Goldstein, D. (2012). The schoolmaster. *The Atlantic*. Retrieved from http://www.theatlantic.com/magazine/archive/2012/10/the-schoolmaster/309091/.

Herbers, J. E., Cutuli, J.J., Supkoff, L.M., Heistad, D., Chan, C.K., Hinz, E. & Masten, A.S. (2012). Early reading skills and academic achievement trajectories of students facing poverty, homelessness, and high residential mobility. *Educational Researcher*, *41* (9), 366–374.

Janks, H. (2011). *The importance of critical literacy*. Keynote address presented at the 10th conference of the International Association of Teachers of English, Auckland, New Zealand.

Lorin, J. (2011). College board leader paid more than Harvard's. *Bloomberg News*. Retrieved from http://www.bloomberg.com/news/2011-08-26/nonprofit-head-of-college-board-paid-more-than-harvard-s-leader.html.

Luke, A. (1995). Text and discourse in education: An introduction to critical discourse analysis. *Review of Research in Education*, *21*, 3–48.

Luke, A. (2012). Critical literacy: Foundational notes. *Theory Into Practice*, *51*, 4–11.

National Center for Education Evaluation and Regional Assistance. (2009). *Reading first impact study final report*. Retrieved from http://ies.ed.gov/ncee/pubs/20094038/index.asp.

No Child Left Behind Act (2001). Retrieved from http://www2.ed.gov/nclb/landing.jhtml?src=ln.

Obradovic, J., Long, J.D., Cutuli, J.J., Chan, C.K., Hinz, E. Heistad, D., & Masten, A.S. (2009). Academic achievement of homeless and highly mobile children in an urban school district: Longitudinal evidence on risk, growth, and resilience. *Development and Psychopathology*, *21*, 493–518.

Chousa mondai wo fumaeta Jugyou aidea rei. (http://www.nier.go.jp/11chousa/23_sho_ koku_jugyourei.pdf)

Suzuki, K. (2005). *Kodomo to tsukuru Taiwa no Kyouiku: Seikatsu shido to Jyugyou.* Tokyo: Yamabuki shoten.

Takeuchi, T. (1994). *Gakkou no Jyouken.* Tokyo: Aoki shoten.

Tanaka, S. (2005). Yowasa no Tetsugaku kara kataru Gakuryoku: Tsuyosa no Gakuryoku kara Yowasa no literacy. In Y. Kudomi & T. Tanaka (Eds.) *Kibou wo tsumugu Gakuryoku* (pp. 248–273). Tokyo: Akashi shoten.

Yoshida, K. (1997). *Feminism Kyouiku jissen no Souzo: Kazoku eno Jiyu.* Tokyo: Aoki shoten.

Partnership for Assessment of Readiness for College and Careers (PARCC). (n.d.) PARCC model content frameworks. Retrieved from http://www.aspendrl. org/portal/browse/DocumentDetail?documentId=1396&download.

RAND Reading Study Group. (2002). *Reading for understanding: Toward an R & D program in reading comprehension.* Santa Monica, CA: RAND Corporation.

Ransom, J. C. (1979). *The new criticism.* Santa Barbara, CA: Praeger.

Robbins, T., Stagman, S. & Smith, S. (2012). Young children at risk. *National Center for Children in Poverty.* Retrieved from http://www.nccp.org/publications/pub_1073. html.

Rosenblatt, L. (1978). *The reader, the text, the poem: The transactional theory of the literary work.* Carbondale, IL: Southern Illinois Press.

Schwartz, R. B. & Robinson, M.A. (2000). Goals 2000 and the standards movement. *Brookings Papers on Education Policy, 2000,* 173–206.

Sirin, S.R. (2005). Socioeconomic status and academic achievement: A meta-analytic review of research. *Review of Educational Research, 75* (3), 417–453.

Smagorinsky, P. (2012). Testing mandates flunk cost benefit analysis. *Washington Post.* 30 June 2012. Retrieved from http://www.washingtonpost.com/blogs/answer-sheet/post/testing-mandates-flunk-cost-benefit-analysis/2012/06/30/gJQACqfsDW_blog. html.

Tyre, P. (2012). The writing revolution. Retrieved from http://www.theatlantic. com/magazine/archive/2012/10/the-writing-revolution/309090/.

Valencia, S., & Pearson, P. D. (1987). Reading assessment: Time for a change. *The Reading Teacher, 40* (8), 726–732.

Vygotsky, L. S. (1978). *Mind in society.* Cambridge, MA: Harvard University Press.

Wertsch, J. V. (1991). *Voices of the mind: A sociocultural approach to mediated action.* Cambridge, MA: Harvard University Press.

Zancanella, D., & Moore, M.T. (in press). The origins and ominous future of the common core standards in English language arts in the United States. In A. Goodwyn, L. Reid & C. Durrant (Eds.) *International perspectives on teaching English in a globalised world.* London, UK: Routledge.

11

WHAT COUNTS AS CRITICAL LITERACY IN THE JAPANESE CONTEXT

Its Possibilities and Practical Approaches Under the Global–National Curriculum

Shinya Takekawa

> The right to learn is
> the right to read and write;
> the right to question and analyze;
> the right to imagine and create;
> the right to read about one's world and to write history;
> the right to have access to educational resources and collective skills.
>
> *The Right to Learn (UNESCO, 1985)*

Introduction

This chapter begins with the above quote from "The Right to Learn," which was ratified more than 20 years ago, for a simple, yet important, reason. That is to say, within the past 20 years, educational movements in Japan have worked against the purpose of this declaration, and currently, the trend of moving away from its principles seems to be increasing. In this chapter I ask, given rising globalization and nationalism, what can be done within education to help the pursuit of an equitable society? A key issue is how critical literacy education is defined and might be incorporated into education.

However, the following two situations illustrate the current lack of critical literacy education in Japanese schools. First, the two words "critical" and "literacy" are rarely used by Japanese teachers in their discussions on curriculum or pedagogy. Even if we consider that the lack of these words is part of the recent political attack on the critical idea of education from neoconservative and neoliberal sectors, as we can confirm in nations and regions in which critical literacy education was promoted as a matter of curriculum, such as Australia, we must acknowledge that the concepts they represent have not permeated Japanese educational practices.

Second, as various data indicate, Japanese children have extremely low senses of self-affirmation, especially when viewed from the perspective of international comparison. Learning in school is not positioned as discovery of oneself and others or as a process by which students can participate in society. For example, results of the Program for International Student Assessment (PISA) exams by the Organization for Economic Cooperation and Development (OECD) show that, among participating nations, Japanese children have the least amount of information on social meaning and values and the least desire to learn in regard to being literate (OECD, 2004). Further, the poverty rate among Japanese children has surpassed 14.9% (UNICEF, 2012) and continues to rise. The hope for learning in school, and about society, is being lost among these children. These statistics show that there are many people who can read and write sufficiently in everyday life in Japan, but whose skills are not sufficient for citizens pursuing social equality.

Although critical literacy education is necessary in Japanese society under such a globalized era in which social gap is growing, the current context of Japanese educational practice does not allow it to be practiced actively. How can this be changed? This chapter will examine how critical literacy education is possible within the political structure that surrounds Japanese classrooms, as well as practical strategies for enacting it.

In the first part of this chapter, I will analyze the political structure that surrounds the pedagogy of Japanese teachers. The analysis will focus on recent developments in the national curriculum, which strongly regulates each teacher's curriculum and teaching methods. Japan's national curriculum has been extremely centralistic and nationalistic, and it strongly constrains what should be taught. However, as neoliberal structural reforms progress, teachers' initiative tends to be stressed in making curriculum and pedagogy. This trend has grown since the results of PISA were released. It looks like a paradoxical situation, but I will analyze it as politics of performativity of teachers by focusing on the recent Plan-Do-Check-Action (PDCA; [Kodama, 2005, 2009]) cycle management of school curriculum. This is the first task of this chapter.

In addition to analyzing the discourses that make teachers politically blind to the current pedagogical situation, I suggest ways of expanding the scope of critical literacy education in Japan by focusing on theories on reading act and agency. After that, I will show a practical approach to critical literacy education in Japan by re-evaluating the pedagogy of Japanese teachers from the viewpoint of critical literacy development. While Japanese educational policy is nationalistic and strongly regulates curriculum, a number of teachers have proposed practical approaches to changing their pedagogy by creating educational content and teaching materials through dialogue with students based on their real-life situations and the conflicts therein. These approaches put emphasis on requiring students to be critical of and responsible for relevant issues through the acquisition of each subject's knowledge and skills simultaneously. I will characterize such an approach as a possible model of critical literacy in Japan, one that is based on "fragility" or "vulnerability."

Finally, I will present the concept of "unlearning" as a key concept through which teachers can develop critical literacy practices in Japanese educational contexts. Spivak (1988) has described this concept, which she argues is necessary in order for intellectuals to investigate the relationship of knowledge and power, and be critically aware of the privilege of the knowledge they have learned. I will suggest that it is inevitable for teachers to learn and unlearn some educational content as they reinterpret the content within the social and political contexts of their classrooms.

Globalization and Nationalism in Japan's Curriculum Policy

In East Asia, including Japan, education has been reformed and expanded under centralized regulations aimed at rapid modernization. These reforms brought about the popularization of school education, and school is now regarded as a way to rise in the socioeconomic hierarchy. As a result, learning in school has become competitive in nature. As we can confirm in countries such as South Korea and Japan, the system of education has emphasized testing, focusing on high-school and university entrance exams, which has resulted in intensely competitive learning aimed at inculcating students with as much information as possible. In the case of Japan, a strong centralized structure has been developed in which the course of study, which is said to have legal binding force as the national curriculum, regulates school textbooks; the textbooks control the curriculum of each school, further restricting the lessons taught within classrooms. Emphasis is placed on the curriculum content and how teachers can work to implement it "faithfully" in class. There is no room for education based on alternative concepts such as critical literacy.

Recently, however, a few changes have occurred following PISA results. The focus of curriculum control is rapidly shifting from regulating educational content and the implementation process to performance management of teachers via the PDCA cycle, which focuses on accountability (Kodama, 2005, 2009). PDCA cycles are ostensibly progressing as independent initiatives at local and school levels under discourses such as the "autonomy of teachers" and "individuality of schools," and it looks like it might offer teachers more freedom to teach what they want to teach and to define and enact critical literacy in their local contexts. But what is actually happening in Japanese schools is the opposite. They continue to be dominated by a test-accountability system, and depoliticization and deprofessionalization of teachers continue. To find room for critical literacy in Japanese schools, we need to understand these developments within the politics of performativity in which teachers realize globalization and nationalism subjectively. To do this, I now turn to my analysis of the present circumstances of the curriculum test structure of Japanese schools.

Reaction and Remedy—After PISA

When we view the circumstances of classroom teaching in Japan as an arena in which globalization and nationalism commingle, the impact of PISA has been significant. The intense reaction to PISA occurred after a 2003 survey, in which Japan's ranking declined considerably in comparison to its previous rankings and continued to descend in surveys thereafter. Even though the results of PISA showed a more serious state of affairs regarding the difference in literacy between youth of different socioeconomic statuses (SES), conservative politicians, educational researchers, and the media turned public attention to the overall fall in the ranking among nations. This drew out further debate concerning the child-centered national curriculum, which had previously been criticized, and it accelerated the change of direction to cramming in "basic" learning in math and language arts. Simultaneously, on an educational policy level, training children for the PISA model was emphasized, and the Ministry of Education, Culture, Sports, Science and Technology presented teaching material and lesson plans for PISA literacy (Ministry of Education, Culture, Sports, Science & Technology, 2006). However, their characteristics were far from the concepts of literacy proposed by PISA in terms of politics and quality of learning.

As mentioned above, PISA's concept of literacy was depoliticized when it was introduced to Japan. As is well known, PISA is based on the OECD DeSeCo project, which examines the knowledge and skills that each person should acquire in a globalized society, and is the test used to assess the competency to "use tools interactively" within the three key competencies displayed there. The DeSeCo project was structured within the social democratic politics called "The Third Way" (Giddens, 1998), and this is reflected in PISA's concept of literacy (Rychen & Salganik, 2003), defined as "Reading literacy is understanding, using, and reflecting on written texts, in order to achieve one's goals, to develop one's knowledge and potential, and to participate in society" (OECD, 1999, p. 20). It is literacy for constructive, concerned, and reflective citizens. However, the Japanese educational response, particularly by the Ministry of Education, received this as just a neutral and general language use competency. The definition of PISA literacy characterized within the context of socio-democratic societies, and as a useful indicator of low-SES students' literacy competencies, was depoliticized.

This depoliticization of literacy has led to a skill-based approach to teaching reading. For example, the National Institute of Educational Policy (2011) proposed a lesson plan to develop a supposed PISA style of literacy. To teach students to read newspapers effectively to obtain necessary information, students are supposed to read and compare newspapers, and report on the different editing methods and styles of writing articles. In this lesson plan, the objective for students to be able to "read effectively" is replaced by the one in which they acquire a general skill for extracting information (e.g., editing methods and styles of writing articles). Moreover, objectives regarding learning about socio-cultural and political contexts of texts have been removed. In this way, the act of reading that should be situated and comprehensive is effaced, and reading is considered a set of operational skills. Furthermore, each skill that enables insight into the text is standardized and taught. Thus, PISA's concept of literacy as it has been actualized in Japan consists of basic learning such as vocabulary, mathematical ability, and study skills, which are decontextual and apolitical; these changes permeate the classroom through the national test.

Since 2007, an annual national test has been given to sixth- and ninth-grade students. This test includes questions to assess students' "basic" academic abilities as mentioned above, as well as questions that require logical thinking related to Japanese and mathematics (science was added in 2012) as separate tests. The results are shown as average scores and rankings of the prefectures for each type of test. Matsushita (2012) points out that the purpose of the test as a nationwide survey of academic ability is to evaluate children's academic ability, as stated in the official explanation of the test aim given by the Ministry of Education; the intended purpose is to spread the evaluation system of the PDCA cycle out to boards of education and schools. This will be discussed further below. Here, it suffices to say that the national achievement test functions as a means to performatively assign educational goals to school management and curriculum content. Therefore, in 2008, the national curriculum was revised to emphasize the two components of thorough acquirement of "fundamental basics" and use of knowledge in the school curriculum, components that correspond to the two types of nationwide tests.

The Ministry of Education has claimed that the new national curriculum corresponds to PISA's concept of literacy, and it was also designed to correspond to global standards. Koyasu (2008) indicates that such dual and phased learning has led to cramming basic knowledge and patterned skills. He also points out that such learning will expand the existing socioeconomic gaps in students' literacy acquisition. Japan's style of cramming learning, which is typical of some East Asian countries, has certainly been a form of "banking education," as described by Paulo Freire (1996). In PISA's concept of literacy, educators are expected to take a critical stance against political characteristics as they correspond to globalization; the notion allows for an attempt to change the traditional learning style of the Japanese classroom into a practice of reading and thinking critically. Yet, what is currently progressing is a system of banking education which supposedly corresponds to globalization.

Quality Management With the PDCA Cycle

What kind of countermeasures are Japanese teachers coming up with to address or meet the curriculum policies mentioned above? The aim evaluation system of the PDCA cycle has been adopted in recent years to manage the curriculum-test structure. PDCA was a method of quality management proposed by Walter A. Shewhart and Edwards Deming in the United States after World War II (Deming, 1986; Shewhart, 1986). These quality management systems are directly imported from business models as a quality assurance system for education.

In Japan, the government has the exclusive power to decide the "quality" of goals in the educational system. In 2006, the Fundamentals of Education Act, a law on the constitutional placement of education, was revised to include detailed goals for student abilities. In response, the School Education Law, which regulates school education, stipulated that students should acquire decontextualized skills and knowledge, as previously pointed out, at each school level, and the law incorporated school management improvement obligations towards that goal. The legal system was changed to allow the government to be involved not only in the aims of school education but also in internal matters such as educational goals and content. From a practical point of view, in 2006 the Ministry of Education presented guidelines for school evaluation to be used by each school for continuous evaluation and improvement of educational activities based on the PDCA cycle (Ministry of Education, Culture, Sports, Science, & Technology, 2010). The guidelines suggest using the results of the national test as indicators with which to evaluate curriculum and pedagogy.

As Nakajima (2007) points out, the PDCA cycle in Japan has become a structure in which: (1) the national government decides the attainment goal of school; (2) each regional educational board and school are required to accomplish that goal; (3) the national government evaluates whether or not the goal has been achieved; and (4) the government suggests improvements to be made by the educational board and school on the basis of that evaluation, and by seizing the check and action initiative, functions as a system that manages school education. Even though decentralization and local autonomy of schools are emphasized, the PDCA cycle actually functions as a mechanism for schools and teachers to "voluntarily" accept excessive burdens. For example, at one school, on the basis of the "voluntary decision" of the principal, students who had low learning performance and/or slight disabilities were made to stay at home on the day of a standardized test, and the teachers supervising the test tacitly pointed out students' mistakes if they found incorrect answers (*Chunichi Shimbun Daily* newspaper, 2007, July 8, p. 39). This directly indicates high demands and high stress placed on schools and educators through the PDCA cycle.

From the perspectives of globalization and nationalism, literacy development is currently defined in Japan from the viewpoint of individualized, decontextualized, and depoliticized ability, and quantitative evaluation of its strength. Some considerations on how to emancipate teachers and students from this kind of education, and the practical conditions for such emancipation, are the issues that research on critical literacy should pursue. To find room for critical literacy in the Japanese classroom, I will next focus on some arguments about language and the social construction of subjectivity.

Reading as Agency

Here, I want to examine a theoretical framework that can make room for Japanese teachers to teach critical literacy in their classrooms under the recent global–national politics. A major possibility is the agency of teachers and children on a performative level. In contrast to the rational subjects imagined by modern society and schools, we live in various social relationships that are interrelated in reality, and these interrelationships allow for performative freedom. From such a perspective, it is absolutely impossible to control the performance of people completely in such a reality.

Bakhtin, a linguist and Marxist during the Soviet Union era, sought to surmount binary understandings of language from the viewpoint of either "individualistic subjectivism" or "abstract objectivism"—the dominant trend in linguistics in the beginning of the twentieth century—with his claim that the actual unit of language is the "utterance" (Voloshinov 1929/1986). By focusing on utterances, Bakhtin tried to understand the meaning of language as social interaction—dialogue, as he called it—not linguistic structure as prescriptive systems or as individual psychological issues. Moreover, Bakhtin pointed out that the act of making an utterance in social interaction, supposing that ideology only appears through symbols (language), exhibits the conditions of an ideological conflict. He labeled the phenomenon of language use, including ideological accents in multi-directions, "polyphony" (Bahktin, 1984). However, regardless of the polyphonic characteristics of language, the reason why various ideological interests are not actualized is because the dominant ideology is "accentuating yesterday's truth as to make it appear today's" (Bahtin, 1984, pp. 22–23). Bahktin's view of language use leads to pedagogical questions such as, how are fissures in the meaning of texts made? And how can polyphonic characteristics, of language be actualized? But Bakhtin did not propose such strategies.

Hall's (1996) "encoding/decoding" theory of the sophisticated polyphonic characteristics of language and meaning is useful here. He examines the political mechanisms surrounding insight into texts and its oppositional strategies regarding the receptive process of the media. His theory criticizes the mass communication theory of the early 1970s that considers the relationship of the sender and receiver of a message in a linear relationship. The encoding/decoding theory proposes a framework in which the communication process is regarded as an "articulation," where aspects such as production, reproduction, distribution, and consumption are elaborately intertwined. Hall acknowledges the relative autonomy of decoding messages, but his main point rests on the fact that messages are not completely free from the surrounding politics, namely, the significance of the sender or the structure of the place where the message is received and decoded.

In order to analyze the political relation between encoding and decoding messages, Hall presented three positions of decoding: dominant-hegemonic, negotiated, and oppositional. This model criticizes the economic determinist theory of orthodox Marxism and views hegemony as the enforcement of authority, as stated by Gramsci (1994). With this understanding, Hall indicated the mechanisms of dominant meaning construction being generated in the text and noted the further possibility of oppositional insights against it. In this case, the three positions of insight are not theorized as given but are duly perceived as being politically constructed through the act of reading.

An understanding of such subject positions is currently explained by the concept of agency. Giddens (1979) theorized autonomy as a force that depends on neither structuralism nor subjectivism; it relies instead on the notion of agency. Giddens (1984) defined agency as the actor who is able to act otherwise at any phase in a given sequence of conduct, and to intervene in the world. Butler (1990) expanded on the concept, pointing out implications of agency-like discursive practice. Butler aimed at resolving binary opposition itself, such as biological sex or social gender, while explaining sexual identity. This means that sexual difference will not be added to cultural interpretations called "gender" with "body" and "sex" as the foundation, but that gender is the act of performing discourse; it is understood that "sex" is constructed through that discursive practice. Butler wrote the following:

> In this sense, *gender* is not a noun, but neither is it a set of free-floating attributes, for we have seen that the substantive effect of gender is performatively produced and compelled by regulatory practices of gender coherence . . . gender is always a doing, though not a doing by a subject who might be said to preexist the deed.
>
> *(Butler, 1990, pp. 24–25)*

As mentioned, the subject position is not an actual state that exists as given; rather it is understood because of its discursive practices, in Butler's concept of agency. Therefore, we can take active roles in the speech act, such as shifting or reversing the meaning of language. It makes room for teaching critical literacy, where students can potentially create fissures in the dominant meanings of language, rename them, and reweave the politics of relationships constructed by language.

The theories of both Bakhtin and Butler focus on autonomy at the level of the act of using language and making meaning. Converting these political mechanisms into an educational strategy is the task of research of critical literacy. In what follows, I want to examine a practical and possible approach in the Japanese context, along with examples of teachers' work in Japan.

Possible Approaches to Developing Critical Literacy in the Japanese Context

Making the performative relationship around the meaning of language a prerequisite, what kind of critical literacy is necessary for us, and what kind can be conceptualized? As I mentioned above, in recent educational policies in Japan, literacy is predominantly defined from the viewpoint of *individualized, decontextualized*, and *depoliticized* ability, and from the matter of the *quantitative evaluation* of its strength. Here, I would like to draw a fundamental oppositional principle to change such a definition into a possible approach for critical literacy by analyzing a case of classroom teaching. I would define this approach as *weakness, fragility*, or *vulnerability*.

Tanaka (2005) points out that, under globalization and nationalism, the dominant discourse requires "strength" for schools, families, and children, but he suggests that the meaning of being "vulnerable" should be reconsidered. Being vulnerable and weak should not be considered as a lack of strength; these should be located as a strong foundation to develop literacy. Tanaka's argument opens a different point of view to the resistant educational practice approach, which emphasizes the struggle against dominant power, and has critical theory and Marxism as its theoretical foundations (especially in a pedagogy of resistance) (Giroux, 1983).

Iwakawa (2005) notes that PISA's concept of literacy includes promoting citizens' skills of political and social participation, but also indicates that there needs to be caution because it includes the interests of global competition and the role of human capital within such a situation. In contrast to the emphasis on neoliberal self-actualization, he suggests that it is necessary to position "responsibility" as learning. In his definition, the term responsibility means an ability to respond to the voice of the other positively. For this to happen, we must consider what students are looking at, what they are feeling, and what kinds of power are influencing, and perhaps damaging, their lives and social relations. Moreover, with such a consideration, teachers should develop various approaches not for training children to acquire decontextualized skills, but for a process in which students reconstruct their recognition and relationships in their lives in and out of school.

In the history of education in Japan, educational practices have not used the term "critical literacy," but from the point of view described above, many practices are conceptually similar. I want to pick up and show two brief examples of teaching here, and analyze them as possibilities for critical literacy education in Japan. In the first, I highlight the work of Kazuo Suzuki, a primary-school teacher in Japan, who develops classroom teaching in which students critically learn the knowledge and skills of each subject's content through their own experiences and real context of their lives (Suzuki, 2005). His pedagogy is characterized by his strong focus on students who are socioeconomically and culturally marginalized, and who receive the impact of a violent social structure directly; he organizes learning to locate such students as prisms through which to rewrite knowledge and reconstruct micropolitical relationships among students.

The story of *Gongitsune* (*Gon, the Little Fox*) has long been published in Japanese textbooks. The lesson that uses this reading traditionally aims for students to understand it as a tragedy, because the poor farmer Hyouju and Gon the fox cannot understand each other. In one class, a student nicknamed Moo remarked,

"This story is boring" (p. 114). In response, Suzuki asked other children to think about why Moo made this comment. When the teacher and other children considered the meaning of Moo's remark in the context of his daily life in the community and his family background, they realized that he was reading the story as one about the importance of the marginalized people knowing and understanding each other. Suzuki communicated with Moo to help him become aware of the meaning of his message by himself. In this lesson, students read the text while reading their context with each other, and through this process, they read deeply into their own worlds while concurrently making the story the object of recognition. Simultaneously, they rewrote the text as their own, understood the dominant coding of the text, and felt both the text and context of others. In this learning process, the real relationship with others, the world, and oneself was reconstructed. In this way, communication in Suzuki's classroom became *responsible.*

Kazuko Yoshida, who was a teacher of commercial high school in Japan, presented a dialogical approach to critical practice (Yoshida, 1997). Commercial high school in Japan was established for vocational education, and the population includes many students who have low achievement with regard to learning; most students are girls. Yoshida recognized that such students live as the multilayered minority, as women, youth, and non-elite, thus they need to critically explore the status quo from the context of their lives, and reconstruct their positionality in the world. In order to organize such learning, Yoshida emphasized dialogue with students, and picked up the issues of sexuality in Japanese families in her class, because she found that the traditional patriarchal norm and discourses of family caused many conflicts in students' lives. Yoshida succeeded in helping her students be critically aware of their own diverse and contradictory identities by confirming the realities of our society, which includes many minorities (e.g., same-sex couples, unmarried mothers, *de facto* marriage). She is remarkable when she suggests that critical literacy practices should let students recognize the relationships between majority and minority as well as the conflicts among minorities.

Although these cases of teaching are located in the lineage of the "Seikatsu-tsuzurikata" pedagogy of writing in Japan, and not based on the theories of critical literacy, I argue that they can serve as a uniquely Japanese form of critical literacy, with a reliance on *responsibility* and *vulnerability.* The approach focuses on viewing life from the perspective of learning in school and conceptualizing learning from life. The life that becomes the object of recognition includes things and phenomena that have been materialized in relation to the students. It is an approach that expands critical recognition of the macrosocial structure while reforming real relationships within the classroom. In this approach, each subject's content mediates between students' critical recognition and reweaving the relationships in which the learner is placed. What makes this approach possible is an educational culture among teachers which emphasizes dialogue with the voices of marginalized students and a high quality of collaborative learning. Such voices are not coherent but more based on weakness, fragility, and vulnerability.

The teaching of both teachers showed that the dialogue with such voices makes a difference in their critical recognition. They reconstructed not only relationships between students and the world, but also knowledge and skills of the subject area. It can be said that, upon progressing in the study of a subject, the lesson will be structured with the subtext that the children create as an indispensable factor. Moreover, in progressing with such studies, Suzuki and Yoshida decided on the issue, setting, and method of learning with students, and focused on making the children aware of themselves as the authors of their lives. Tsunekazu Takeuchi (1994) argued the necessity of critical learning that includes critical learning activities, critical study of the method of learning, and self-governing education, and Suzuki and Yoshida's practice reinforce that point, so the accumulation of such initiatives should be evaluated as a beneficial inheritance of the educational practice in Japan.

Their approaches do not represent all possibilities of critical literacy education in Japan. However, Japanese teachers tend to be conscious of the situations of students who come to school from unstable family and various social backgrounds, and thus, the approach of organizing teaching that begins with a critical recognition of the state of such marginalization can potentially become widely practiced. I would like to stress again that it would be critical for Japanese teachers to begin by recognizing what students know, what they feel conflicted about, and how they think in everyday life, to become aware of the critical value of such a dialogue.

In Conclusion: Unlearning Critical Literacy

As argued, even in the Japanese classroom, which is in a centralized and extremely nationalistic environment, there exists the possibility of developing teaching for critical literacy. To actualize this possibility, the conscientization (Freire, 1996) of teachers is essential. Finally, I want to mention the concept of "unlearning" as a form of it for teachers.

Gayatri Spivak suggests that learning and obtaining knowledge is a privilege, and simultaneously, that nothing else was learned; thus, "unlearning" is the concept of disrupting the privilege of knowledge on your own by learning that there is much lost from that privilege (Spivak, 1988; Landry & Maclean, 1996). This does not mean one should stop learning or forget what has already been learned. Rather, we should consider what was not learned in the process of learning something and redraw the boundaries of knowledge accordingly.

Spivak's argument is stated in the context of postcolonial research, but it provides a strong reason to promote critical literacy education and sounds an alarm bell: If people do not acquire language, it is impossible to have exchanges with others, participate in society, or to have self-recognition. However, language acquisition also means incorporating oneself into the structure of the dominant system of history and politics. It might be an incomprehensible position for those who believe that increasing and strengthening knowledge and skills is the mission of school education, but questioning whether this type of education is really rich education is the aim of critical research. Simultaneously, the gaze of unlearning must be turned towards critical literacy itself. How to define critical literacy is highly controversial and constitutes a political issue, but whatever it may be, it is necessary for the teacher to unlearn it. Critical literacy must be regarded as a present progressive process at all times.

What does it mean for the teacher to encourage unlearning to conceptualize teaching? It means to interrogate again the connections among and between humans and the world in the past, anticipate seeing a different state, and conceptualize dialogical activities and interactions with people (Koyasu, 2006). This task is no more difficult than conducting a prepackaged lesson. It is the same as looking at the front of a coin and viewing it from the back and the side. It is important to remember that looking at the front of the coin is not the only way to view it. Political implications that exist in the background of individual actions, the explicit that exists behind the implicit, reproductive labor that exists behind productive labor, the discursive that is in the background of experiential things (and experiential things that are in the background of the discursive)—unlearning critical literacy is to go back and forth to illuminate these things.

References

Bahktin, M. (1984). *Problems of Dostoevsky's poetics*, C. Emerson Trans. Minneapolis, MN: University of Minnesota Press.

Butler, J. (1990). *Gender trouble: Feminism and the subversion of identity*. New York, NY: Routledge.

Deming, W.E. (1986). *Out of the crisis*. Cambridge, UK: Cambridge University Press.

Freire, P. (1996). *Pedagogy of the oppressed*. M. A. Ramos Trans. New York, NY: Continuum.

Giddens, A. (1979). *Central problems in social theory*. London, UK: Macmillan.

Giddens, A. (1984). *The constitution of society: Outline of the theory of structuration*. Berkeley, CA: University of California Press.

Giddens, A. (1998). *The third way: The renewal of social democracy*. Cambridge, UK: Polity Press.

Giroux, H.A. (1983). *Theory and resistance in education: A pedagogy for the opposition*. South Hadley, MA: Bergin & Garvey.

Gramsci, A. (1994). *Letters from prison*, Vol. 1, Vol. 2. Edited by F. Rosengarten; Translated by R. Rosenthal. New York, NY: Columbia University Press.

Hall, S. (1996). Encoding/decoding. In S. Hall, D. Hobson, A. Lowe, & P. Willis (Eds.) *Culture, media, language: Working papers in cultural studies 1972–1979* (pp. 128–138). London, UK: Routledge.

Landry, D. & Maclean, G. (Eds.). (1996). *The Spivak reader: Selected works of Gayatri Chakravorty Spivak*. New York, NY: Routledge.

OECD (1999). *Measuring student knowledge and skills: A new framework for assessment.* http://
www.oecd.org/edu/preschoolandschool/programmeforinternationalstudentassess-
mentpisa/33693997.pdf.

OECD (2004). *Learning for tomorrow's world: First results from PISA 2003* (available on
OECD website: http://www.oecd.org/education/school/programmeforinternation-
alstudentassessmentpisa/34002216.pdf.

Rychen, D.S. and Salganik, L.H. (Eds). (2003). *Key competencies for a successful life and a well-
functioning society.* Cambridge, MA: Hogrefe & Huber.

Shewhart, W. A. (1986). *Statistical method from the viewpoint of quality control.* New York,
NY: Dover.

Spivak, G. (1988). Can the subaltern speak? In C. Nelson & L. Grossberg (Eds.) *Marxism
and the interpretation of culture* (pp. 271–316). Urbana, IL: The Board of Trustees of the
University of Illinois.

UNESCO (1985). *Final report. Fourth International Conference on Adult Education.* Retrieved
from: www.unesco.org/education/uie/confintea/paris_e.pdf.

UNICEF (2012). *Measuring child poverty: New league tables of child poverty in the world rich
countries.* http://www.unicef-irc.org/publications/pdf/rc10_eng.pdf.

Voloshinov, V.N. (1929/1986). *Marxism and the philosophy of language.* L. Matejka & I.R.
Titunik, Trans. Cambridge, MA: Harvard University Press.

(Below are all written and published in Japan.)

Chunichi Shimbun Daily newspaper. (2007), July 8, p. 39.

Iwakawa, N. (2005). Kyouiku niokeru Chikara no Datsukouchiku: Jiko jitsugen kara Out-
oukanousei e. In Y. Kudomi & T. Tanaka (Eds.). *Kibou wo tsumugu Gakuryoku* (pp.
220–247). Tokyo: Akashi shoten.

Kodama, S. (2005). Gakuryoku chousa no Shisoushi teki bunmyaku: Atarashi Kokka
tousei ka soretomo Fukushi kokka no Saiteigi ka. In *Kyouiku kakusa no Hassei Kai-
shou ni kansuru Chousa houkoku sho* (pp. 111–120). Tokyo, Japan: Benesse Educational
Research & Development Center.

Kodama, S. (2009). Performativity and the afformative in educational reform: Toward the
new politics of education. In *Kyouikugaku kenkyu* (pp. 412–422), 76(4). Tokyo, Japan:
Japanese Educational Research Association.

Koyasu, J. (2006). *Han Kyouiku nyumon: Kyouikukatei no anran.* Tokyo: Hakutaku sha.

Koyasu, J. (2008). Kuruma no Ryourin towa nani ka: Kakujitsu na Shutoku to Katsuyou
no Mondaiten. In T. Takeuchi, T. Takeuchi, J. Koyasu, et al. (Eds.) *Gakushu shidouy-
ouryou wo Yomu shiten* (pp. 27–38). Tokyo: Hakutaku sha.

Matsushita, K. (2012). Gakkou wa naze konnanimo Hyouka mamire nanoka: Kyouiku no
global ka no hatashita yakuwari. In Group Didaktika (Eds.) *Kyoushi ni narukoto Kyoushi
de ari tsuzukeru koto* (pp. 23–45). Tokyo: Keisou shobou.

Ministry of Education, Culture, Sports, Science & Technology. (2006). *Dokkai ryoku kou-
jyou ni kansuru Shidou shiryo,* Tokyo: Touyou kan shuppan sha.

Ministry of Education, Culture, Sports, Science & Technology. (2010). *Gakkou hyouka
gaidorain* (http://www.mext.go.jp/a_menu/shotou/gakko-hyoka/index.htm)

Nakajima, T. (2007). Kyouiku kihonhou Kaisei gono Shin jiyu shugi Kyouiku: PDCA
saikuru ni Housetsu sareru Kyouiku genba. In Kyouiku kagku kenkyu kai (Eds.). *Kyouiku,* No. 739 (pp. 27–32). Tokyo: Kokudo sha.

National Institute of Educational Policy (2011). *Heisei 23 nendo Shougakkou Kokugo no*

12

STANDARDIZING, AND ERASING, CRITICAL LITERACY IN HIGH-STAKES SETTINGS*

Jessica Zacher Pandya

We find ourselves in the midst of intense pressures for assessment and account-ability in education systems around the globe, as other authors in this book attest. In the United States, the national urge to hold teachers accountable for student learning is visible in the proliferation of "value-added" models that enable admin-istrators and parents to examine the progress students make on standardized tests in individual teachers' classrooms (Baker et al., 2010; Felch, Song, & Smith, 2010). While there is still an ongoing debate about the merits of publicizing test scores by teacher name, a debate symptomatic of what I have recently called a national obsession with accountability (Zacher Pandya, 2011), more and more school districts and teachers' unions have given in to state and federal pressure to use test scores as a means of measuring the value teachers add to students' learning. In this chapter, I focus on the work of a teacher in just such a high-stakes setting, one where students were supposed to acquire critical literacy skills by making in-depth inquiries into various curricular subjects, and where teachers were trained to help students through the standardized process. As the title of this chapter sug-gests, this pedagogical plan—which I describe herein—was a way of attempting to standardize the teaching of critical literacy skills. Unfortunately, in the end, the plan erased more critical literacy opportunities for children in language arts classes than it afforded.

Advocates of increased accountability see classroom teaching as a sort of black box, dangerous in its opacity. Structured curricula like *Houghton Mifflin Reading:*

* This chapter is an expanded version of: Zacher Pandya, J. (2012). Mandating and stand-ardizing the teaching of critical literacy skills: A cautionary tale. *Theory Into Practice, 51* (1), 20–26. DOI: 10.1080/00405841.2012.636330. Reprinted by permission of Taylor & Francis (http://www.tandfonline.com).

A Legacy of Literacy (Houghton Mifflin, 2003) and *Open Court Reading* (SRA/ McGraw-Hill, 2005) offer compelling alternatives to the black box via the illusion of accountability: if teachers simply follow the "research-based" instructions in the teacher's edition, then outsiders will know exactly what kind of instruction students have received. This was the thinking underlying the unit I will describe here: if teachers were given a precise structure through which to help students, their students could, at the least, become critical consumers of information. In this case, however, the implementation of the structured program looked different in each classroom I visited at the school, depending on the teacher's practices and the level and length of support they received from other school staff, as I discuss below.

To explore the problems inherent in trying to standardize individuals' processes of inquiry, I describe and critique the implementation of the "Inquiry" component of the *Open Court Reading* program that was designed to teach children "inquiry and higher-order thinking" skills through a "proven structure" (SRA/McGraw-Hill, 2002, p. 38). I enclose the term "Inquiry" in quotation marks when I discuss it as a component of the *Open Court Reading* program to distinguish the prepackaged version from other, less commodified, methods of inquiry. According to supplemental materials and the *Open Court Reading* teacher's edition, the intended outcome of the "Inquiry" component is the production of knowledgeable "consumers" of information—what some might term critically literate children (see, for example, past work on critical media literacy [Alvermann, Moon, & Hagood, 1999; Morrell, 2002]).

We know that the teaching of critical literacy skills, and engagement with critical literacy practices, involves questioning power relations in the world through, and with, texts, and asking potentially revolutionary questions about representation, language, and social justice (Comber, Thompon, & Wells, 2001; Janks, 2010; Rogers, Mosely, & Folkes, 2009, and Chapter 3, this volume). As many authors in this volume alone attest, teachers can approach critical literacy from a variety of stances (Vasquez, Chapter 13, this volume) and dimensions (Flint & Laman, Chapter 6, this volume), but most educators know they will be entering into uncharted, and sometimes uncomfortable, territory in this process. When a publisher like SRA/McGraw-Hill takes on the task of helping teachers help their students ask questions—help them inquire into their worlds, or at least into the topics presented in the curriculum—they too have had some ideas about what *kinds* of questions children might ask.

I was reading this particular *Open Court Reading* teacher's edition while undertaking a year-long ethnographic study of English language learners' literacy practices in a structured-curriculum classroom. At the school, students and teachers underwent 35 tests per year, were required to use swiftly moving curricular pacing charts, and were required to submit to heavy administrative oversight. In the following pages, I will use scenes from a fourth-grade classroom to argue that the attempt to mandate and standardize the teaching of critical literacy skills—including the ability to ask questions to learn more about the topic being taught, as well as to discern the validity of different sources of information, and to understand the ways different sources positioned readers and consumers—was, at best, an ill-fated endeavor. Indeed, this particular approach to critical literacy not only failed to meet its stated objectives to turn children into informed consumers of texts, but also, as I explain at the end of this chapter, compromised learning and teaching more generally for students *and* teachers. This was mostly due to the highly structured nature of the curriculum, whose implementation simultaneously deprofessionalized teachers and subtracted learning opportunities for students (Arya, Laster, & Lin, 2005; Fang, Fu, & Lamme, 2004; McCarthey, 2009; Samway & Pease-Alvarez, 2005). Some teachers and researchers have found spaces for critical literacy in similar settings (Paugh, Carey, King-Jackson, & Russell, 2007), but I argue that this systematic, top-down attempt to enforce critical literacy skill teaching failed to inculcate the hoped-for skills.

I designed the larger study from a sociocultural and critical perspective, foregrounding the social and mediational aspects of literacy practices (Bakhtin, 1981; Vygotsky, 1986). In it, I aimed to understand the purposes and goals of the literacy practices engendered by the mandated curriculum itself (Luke, 1988). I also documented the effects of these goals on students' English language and literacy acquisition (see August & Shanahan, 2006; Menken, 2006). Several scholars have recently begun to interrogate the kinds of teaching and learning taking place in classrooms with highly structured language arts curricula (Arya, Laster, & Lin, 2005; Valli & Chambliss, 2007; Wiltz & Wilson, 2006), and many have investigated the teaching of critical inquiry (Berghoff, Egawa, Harste, & Hoonan, 2000; Comber, 2001; O'Brien, 2001; Short & Burke, 2001). However, few have investigated the use of structured curricula with English language learners (Ruiz & Morales-Ellis, 2005; Zacher Pandya, 2011), and fewer still have examined such explicit attempts to standardize the teaching of critical literacy skills with this population.

Six (Plus Eleven More) Steps to Inquiry: The Scripting of Critical Literacy

Producing "Genuine Research" via a Scripted Plan

I first heard about *Open Court Reading's* inquiry component from a school district language arts coordinator eager to show me the best teaching in the district (to protect the anonymity of research subjects, all names used in this chapter are pseudonyms). I was taken on a tour of Laurel Elementary, a school saturated with high-stakes tests and heavy curricular oversight by the principal and the school's literacy coaches. There, I met Ms. Romano, a fourth-grade teacher who had recently completed an "inquiry cycle" with her 28 students, 20 of whom were English language learners of a range of oral and written language proficiencies.

The school's literacy coach would work with a teacher during the first inquiry cycle, then offer some help on the second cycle, and then be available only for troubleshooting in the third cycle—a gradual release of responsibility. However, since there was so much *Open Court Reading* material to cover without even trying the inquiry component, teachers tended not to do it unless the coach was a frequent and visible supporter of the process.

Like other structured language arts curricula, the *Open Court Reading* program's daily and weekly lessons were divided into three parts: First, "Preparing to Read," a "carefully crafted sequence" (SRA/McGraw-Hill, 2002, p. x) of lessons about sounds and letters, phonemic awareness, phonics, fluency, and word knowledge. Once the teacher and students made it through the 5–30 minutes of these daily preparatory activities, they were to turn to part two, "Reading and Responding." The reading comprehension skills and strategies lessons in this segment could take from half an hour to 2 hours, depending on the content, the methods, and the amount of time the school required the teacher to use the program every day. "Inquiry" lessons linked directly to the unit's topic were supposed to follow and build on the comprehension lessons in the "Reading and Responding" segment. On paper, they might be done weekly, or daily, depending on the structure the school's literacy coach chose. However, they were seen as so cumbersome and time-consuming that they were seldom taught unless the teacher had outside help and oversight.

The third and final section of daily lessons—which took on average another 30 minutes—was euphemistically titled "Language Arts" and included spelling; vocabulary; writing process strategies; "writer's craft"; English language conventions; grammar, usage, and mechanics; listening, speaking, and viewing; penmanship; and basic computer skills (SRA/McGraw-Hill, 2002, pp. x–xi). The attractiveness of such curriculum stems partly from these comprehensive, even exhaustive, lists of activities, broken down into seemingly manageable and seemingly logical parts. However, as we now know, it's not only the content of the curriculum, but the way teachers are made to teach it (including pacing and emphasis on some parts over others) and the attendant, and in many cases all-consuming, tests that assess students' learning of the skills and content (cf. McCarthey, 2009; Valli & Chambliss, 2007).

For those like Ms. Romano lucky enough to have an on-site literacy coach, "Inquiry" still did not happen as regularly as every other aspect of the program. Actually, in the year I spent in her room collecting data, her students completed five *Open Court Reading* units, but only one "Inquiry" cycle. *Open Court Reading's* "Inquiry" process is also referred to as "investigation" and "investigating through research." It is described in great detail in each Teacher's Edition's "Program Appendix" (SRA/McGraw-Hill, 2002, pp. 36–39), where its purpose is explained thusly: to allow teachers to "capitalize on students' questions and natural curiosity by using a proven structure" (p. 38). The "proven structure," the target of most of my criticism, is alleged to help "preserve the open-ended character of real research" while preventing students from getting "lost or bogged down." The authors unironically distinguish their process from the "conventional [inquiry or research] approach" with its "series of steps" from "select a topic, narrow the topic, collect materials, take notes, outline, and write." Such mundane inquiry, they say, "does not constitute research in a meaningful sense," while their six-step process does. They suggest that "even elementary school students can produce works of genuine research—research that seeks answers to real questions or solutions to real problems" (p. 38). The occasional hint of condescension visible in most structured curricula—the insinuation that teachers, and students, need outside guidance to plan instruction and to learn—is more visible in the inquiry process in this case, where students are simultaneously positioned as inquirers and as objects who need to be acted upon by the teacher, echoing Freire's (2000) descriptions of banking education practices and behaviors.

To produce this "genuine research," teachers are required to guide their students through a research cycle of six steps:

1. Decide on a problem or question to research.
2. Formulate an idea or conjecture about the research problem.
3. Identify needs and make plans.
4. Reevaluate the problem or question based on what we have learned so far and the feedback we have received.
5. Revise the idea or conjecture.
6. Identify new needs and make new plans (SRA/McGraw-Hill, 2002, p. 38).

In the teacher's edition, after these six steps, there are *11* further steps that constitute the "procedure for choosing a problem to research" (pp. 38–39). They relate mostly to teacher actions:

1. First, teachers should "discuss with students the nature of the unit".
2. And then "the schedule" they "have planned for their investigations".
3. Then "have students talk about things they wonder about that are related to the unit subject".
4. The teacher next brainstorms "possible questions for students to think about".
5. And models "for students the difference between a research topic and a research problem or question".
6. & 7. Are reminders that "a good research problem or question not only requires students to consult a variety of sources but is engaging and adds to the group's knowledge of the concepts" and that the question should serve "only as a guide for research".
8. Teachers should have students "elaborate on their reasons for wanting to research their stated problems".

9.   Teachers should remember that, "at this stage, students' ideas will be of a very vague and limited sort." They are to "have students present their proposed problems or questions, along with reasons for their choices, and have an open discussion of how promising proposed questions are".

10. & 11. Finally, the teacher should help students form research groups in the way they "find best" for their class.

These 11 stages are just details of step one of the larger inquiry cycle, which ends with students making projects, PowerPoints, posters, or books with which to share their findings with the class. These artifacts are meant to be to enrich the class's knowledge base about the *Open Court Reading* unit's broader topic. Many critical literacy practitioners describe all sorts of artifacts children might produce to share what they have learned in their inquiries (Comber & Nixon, Chapter 7, this volume; Stevens & Bean, 2007), and when I first heard about the inquiry process I thought I might see more such student-generated work. However, the work I saw tended to echo the format and contents of other school reports, not to show children positioning themselves as, for example, discerning consumers of information. I discuss some of the sticking points in the scripted inquiry process that led to these rather uncritical products below.

Sticking Points at Steps One, Two, and Three of an Actual "Inquiry" Unit

The school's literacy coach had modified the six steps and made a portable poster of "inquiry directions" that she used when she taught inquiry classes:

1. Ask questions.
2. Make conjectures.
3. Needs and plans.
4. Investigate (also called "research").
5. Revise conjectures.
6. Present information.

Although both the official and the more local (but still highly scripted) processes seem smooth on paper, in practice there were some sticking points. These are points at which, in an ideal world, actual critical literacy practices, such as interrogating the purpose and structure of the inquiry process itself, would have occurred. They did not. To illustrate some of these failures, I'll describe some sticking points Ms. Romano and her students encountered in the first three steps of the process. In Ms. Romano's fourth-grade room, students had grouped themselves based on the medicine-related problems they wanted to research for the unit "From Mystery to Medicine." These were the approved questions:

"What is cancer?"
"What is diabetes?"
"Why do we need our muscles?"
"How does the stomach work?"
"How does the heart work?"
"How does the brain work?"

The first complication in the six-step plan that I saw was the issue of making sure students had crafted appropriate research questions. One girl's mother had died from cancer when the girl was 2 years old—the question about cancer was her invention; also, a few children had diabetic relatives, which accounted for the second question. Overall, the questions seemed to reflect students' interests and lifeworlds, as well as the topic of the unit on the history of medicine. However, Ms. Romano told me that she had already made sure students' "problems," or questions, were linked to the unit, researchable, and answerable, according to her own unstated (to me) criteria. She had also already weeded out questions that were unrelated, unresearchable (in her opinion), and unanswerable (by fourth-grade students, again in her opinion).

Ms. Romano and her students came to the second sticking point when students had to move to step two: "Formulate an idea or conjecture about the research problem" (SRA/McGraw-Hill, 2002, p. 38). Earlier that year, I had seen Ms. Forrest, the literacy coach, explain "conjecture" to second-grade students with analogies. She wrote "estimate/math," "hypothesis/science," and "conjecture/inquiry" on the board, and said, "conjecture is to inquiry as estimate is to math" and repeated the phrase for "hypothesis" and "science." These analogies, which were meant in part to help English learners acquire what the school referred to "the language of the discipline"—of math and science, presumably—seemed only to confuse, judging from the silence of the class after the analogies were introduced. The students had voted as a class to inquire into how to "show kindness to the Earth." Ms. Forrest asked the group, "How can you be kind to the Earth? What's your conjecture?" Students eventually caught on to the idea that Ms. Forrest wanted them to hazard a guess, and some of them did so.

On this occasion, Ms. Romano had her students read aloud the definition of "conjecture" that she had borrowed from Ms. Forrest and written on the board: "A conjecture is a scholarly guess based upon your prior knowledge." Then she had them "read it one more time." After their recitation, she asked, "What's prior knowledge, Lucas?" Lucas, an intermediate English language learner, replied, "Like you're guessing, like a prediction." Ms. Romano said "Yes, but what's prior knowledge?" and Daniel, a former English language learner reclassified in third grade as a "fluent English proficient" speaker, tried: "Prior knowledge is like the words." Unable to get a student to define "prior knowledge" satisfactorily, Ms. Romano said it herself: "What you already know," and wrote her definition beneath the definition of "conjecture" already written on the board. She asked her students, "Do you know anything [about your topics] already?" and two children said "No." She continued, "About your question?" and then she said, "We're going to write, but first we're going to talk about it, we're going to share our brains by talking." She asked them if their discussion now had to be about "the right answer" and answered herself, saying, "No, it's a guess."

For the next 5 minutes, students talked over their "guesses" about what they might learn about their questions. It was not easy for students to stay focused on their questions, and some wanted to move ahead to step three, "identify needs and make plans." For instance, at the table of girls working on "How does the stomach work," Andrea, an intermediate English language learner, suggested to her tablemates, "We could, like, make a plan." Her friend and co-inquirer Rosa (also identified as an intermediate-level English language learner) echoed Ms. Romano, saying, "But it doesn't need to be right or wrong." Rosa was referring to Ms. Romano's reminder that their discussion and questions—not the plan itself—did not need to be right or wrong. Monique, the only African-American girl in the class and one of few native English speakers, said, "When you go to the doctor—" but Andrea interrupted, saying, "If we went to the doctor, she could tell us like how does the stomach work." Ms. Romano had been walking around the room, listening to and editing questions and ideas. She came over and reminded the girls that they were supposed to be working on a "conjecture . . . about how your stomach works." The girls looked at each other, and then, temporarily abandoning her ideas about visiting the doctor, Andrea smiled at Ms. Romano and said slowly "your stomach . . ." Ms. Romano prompted her to add "I think," and Andrea said, "*I think* that your stomach works when you're eating." Ms. Romano said "Oh! You may be right!" She then asked Monique about her ideas. The stomach works, Monique guessed, "by taking care of food, and you get the aches when you put bad food in it." After a moment listening to more of their guesses, Ms. Romano told the class that each table would "need to have a conjecture on a sticky note for me in two minutes."

The girls gathered their pencils and Rosa got control of the sticky notes. She began to write and speak, saying, "we think the stomach—"

Andrea supplied, "the stomach works."

Rosa interrupted, "no, we think—" at the same time that Andrea said "we think—"

Rosa said, "we think that the stomach's—"

Monique said "the stomach's—"

Andrea said "the stomach works—"

After a pause, Rosa asked, "What did you say, Andrea?" Andrea replied, "I think the stomach works with eating, it's gobbling it." Ms. Romano, listening in again, asked if this was a "team conjecture," and Andrea said that no, it was her own. Ms. Romano had to go help at another table and left the girls to their own devices, not providing further instructions on how to arrive at a "team conjecture" instead of individual ones.

Rosa wrote down Andrea's conjecture on the group's sticky note, and Rosa and Andrea spent the next 10 minutes following Ms. Romano's directions about where to write their names on their group folder, where to put the sticky with their team's conjecture, where to write the date, where to write a single word about their topic, etcetera. Monique busied herself with her own papers and did not say anything else. As students worked on these little tasks, Ms. Romano told the class that "neatness was paramount, that means really important," throughout the inquiry process. Her emphasis on neatness was meant to help students get and stay organized, but it often seemed to me to take precedence over the content of the projects—perhaps because it is easier for a busy teacher to do a visual check for organization than for evidence of more complex critical literacy practices.

The last sticking point I want to address in this supposedly smooth process occurred when students moved to make plans as a group; the ideal collective thinking and planning process had already broken down here, and would only become more driven by Rosa and Andrea, and less by the other students, over time. Groups had to fill in charts about their "needs"—i.e., what they needed to gather to learn about their question—and their "plans"—i.e., what they were going to do to learn more. Ms. Romano started by asking her students to write a list of their "resource needs," explaining that, "Resources are how, where you find information." She told the class that their job was "to make a list of resources." She had them do one together as a class first—before letting them work on their own—and the first thing someone said was "dictionary." She said "No, that's for finding words out, so don't write dictionary."

The larger class list included the *Open Court* book, their science book, the internet, radio, newspapers, museum, observations, and "people" (as in people to interview and learn from). After the class had generated this list, instead of asking students for more specifics on how they might use these resources, Ms. Romano had students choose what resources they would use; she did this by making them write "books" and one other resource on a sticky note. She said, "If you pick it [whatever resource, aside from books], you have to do it." With this momentary chance to choose, students unwittingly gave up the opportunity to learn from multiple sources, and instead narrowed their "inquiry" to "books" and one other "resource." The pressure to choose quickly, combined with the lure of the computer, lead most students to choose the internet, relegating other potential resources to secondary statuses.

Evaluating Standardized Inquiry: Success and Failures

As I watched this process unfold, I was struck by one positive aspect: English language learners were certainly using content-area vocabulary, and (when prompted) were doing their best to use the frames their teacher had given them, such as "I think that . . ." and "My guess is. . . ." When Ms. Romano was not around to press for content-oriented talk, conversations often reverted to procedural discussions about what needed to be done to fulfill the assignment or to organize their work neatly. Overall, however, the negative outcomes of this and other inquiry lessons far outweighed the positives.

The first of three main problems I saw in the inquiry process was one common to many other classroom activities in this structured, test-heavy class: students got confused about which step in the teacher's plan they ought to be "on." These girls' attempts to move on to step three, "needs and plans" without dwelling on the second step, "make conjectures," was therefore not out of the ordinary, though delays caused by errant students caused teachers to spend even more time making sure students were on task and doing the "right" step (cf. Dyson, 2006). Regardless of the intent behind the inquiry process, the teacher's manual-given plan automatically positioned students as objects in the learning process, as people who needed to wait to be told what to do when, and to follow orders. Ms. Romano was used to following steps and having her students follow steps in other lessons in the curriculum—indeed, she and her colleagues had attended workshops in the Ruby Payne (2001) style, in which they learned that poor children need steps and clear direction to follow in order to learn in school (see Bomer, Dworin, May, & Semingson, 2008; and Gorski, 2006, for critiques of this deterministic, classist ideology).

A second result was the further deskilling of teachers. Ms. Romano and her students had had to be trained in the inquiry process by the literacy coach (who had in turn been trained by a district coach), in a series of lessons that made Ms. Romano's own lack of ability to help students inquire clear to her. She was then required to make her students follow the plan and stick to the six-step cycle—again, highlighting the publishers' opinion that she and her students were not capable of inquiring on their own. In what was ostensibly a time for students to work independently, Ms. Romano had to go from table to table checking to make sure students were on the right step and were making correct guesses (pardon me: conjectures!). She told me that she appreciated the potential of the inquiry process for students to work and think independently, but in practice, she was unable to engage in discussions of ideas aside from a few quick initiate–reply–evaluate (I–R–E) exchanges (Cazden & Mehan, 1989) because she had to police students' progress and keep them on track. Paradoxically, this led to a double loss of control: teachers in classrooms like these are actually deskilled while, and because, they follow directions to make students follow steps (cf. Valli & Chambliss, 2007). This deskilling contributed to banking models of education, since teachers are not able to learn with and from their students, but are positioned by the curriculum as dehumanized, and dehumanizing, agents of control.

The third, and arguably worst, aspect of attempting to standardize critical literacy and inquiry was that adults made students' difficult and out-of-bounds inquiries inappropriate through a combination of outright rejection of ideas and subtle maneuvering. The pressure to conform to the cycle, and to push students to do the same, drained the process of any potential for the development of critical literacy skills. As noted above (in steps 1–11 of the "procedure for choosing a problem to research" [SRA/McGraw-Hill, 2002, pp. 38–39]), the teacher's manual offered many hints about how teachers might elide questions that they perceived as too hard or complex to research. Thus, what might have been at the least a student-driven exploration of the workings of the stomach, and might have turned into more of a critical literacy activity if students were even allowed to make judgments about the veracity and utility of information they gathered from different sources, turned into an exercise in keeping on track, and in being on the right step in the right moment.

Creating Space for Critical Literacy in the Highly Structured Classroom

So, how can teachers engage in critical literacy practices in scripted/highly structured settings like this one? Despite my disparaging discussion of the implementation of the *Open Court Reading* Inquiry cycle, conducting student-centered inquiry in structured curriculum classrooms is not impossible. Teachers must advocate for their students' and their own intellectual freedom. They can begin by showing administrators and literacy coaches what is lost when students are forced into such narrow curricular regimes. Teachers must make conscious, informed decisions about which parts of the given curriculum they will use, and why, as well as which parts they will jettison, and why. They should consult with colleagues, literacy coaches, and their administrators for advice, guidance, and (repeating my first point about advocacy) to explain why change is necessary and why critical literacy activities are valuable for their students.

Teachers can start making changes in their classroom teaching by asking themselves how much control they need to have over classroom discussions and investigations. Vasquez (2001) explored how she dealt with control issues that arose in the midst of critical literacy activities; Ms. Romano would need to be willing to forgo some control in order to release herself and her students from the need to follow pedantic, prescriptive steps. In the classroom, a synergistic blend of overlapping research "steps," including discussion, writing, questioning, thinking, and revising of questions, should be privileged over adherence to any set of precise steps. Teachers working with Kersten & Pardo (2007) negotiated their school's high-stakes requirements and lesson plans to create innovative literacy practices. Ms. Romano could have gone off script and let her students make "conjectures" and "plans" at the same time, or she could have improvised to respond to her student's immediate questions and needs. In a reversal of Ms. Romano's situation in which the literacy coach called the shots about "inquiry," Paugh, Carey, King-Jackson, and Russell (2007) show a teacher working with her school's literacy coach to shift interactional patterns and classroom workspaces to create critical literacy spaces. And, indeed, Ms. Romano could have tried to work with Ms. Forrest, the literacy coach, to make the inquiry process more flexible and student-centered, and less scripted and narrow.

I do not believe that the majority of teachers in such classrooms are simply forced to distribute what Freebody and Luke (2003) term "narrowly defined sets of psychological and behavioural skills" (p. 57) to their students. Even in a high-stakes climate like the one at Laurel Elementary where Ms. Romano taught, there is room and scope for teachers and students to work together to make inquiries into their lived experiences and the things about which they want to learn. Pennington (2007) suggests that there is space for individual teachers to make agentive changes to their instruction through curricular improvisation. Refuting pseudocritical literacy practices like "Inquiry" units, and branching out into student-centered inquiry projects that offer students real chances to acquire critical literacy skills (see, for example, Berghoff, Egawa, Harste, & Hoonan, 2000), can help ensure that critical literacy has a place even in classrooms where teachers must use structured curricula.

Ultimately, I recommend a new kind of curricular mandate: that *teachers* plan the kind of language arts instruction they think best fits their students' needs, which may or may not include critical literacy activities. They can use the resources offered by structured programs like *Open Court Reading*, or any other mandated curriculum, but they should be allowed to create inquiry processes that work with and for their students. Forcing scripted "Inquiry" on teachers and students, and assuming that the process will help students acquire critical thinking skills and engage in critical literacy practices, only produces the opposite: students (and teachers) who meekly follow directions and try to offer their teacher or literacy coach the "right" answer. Such negative outcomes are only exacerbated in high-stakes settings like Ms. Romano's classroom and school, where teachers and students are already focused on getting the right answers for tests and evaluations. In such intellectually confining circumstances, it is no wonder that attempts to standardize critical literacy only result in its erasure.

References

Alvermann, D., Moon, J., & Hagood, M. (1999). *Popular culture in the classroom: Teaching and researching critical media literacy.* Newark, DE: International Reading Association.

Arya, P., Laster, B., & Lin, L. (2005). An open look at the Open Court program. In B. Altwerger (Ed.) *Reading for profit: How the bottom line leaves kids behind* (pp. 128–141). Portsmouth, NH: Heinemann.

August, D. & Shanahan, T. (Eds.) (2006). *Developing literacy in second-language learners: Report of the National Literacy Panel on Language Minority Children and Youth.* Mahwah, NJ: Erlbaum.

Baker, E., Barton, P., Darling-Hammond, L., Haertel, E., Ladd, H., Linn, R., Ravitch, D., Rothstein, R., Shavelson, R., & Shepard, L. (2010). *Problems with the use of student test scores to evaluate teachers.* Washington, DC: Economic Policy Institute.

Bakhtin, M. M. (1981). Discourse in the novel. In M. Holquist (Ed.) *The dialogic imagination.* C. Emerson & M. Holquist, Trans. (pp. 259–422). Austin, TX: University of Texas Press.

Berghoff, B., Egawa, K. A., Harste, J. C., & Hoonan, B. T. (2000). *Beyond reading and writing: Inquiry curriculum, and multiple ways of knowing*. Urbana, IL: National Council of Teachers of English.

Bomer, R., Dworin, J., May, L., & Semingson, P. (2008). Miseducating teachers about the poor: A critical analysis of Ruby Payne's claims about poverty. *Teachers College Record*, *10* (11). Retrieved from http://www.tcrecord.org/content.asp?ContentsId=14591.

Cazden, C. & Mehan, H. (1989). Principles for sociology and anthropology: Context, code, classroom, and culture. In C. Cazden & H. Mehan (Eds.) *Knowledge base for the beginning teacher* (pp. 47–57). Oxford, UK: Pergamon.

Comber, B. (2001). Critical inquiry or safe literacies: Who's allowed to ask which questions? In S. Boran & B. Comber (Eds.) *Critiquing whole language and classroom inquiry* (pp. 81–102). Urbana, IL: National Council of Teachers of English.

Comber, P., Thomson, P., & Wells, M. (2001). Critical literacy finds a "place": Writing and social action in a low-income Australian grade 2/3 classroom. *The Elementary School Journal*, *101* (4), 451–464.

Dyson, A.H. (2006). On saying it right (write): "Fix-Its" in the foundations of learning to write. *Research in the Teaching of English*, *41*, 8–42.

Fang, Z., Fu, D., & Lamme, L. L. (2004). From scripted instruction to teacher empowerment: Supporting literacy teachers to make pedagogical transitions. *Literacy*, *38* (1), 58–64.

Felch, J., Song, J., & Smith, D. (2010, August 14). Who's teaching L.A.'s kids? http://www.latimes.com/news/local/la-me-teachers-value-20100815,0,258862,full.story.

Freebody, P. & Luke, A. (2003). Literacy as engaging with new forms of life: The Four roles model. In G. Bull & M. Anstey (Eds.) *The literacy lexicon*, 2nd edn (pp. 51–66). Melbourne, Australia: Pearson Education Australia.

Freire, P. (2000). *Pedagogy of the oppressed*. New York, NY: Continuum.

Gorski, P. (2006, February 9). The classist underpinnings of Ruby Payne's framework. *Teachers college record*. Retrieved from http://www.tcrecord.org, ID number: 12322.

Houghton Mifflin. (2003). *Houghton Mifflin reading: A legacy of literacy*. Boston, MA: Houghton Mifflin Company.

Janks, H. (2010). *Literacy and power*. London, UK: Routledge.

Kersten, J. & Pardo, L. (2007). Finessing and hybridizing: Innovative literacy practices in Reading First classrooms. *The Reading Teacher 61* (2), 146–154.

Luke, A. (1988). *Literacy, textbooks, and ideology: Postwar literacy instruction and the mythology of Dick and Jan e*. New York, NY: Falmer Press.

McCarthey, S. (2009). The impact of No Child Left Behind on teachers' writing instruction. *Written Communication*, *25* (4), 462–505.

Menken, K. (2006). Teaching to the test: How No Child Left Behind impacts language policy, curriculum, and instruction for English language learners. *Bilingual Research Journal*, *30*, 521–546.

Morrell, E. (2002). Toward a critical pedagogy of popular culture: Literacy development among urban youth. *Journal of Adolescent & Adult Literacy*, *46* (1), 72–77.

O'Brien, J. (2001). "I knew that already": How children's books limit inquiry. In S. Boran & B. Comber (Eds.) *Critiquing whole language and classroom inquiry* (pp. 142–168). Urbana, IL: National Council of Teachers of English.

Paugh, P., Carey, J., King-Jackson, V., & Russell, S. (2007). Negotiating the literacy block: Constructing spaces for critical literacy in a high-stakes setting. *Language Arts*, *85* (1), 31–42.

Payne, R. (2001). *A framework for understanding poverty*. Highlands, TX: Aha! Process.

Pennington, J.L. (2007). Re-viewing NCLB through the figured worlds of policy and teaching: Creating a space for teacher agency and improvisation. *Language Arts, 84* (5), 465–474.

Rogers, R., Mosely, M., & Folkes, A. (2009). Standing up to Neoliberalism through critical literacy education. *Language Arts, 87* (2), 127–138.

Ruiz, N. & Morales-Ellis, L. (2005). "Gracias por la oportunidad, pero voy a buscar otro trabajo . . ." A beginning teacher resists high-stakes curriculum. In B. Altwerger (Ed.), *Reading for profit: How the bottom line leaves kids behind* (pp. 199–215). Portsmouth, NH: Heinemann.

Samway, K. D. & Pease-Alvarez, L. (2005) Teachers' perspectives on Open Court. In B. Altwerger (Ed.) *Reading for profit: How the bottom line leaves kids behind* (pp. 142–155). Portsmouth, NH: Heinemann.

Short, K. & Burke, C. (2001). Curriculum as inquiry. In S. Boran & B. Comber (Eds.) *Critiquing whole language and classroom inquiry* (pp. 18–41). Urbana, IL: National Council of Teachers of English.

SRA/McGraw-Hill. (2002). *Open court reading: Teacher's edition, level 4, unit 1.* Columbus, OH: SRA/McGraw-Hill.

SRA/McGraw-Hill. (2005). *Open court reading.* Columbus, OH: SRA/McGraw-Hill.

Stevens, L. & Bean, T. (2007). *Critical literacy: Context, research and practice in the K-12 classroom.* Thousand Oaks, CA: Sage Publications.

Valli, L. & Chambliss, M. (2007). Creating classroom cultures: One teacher, two lessons, and a high-stakes test. *Anthropology & Education Quarterly, 38* (1), 57–75.

Vasquez, V. (2001). Constructing a critical curriculum with young children. In Comber, B. & Simpson, A. (Eds.). (2001) *Negotiating critical literacies in classrooms* (pp. 55–66). Mahwah, NJ: Erlbaum.

Vygotsky, L. (1986). *Thought and language.* A. Kozulin, Trans. Cambridge, MA: MIT Press.

Wiltz, N. & Wilson, G. P. (2006). An inquiry into children's reading in one urban school using SRA reading mastery (direct instruction). *Journal of Literacy Research, 37,* 493–528.

Zacher Pandya, J. (2011). *Overtested: How high-stakes accountability fails English language learners.* New York, NY: Teachers College Press.

13

INQUIRY INTO THE INCIDENTAL UNFOLDING OF SOCIAL JUSTICE ISSUES

20 Years of Seeking Out Possibilities for Critical Literacies

Vivian Maria Vasquez

Negotiating Critical Literacies Using Children's Artifacts of Learning

One of the key tenets of critical literacy (Larson & Marsh, 2005; Vasquez, 2010) is that it works to disrupt normalized social practices. Another tenet, which I have promoted through the years, is that critical literacies need to be lived (Vasquez, 2001, 2004; Vasquez, Muise, Nakai, Shear, & Heffernan, 2003; Vasquez & Felderman, 2013). In keeping with these tenets I have crafted this chapter in such a way that it somewhat disrupts the normalized format of academic writing by creating an audit trail (Harste & Vasquez, 1998; Vasquez, 2004) of my inquiry into critical literacy, beginning in 1993. To create this audit trail I will use artifacts that represent significant "critical literacy" moments in my life as a teacher researcher and academic researcher. These artifacts are material objects such as a child's writing or drawing, a book cover, a photograph, and other such items that work semiotically to embody a past experience or event. My intent in doing this is to show and tell about how and why, 20 years later, critical literacies continue to have relevance in my work with classroom teachers and young children.

The first artifact in my audit trail is a pair of letters, written by Marianne and Eric (the children's names throughout this chapter are pseudonyms) in 1993 (Figures 13.1 and 13.2 – Artifact 1). This pair of letters represents the first pieces of data that I analyzed as I began my exploration into critical literacies in the early 1990s. At the time I was in a public school setting, working as a first- and second-grade teacher in an ethnically diverse community located about 20 minutes outside of Toronto, Ontario, Canada. At the time, I was completing a Masters degree in Literacy Education. One of the courses for this degree was held at the University of South Australia, where Barbara Comber was teaching. (For more on Comber, refer to Comber, 1992, 1993; Comber & O'Brien, 1993.) It was that summer, while working with Barbara, that I first became interested in exploring critical literacy. In particular the work done by Comber and O'Brien (1993) on analyzing everyday text fascinated me. In this critical literacy work, O'Brien (1994) created spaces for her 5–7-year-old students to attend "to the way language is used to construct reality, and to the critical issue of the positioning of readers in and by texts" (p. 45). At the time, this kind of work with children pushed at my definition of critical literacy that "involved taking action to resist, and to expose the discourse of dominant cultures" (Vasquez, 1994, p. 39).

Research as a Way of Teaching

I entered into the world of critical literacy as a preschool and elementary school teacher who had learned to use researching as a way of teaching, from books I had read (Bissex, 1985; Brice Heath, 1983; Harste, Woodward, & Burke, 1984) as well as from professional development events. I also entered into the world of critical literacy having experienced racism and othering as well as bullying as a child. However, it was an incident that took place during my first year of teaching that opened my eyes to the importance of creating curriculum based on "kid-watching" (Goodman, 1978). In a paper (Vasquez, 2013) describing this incident, I wrote,

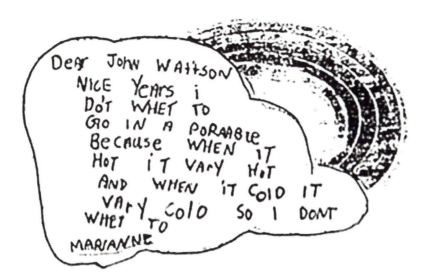

FIGURES 13.1 Artifact 1, children's letters.

Note: "Dear John Wattson Next year I don't want to go in a portable because when it hot it very hot and when it cold it very cold so I don't want to. Marianne

FIGURES 13.2 Artifact 1, children's letters.

Note: Dear Mrs. Ciuffo. Could you please tell me Why do we only have French time. Why can't we have different language like Spanish & Chinese so if we have a friend that can't speak our language then if we can speak their language we can speak to each other. Can you please write back to me.

Early in my career, while teaching first grade, at a time when learning centers were all the rage, I experienced a literacy event with 6-year-old Kevin who opened my eyes to how much I could learn from my students. During writing time one day, I noticed Kevin was drawing. "Kevin, it's writing time and during writing time I expect you to write," I said. He responded, "But Miss Vasquez if I don't draw then I won't know what to write about." I left Kevin alone that day and watched as he drew and then wrote and then drew and then wrote some more. He taught me to watch more closely and to interpret and re-interpret what I was observing and then use my interpretations and analysis of those observations to construct powerful learning opportunities for my students. On that day I realized how powerful it would be to use research as a way of teaching (p. 80).

Reflecting on my experience with Kevin pushed me to consider how I could use "kid-watching" as a way to organically negotiate and create opportunities for critical literacies from my students' inquiry questions and topics of interest. Informed by the scholarship of groundbreaking researchers of literacy, such as Haas Dyson (1989), Bissex (1985) and Harste, Woodward, & Burke (1984), I decided to revisit existing data from my classroom, with the intent of examining where opportunities for critical literacies may have been possible, as a way of helping me imagine how I might go about creating spaces for critical literacy from my students' interests. In particular I was interested in teaching my students how to read texts critically, in relation to the ways in which they work to position readers (Janks, 1993), and write texts critically, as a step towards positioning themselves differently in the world (Vasquez, 1994).

When I revisited letters (Figures 13.1 and 13.2; Artifact 1) written by a group of 6–8-year-old children with whom I worked, during the year leading up to my summer in Australia, I realized I was engaging in what could be called a naïve form of literacy (Lankshear, 1989; Comber, 1993). That is a form of literacy that protects and maintains the status quo and in doing so maintains the conditions within which subordinate groups are disadvantaged. Marianne and Eric, through the letters they wrote, were attempting to write themselves into a different existence. Davies (1993) reminds us that in learning to read and write children also learn to exist within the particular authority relations of the classroom. They also learn a different way of positioning themselves and being positioned into the storylines of the worlds they inhabit. At the time I did not have the theoretical tools to understand this and instead treated their letters as examples of writing for a particular audience rather than writing to disrupt problematic normalized social practices. It was clear to me I had missed an opportunity for critical literacy, because my focus was on helping them participate with text and use text without engaging in the analysis of text (Luke & Freebody, 1999). It was at this time that I began to explore ways of using critical literacy as a frame through which to participate in the world (Vasquez, 2004, 2010; Vasquez & Felderman, 2013). I asked myself: How might I capture my students' interests as they participate in the world around them, and then use those interests as text to build a curriculum that has significance in their lives?

The year following my analysis of the children's letters, I was transferred to a classroom for 3–5-year-olds. From the start of that school year, my plan was to create spaces for critical literacy using my students' interests, questions, passions, and desires. Our school was pre-K to eighth grade, with approximately 800 students. It was located in a middle-income neighborhood in a suburb of Toronto, Ontario, Canada. In our class of 18 students, we had 11 ethnicities represented, including children from Malta, the Philippines, and Peru.

The second artifact in my audit trail is a letter written to a librarian after a brief conversation between two children from the class (Figure 13.3). The children had been looking for a book on the Philippines to support Emma, a new student in the class, whose family had just moved to Canada from the Philippines. Their quest was met with frustration when they learned there were no books with characters who might be identified as Filipino, nor were there any resource books on the Philippines. In that moment some of the children experienced the notion of being other, of not having spaces and opportunities to belong. They shared their concern with the rest of the class during a class meeting.

I decided to use the incident as an opportunity to create a space for some critical literacy work by suggesting a class project focusing on the question, "Do we see ourselves in books that are in our school library?" Only the children who identified as White immediately found themselves represented in many of the books. The children and I were therefore disturbed when we searched through the shelves of our school library over the next few weeks and discovered the following:

- There were no books on the Philippines.
- The books on Peru were outdated and were published in the 1970s.
- There were no books on Malta.

FIGURE 13.3   Artifact 2: A letter to the librarian.

Note: Dear Our class did research in the library on books. This is what we found out. The other paper has books you should buy.

While discussing possible ways of acting on this newly named issue, a group of students suggested writing a letter to our school librarian. The letter was meant to alert the librarian to the research we had done that revealed a lack of diversity in the children's books available in the library. Together with the letter, we included a list of books with characters from diverse ethnicities and backgrounds and bilingual books that could be purchased for the school. The list was created by one of the boys in the class with his parents. When presented with the findings, the librarian appeared genuinely disturbed. She was therefore very receptive to receiving our list. Apparently she had not thought about the marginalization of certain individuals and groups of students when they are unable to see themselves in books and other texts used in school. She immediately worked on ordering books to address our concerns. She also began rethinking the decisions she made regarding which books to display based on who was represented and not represented by those books.

We included this project in a class newsletter sent home to the children's families. From the newsletter, Mena and her family began to explore how different cultures are represented by the way in which books are displayed at local bookstores. She and her parents talked to the manager of their neighborhood bookstore, emphasizing the need for books that represent diverse cultures to be available all year, and not just for special events such as Black History Month or Women's History Month. Anthony and his mother questioned why children's literature was hidden in the back corner of their local bookstore and why a computer used to locate books was not available in the children's section as it was in other areas. It was amazing to learn about ways that my students had taken what they had learned in the classroom into their homes to engage in projects with their parents.

I found this critical literacy experience to be powerful because it had real-world effects. The children's actions led them to highlight the lack of diversity in the books at the school library as problematic. In the end, bringing this to the awareness of the school librarian led to the purchase of more diverse children's literature. Sharing our project with the children's families resulted in extending the learning beyond the four walls of our classroom into some of the children's homes and the community.

The year after the letter to the librarian was written, I once again had the opportunity to work with a prekindergarten class of 3–5-year-olds. Before the start of the new school year I took a look back and analyzed the data I had produced over the course of the previous year. What resulted was a realization that, although I had been much more successful at creating spaces for critical literacy, the moments spent engaging in critical literacy work were disconnected and isolated instances of learning. It was as though critical literacy was dropping in and out of our curriculum. With a new year ahead of me I decided to explore ways of creating generative and ongoing spaces for critical literacy. To do this I asked the following questions:

1. How might we frame all that we do in the classroom from a critical literacy perspective?
2. How might we live a critical literacy curriculum throughout the school year?

The first step in answering these questions was to articulate better, for myself and those interested, what I felt were key tenets that comprised my critical literacy toolkit. I will not outline those tenets here as I have written about them elsewhere (Vasquez, 2010; Vasquez & Felderman, 2013; Vasquez, Tate, & Harste, 2013).

Artifact 3 (Figure 13.4) is a photo of part of what I began referring to as an audit trail of learning (Vasquez, 2004). This trail was comprised of different artifacts representing the various projects my students and I took on from the first day of class to the last day of class. After each project the group discussed what to post on the audit trail to remind us of the work we had done (e.g., photographs, transcripts of a conversations, drawings, cutouts from a magazines). It became a visual articulation of our thinking, learning, and researching over the course of a school year. The audit trail represented how one issue seamlessly flowed into the next and how our critical literacy journeys were intimately connected and also cross-curricular. For instance, at one point in time the children problematized the highly carnist diet inadvertently followed by our school. This happened when they discovered that one of children in the class, and his family, were not able to eat anything at the school barbecue because they were vegetarian. The result was a social action project that involved surveying our school population regarding food lifestyle choices and a letter-writing campaign to ensure that vegetarian options were available at school events not only in our own setting but in other schools within our district as well. In the end, vegetarian options became available for all events in our school, including faculty events and meetings.

While researching vegetarian issues, the children discovered we had no books about being a vegetarian in our school library, even though we had vegetarian families in our school. This generated another social action project aimed at

FIGURE 13.4   Artifact 3: An audit trail of learning.

disrupting the dominance of children's books, such as recipe books and books focused on food and eating that represented carnist lifestyles. That social action project then resulted in a conversation about inequality and inequitable ways of being, which generated projects dealing with ways that the prekindergarten children were being marginalized in our school by not allowing them to participate in many of our "school community" events. These projects were represented on our audit trail by different artifacts of learning, such as copies of the letters the children had written or a book cover from one of the books they read pertaining to a particular study. This work represents only a small portion of the generative and seamless learning that took place throughout the year. As my year with these children ended I transitioned into the life of academia, and I used the existing data, from the year of the audit trail, in my research. My transition into researching in academia was seamless as a result of my experiences as a teacher researcher.

One of the things that stood out from analyzing the audit trail data was an understanding of how young children read the word and the world (Freire, 1970) and how capitalizing on this understanding helped me to find ways to support them in challenging, critiquing, and redesigning historical and existing dominant narratives that work to "devalue their experiences" (Janks and Vasquez, 2011, p. 2). To have been able to do this across the curriculum added to the power and pleasure of our learning endeavors since, at the time, most of what had been written about with regard to critical literacy practice had focused primarily on reading and language arts (Morgan, 1997; Fehring and Green, 2001).

Most recently I have focused my work at the intersection of critical literacy and technology (Vasquez, 2013), in particular working in early childhood settings with children between the ages of 4 and 8. Artifact 4 is a drawing that was created by my son when he was 4 years old. It was made when his preschool teacher asked him to draw a picture of his family. This is what he drew (Figure 13.5). When he brought the drawing home I asked him to tell me about it. He had drawn my husband, himself, and me holding iPod Touches. When I asked him about the different-colored dots on the iPods he told me that he drew different-colored dots to show we have different "apps" (applications) on our iPods because, he said, we each have different interests. This to me is a clear demonstration of the ways in which children today are born and quickly introduced into a world in which new technologies and new forms of communication are widespread. The result is the ability to participate in the world with new ways of thinking, being, and doing, which impact their lives at home and at school. This incident, along with a few other instances of interacting with children in relation to their interest in technology, generated a curiosity as to the role technology could play in creating spaces for critical literacy.

My recent work therefore focuses on an exploration of the "technoliteracies" (Marsh, 2002, p. 127) with which young children might engage in the world from a critical literacies perspective. Marsh argues that the multimodal textual competencies and semiotic choices of children, referred to by Luke (2007) as netizens, are not given sufficient space within current curriculum frameworks to

FIGURE 13.5   Artifact 4: The iPod family.

support their learning. How then do we provide this space while building from the interests of the children? Along with a colleague, Carol Felderman, I sought to explore how classroom teachers have reshaped curriculum with new technologies in mind (Vasquez & Felderman, 2013). In spite of the fact that "teachers of young children are asked to teach to the test in ways that take away opportunities for holistic, thoughtful, play-oriented practices" (Early Childhood Education Assembly, 2007), what we found were classrooms where teachers of young children had used their students' inquiry questions to create spaces for critical literacy and use technological tools to research, communicate, design and redesign, and make accessible their projects to a broader global audience.

For instance, a colleague of ours shared an experience she had with a preschool class in Georgia. The children, frustrated with the trash accumulating along the river by the playground at their school, decided to take action. The problem was that there was a fence separating the playground from the river, meaning that they could not get to the trash. For safety reasons, they were not allowed on the other side of the fence. Rather than give up, they turned to the internet to search for information about the water situation in their area, and, specifically they searched for information on water use and water pollution. What they discovered was that much of the water used in the city was from toilet flushing. They followed up by searching online for possible ways to reduce the amount of water used in this way.

What they learned was that putting a sealed plastic container filled with rocks or sand in the toilet tank reduces the amount of water that is needed to flush. The children began a recycling drive and collected small plastic containers like the containers used to hold ready-made icing. After making a bunch of these containers, they distributed them to their families and community members, asking them to put the devices inside the water tanks of their toilets as one way to contribute to the conservation of water and to recycle containers that likely would have ended up in a landfill site. This work is in keeping with a pedagogy that Comber and Nixon (this volume) refer to as "across-curriculum place-based pedagogy," a pedagogy that "allows young people to connect with their places, environments, and each other." The work done by these children cut across content areas such as language arts, science, social studies, and mathematics, and technology was a tool that they used across these areas. The first three are a bit more obvious. Mathematics comes into play as the children measured and calculated the size of the containers and the amount of rock or sand with which to fill each one.

Conclusion

Over the past 20 years, the focus of my work in critical literacy has shifted in organic ways based on the interests of the children with whom I have worked and researched and the context in which I have done this work. My focus started with reading and writing texts critically (Vasquez, 1994, 1998). When I began this work, what I wanted was for my students to be engaged with critical literacies by studying their own interests. I quickly realized this was not enough and that, from a critical literacy perspective, my students needed opportunities to "have a sense of how the text could be different . . . to read the content, form and interests of the text, however unconsciously, in order to be able to redesign it" (Janks and Vasquez, 2011, p. 3). With this shift in understanding I began exploring ways of creating spaces for critical social action across the curriculum (Vasquez, 2010) and then on critical literacy and "the consumption and production of texts broadly defined" (Janks and Vasquez, 2011, p. 1) including the use of technology and new digital tools.

It seems as I continue to participate in a dance of critical literacy that new changes and possibilities come into being. These provide fertile ground upon which to take up the challenges to language and literacy teachers at varying levels of education and in different educational contexts. Hilary Janks and I believe,

> these challenges and possibilities create spaces for new and exciting opportunities to further explore critical literacies . . . and that none of these changes minimise the need for an understanding of the social effects of textual practices. If anything, we would argue that the more complex and multimodal texts become, the more important it is for "readers" to understand the politics of semiosis and the textual instantiations of power.
>
> *(Janks and Vasquez, 2011, p. 2)*

Regardless of the challenges that arise, and the different ways that critical literacies have been taken up over the past 20 years, I continue to believe that the critical literacy work that needs to continue must focus on "understanding the relationship between texts, meaning-making and power in order to undertake transformative social action" (Janks and Vasquez, 2011, p. 1). I also believe this work needs to be based on the needs and desires of particular communities, with a focus on ways individuals and groups within those communities can contribute "to the achievement of a more equitable social order" (Janks and Vasquez, 2011, p. 1).

Carrington (2008) reminds us that:

> For literacy education to make a real difference in the lives and futures of the young people who move in and out of complex social fields and who are growing up in a post-traditional risk society, it is necessary to acknowledge that childhood is not what it used to be and that curricula, school hierarchies, and classrooms cannot, therefore, continue to be what they used to be (p. 164).

The same is true for critical literacy. We have known for some time now that critical literacies achieve life work when the projects taken on by teachers and their students are focused on real-world issues that are important in the particular context in which the children live their lives, and that use the resources currently available. Some of the resources currently available include digital tools. In her definition of young technology users, Wohlwend notes that an identity associated with such users is that they are "curious explorers who willingly play with new media" (Wohlwend, 2009, p. 117). Although on its own curiosity is not enough, Janks (2010) reminds us that the pleasure that comes with new discoveries and opportunities "can renew us" (p. 224). Renewal is particularly attractive given that "change is so rapid, it is difficult to imagine what the landscape will look like by the time the generation currently in school will graduate" (Janks and Vasquez, 2010, p. 2). Perhaps ongoing renewal will keep us imagining and reimagining much-needed spaces for critical literacies.

References

Bissex, G.L. (1985). *Gnys at wrk: A child learns to write and read.* Cambridge, MA: Harvard University Press.

Brice Heath, S. (1983). *Ways with words.* Cambridge, UK: Cambridge University Press.

Carrington, V. (2008). I'm Dylan, I'm not going to say my last name: Some thoughts on childhood, text and new technologies. *British Educational Research Journal, 32* (2), 151–166.

Comber, B. (1992). Critical literacy: A selective review and discussion of the recent literature. *South Australian Educational Leader, 3* (1), 1–10.

Comber, B. (1993). Classroom explorations in critical literacy. *Australian Journal of Language and Literacy, 16* (1), 73–83.

Comber, B. & O'Brien, J. (1993). *Critical literacy: Classroom explorations. Critical Pedagogy Networker, 6,* 1–11.

Davies, B. (1993). *Shards of glass: Children reading and writing beyond gendered identities.* St. Leonards, NSW: Allen & Unwin.

Early Childhood Education Assembly (2007). Retrieved from: http://www.eceassembly. blogspot.com/.

Fehring, H. & Green, P. (Eds.) (2001). *Critical literacy: A collection of articles from the Australian Literacy Educators' Association.* Newark, DE: International Reading Association.

Freire, P. (1970). *Cultural action for freedom.* Cambridge, MA: Harvard Educational Review and Center for the Study of Development and Social Change.

Goodman, Y.M. (1978). Kid-watching: an alternative to testing. *National Elementary School Principal, 57* (4), 41–45.

Haas Dyson, A. (1989) *Multiple worlds of child writers: Friends learning to write.* New York, NY: Teachers College Press.

Harste, J. & Vasquez, V. (1998). The work we do: Journal as audit trail. *Language Arts, 75* (4), 266–276.

Harste, J.C., Woodward, V.A., & Burke, C.L. (1984). *Language stories and literacy lessons.* Portsmouth, NH: Heinemann.

Janks, H. (1993). *Language, identity and power.* Johannesburg, South Africa: Witwatersrand University Press.

Janks, J. (2010). *Literacy and power.* New York, NY: Routledge.

Janks, H. & Vasquez, V. (2010). Critical literacy revisited: Writing as critique. *English Teaching: Practice and Critique, 10* (1), 1–6. Retrieved from http://edlinked.soe.waikato. ac.nz/research/journal/view.php?id=54&p=1.

Janks, H. & Vasquez, V. (2011). Critical literacy revisited: Writing as critique. *English Teaching: Practice and Critique, 10* (1): 1–6. Retrieved from http://edlinked.soe.waikato. ac.nz/research/files/etpc/files/2011v10n1ed.pdf.

Lankshear, C. (1989). Reading and righting wrongs: Literacy and the underclass. *Language and Education, 3* (3).

Larson, J. & Marsh, J. (2005). *Making literacy real.* Thousand Oaks, CA: Sage.

Luke, A. (2007). The body literate: Discourse and inscription in early literacy. In T. Van Dijk (Ed.) *Discourse studies, IV,* pp. 1–22. London, UK: Sage Publications.

Luke, A. & Freebody, P. (1999) Further notes on the Four Resources model. *Reading Online.* http: www.readingonline.org/research/lukefreebody.html.

Marsh, J. (2002). Popular culture, computer games and the primary curriculum. In M. Monteith (Ed.) *Teaching primary literacy through ICT* (pp. 127–143). Buckinghamshire, UK: Open University Press.

Morgan, W. (1997). *Critical literacy in the classroom: The art of the possible.* New York, NY: Routledge.

O'Brien, J. (1994). Show mum you love her. *Reading, 28* (1), 43–46.

Vasquez, V. (1994). A step in the dance of critical literacy. *UKRA Reading, 28* (1), 39–43.

Vasquez, V. (1998). Building equitable communities: Taking social action in a kindergarten classroom. *Talking Points, 9* (2), 3–7.

Vasquez, V. (2001). Constructing a critical curriculum with young children. In B. Comber & A. Simpson (Eds.) *Critical literacy at elementary sites* (pp. 55–66). Mahwah, NJ: Lawrence Erlbaum Associates.

Vasquez, V. (2004). *Negotiating critical literacies with young children.* New York, NY: Routledge.

Vasquez, V. (2010). *Getting beyond I like the book: Creating spaces for critical literacy in K-6 settings.* Newark, DE: International Reading Association.

Vasquez, V. (2013). Children's literature: A critical literacy perspective. In C. Kosnik, R. Simon, P. Williamson, J. Rowsell & C. Beck (Eds.) *Literacy teacher educators: Preparing teachers for a changing world.* New York, NY: Sense Publishers.

Vasquez, V. & Felderman, C. (2013). *Technology and critical literacy in early childhood.* New York, NY: Routledge.

Vasquez, V., Muise, M., Nakai, D., Shear, J., & Heffernan, L. (2003). *Getting beyond I like the book: Creating spaces for critical literacy in K-6 classrooms.* Newark, DE: International Reading Association.

Vasquez, V., Tate, S., & Harste, J.C. (2013). *Negotiating critical literacies with teachers.* New York, NY: Routledge.

Wohlwend, K. (2009). Early adopters: Playing literacies and pretending new technologies in print-centric classrooms. *Journal of Early Childhood Literacy, 9* (2), 117–140.

14

CONCLUSION

Affective and Global Ecologies: New Directions for Critical Literacy

Cynthia Lewis

The contributors to this volume argue that not only is there a continuing need for critically literate citizens in the face of changing economies, policies, and technologies, but that scholars need to expand the focus of contemporary critical literacy by attending to the embodied and sociomaterial dimensions of critical literacy as well as those literacies related to globalization and digital media. In doing so, some authors specifically critique the policies that standardize knowledge and create structural barriers to critical literacy, extending earlier scholarship on critical literacy and acknowledging that, despite its "verbo and logo-centric" foundations (Johnson & Vasudevan, this volume), critical literacy has always included attention to multiple modes and lived experiences.

Using Bakhtin's (1984) theories of carnival as a way of reimagining critical pedagogy, Lensmire (2011) undercuts the seriousness of its rationalist tendencies in light of the historical importance of humor and embodiment in all meaningful and transformative critical projects. Lensmire reminds us that, for decades, Ellsworth (1989), Grande (2004), and others have interrupted the rationalist, male, Western biases of critical pedagogy, insisting that its own ideologies be subject to critique while at the same time supporting its underlying political project. The chapters in this volume offer insightful examples of this work as it relates specifically to critical literacy. That is, the authors advocate the importance of critical literacy as a political project, but also reimagine critical literacy in light of contemporary developments related to embodiment and spatiality, digital technology and globalization, and, finally, standardization.[1]

As might be expected, these themes are not discrete. Globalization especially is an overarching theme that relates directly to the communication flows that result from digital media, which, in turn, have been associated with unprecedented forms of embodiment and affect. As Ellsworth (2004) pointed out, media texts set "representations into motion across emergent contexts," resulting in "new alignments" and "unexpected intensities" (p. 127) that challenge rationalist forms of ideological critique. But, whereas globalization, particularly as related to social media, is associated with heterogeneity and the disruption of dominant, mono-logic discourses, it is also a driving force for homogeneity and standardization (Santos, 2006; Pennycook, 2010), as in, for example, national and international standards of academic achievement.

As a whole, this volume works through the tensions inherent in some of these overlapping concerns. The chapter by Johnson and Vasudevan, for example, shows how stances that appear to be antithetical to critical literacy—e.g., ado-lescent females who appear to desire what advertisers want them to desire—can be viewed as intentionally savvy or humorously parodic in critically literate ways that, in Luke's words (this volume), contribute to "naming and renaming the world."

The foundations of critical literacy that undergird the chapters vary, based on whether the influence taken up is based on Freire's (1970) work or whether it is based on either poststructuralist theory or Hallidayan (1978) systemic linguistics. Luke discusses these foundational influences in his chapter of this volume (see also Morgan's [1997] excellent mapping of these influences in which she distinguishes between work in the Americas influenced by Freire and work in Australia influ-enced by Halliday). In keeping with these influences, I view the chapters in this volume that are more closely aligned with Freire as emphasizing the relationship between social structures and power (Comber & Nixon; Finn; Flint & Laman; Johnson & Vasudevan; Rosario-Ramos & Johnson) and chapters more closely aligned with Halliday as emphasizing the relationship between language and power (Exley, Woods, & Dooley; Janks; Moore, Zancanella & Ávila; Takekawa; Pandya; Vasquez). Social justice serves as the common thread throughout the chapters, no matter the influence, underscoring the ultimate goal of this political project, which several of the authors have been engaged in for decades.

New Directions: Three Themes

Three themes—embodiment/spatiality, digital technologies/globalization, and standardization—resonate throughout the volume to signal the future of critical literacy. I discuss these themes in what follows, occasionally inserting my own work into the conversation as it intersects with the themes developed in the volume.

Embodiment/Spatiality

As previously mentioned, critical literacy has long been critiqued for its rationalist and verbo-centric underpinnings. However, recent scholarship, including four chapters in this volume, has argued for a version of critical literacy that locates the body as central to both the experience of marginalization and to the enactment of counter-narratives. For example, based on a study of the enactment of critical literacy in a creative drama program, my colleagues and I found that embodied play held much potential for student-initiated critical literacy. Critical enactments often took the form of amplification, humor, or parody, which served to disrupt normative bodily habits and ways of being. In this sense, the actors interrupted commonplace notions of space and movement to heighten attention to issues of gender and authority (Doerr-Stevens, Lewis, Ingram, & Asp, in press).

Four chapters in this volume are especially related to the theme of embodiment/spatiality. One of these chapters, by contributors Johnson and Vasudevan, has already been discussed, so I move now to the others. Finn's chapter on social class, meritocracy, and structural inequality in three settings draws on work by Bourdieu, whose concept of habitus is explicitly connected to bodily dispositions as sedimented through structural conditions such as social class. Implicitly the body is implicated throughout this chapter in its focus on privilege/entitlement, regulation/resistance, and collective action as bodily habituses associated respectively with elite boarding schools, working-class public schools, and socialist Sunday schools.

Comber and Nixon's chapter makes visible the central role of space–place in critical literacy. Their account of critical literacy depends on a socio-material framework that assumes bodies constantly interact with the environment and tools or objects. Through this interaction, environments can alienate bodies or draw them in, and students can design spaces that will effect positive change and create a sense of belonging and joy.

The spatial reference point in the chapter by Rosario-Ramos and Johnson is the community. They argue for community-based institutions that foster intergenerational learning as essential to deepening the development of critical literacy. Schools, they contend, have not been effective at teaching socio-political critique, whereas youth are regularly immersed in socio-political critique in community-based organizations that have a social change/equity mission. Unlike many teachers who believe that critical literacy is too difficult for students who are at a "basic" literacy level, the authors of this chapter view marginalized communities as ideal spaces for promoting counter-narratives based on lived, intergenerational histories.

Digital Technologies/Globalization

Scholarship on critical literacy has been profoundly changed by globalization and the expansion of digital technologies. Often the two are intertwined, as in the work of Hull, Stornaiuolo, and Sahni (2010), in which they describe their work at connecting youth from around the world through a site called "space2cre8" (space2cre8.com). Although this work is explicitly about developing cosmopolitanism rather than critical literacy, cosmopolitanism assumes a probing of normative practices and local assumptions in the face of multilingual, multicultural communication, including collaborative video creation among global online peers.

Over a decade ago, Peters and Lankshear (1996) focused on the intersection of critical literacy and technology with an early analysis of the ways that digital texts reposition readers and writers, sometimes opening new spaces for criticality and reframing. The flip side, of course, is that increasingly visual and global culture requires new skills so that critical citizens can "read" the linguistic, visual, and aural signs and symbols that inundate their lives, public and private. As Karen Wohlwend and I indicated in a handbook chapter (2010) on the connection between critical and digital literacies:

> Our challenge is to reinterpret critical literacy for the new commonplace: visual and embodied texts, digital technologies, interactive media, and virtual spaces circulated through global flows that are at once universalizing and fragmenting (p. 189).

Two chapters in this volume, by Janks and Vasquez, do just that. Janks's chapter provides a strong argument for resisting the urge to swoon uncritically over digital affordances and their potential for design. It's easy to fall for the romance of digital production and its impact on youth engagement. I have done so myself. Yet, as Janks makes clear here and elsewhere, design without critique is, at best, incomplete, and, reflective of a naïve view of the author's intention/choice that views the author as a free agent.

In her chapter on the connection between classroom inquiry and critical literacy, Vasquez uses the method she is well known for—an audit trail—to follow the trail of her own movement through 20 years as a critical literacy teacher-scholar who followed her students' interests and desires, which eventually brought her to the intersection of critical literacy and technology. The chapters by Janks and Vasquez both argue that interpreting and producing semiotic texts of all kinds require complex critical practices and an analysis of the relationship between semiosis and power. Globalization has given rise to "complex forms of text production and dissemination" (Janks, this volume) that demand an ever more sophisticated critical literacy.

Standardization

Globalization both interrupts and produces homogenization. Five chapters in the volume deal with the homogenizing effects that take the form of centralized standards, testing, and accountability measures used to compete in the global market. These chapters show how critical literacy can be sustained or defeated in the face of standardization. Takekawa's chapter makes the effects of globalization on Japan's centralized curriculum explicit and illustrates the negative consequences, which include regulation of curriculum and the deprofessionalization of teachers. This chapter also offers examples of teachers who resist such control of their work and who create counter-pedagogies that build on students' experiences.

Of the remaining chapters, two (Moore, Zancanella, & Ávila; Pandya) focus on how standardization limits the enactment of critical literacy and two (Flint & Laman; Exley, Woods, & Dooley) address the way that teachers are able to work around or within standardization to offer students opportunities for critical literacy. Moore, Zancanella, and Ávila argue persuasively that the Common Core State Standard (CCSS) related to text complexity emphasizes texts at the expense of readers and contexts. Given that the CCSS emphasis on text complexity is often lauded as a positive change, compared to previous standards aimed at competence in basic reading skills, this chapter served as a much-needed examination of what gets lost in the process. This chapter also offers an important critical examination of the development of CCSS and the particular interests that have been served by its adoption.

Pandya's chapter demonstrates the dangers of another kind of standardization—the kind that occurs when textbooks institutionalize critical inquiry so that it becomes little more than a technical apparatus or regime of truth delivered through scripted curricula and divorced from any sense of genuine inquiry. This chapter reminds readers that critical literacy is not a curriculum but a practice (or many practices) based on a philosophy of language and its relationship to power, social structure, and the possibility of social transformation.

The possibility for social transformation through poetry writing is the focus of the chapter by Flint & Laman, who describe teachers' efforts to shift their pedagogy from scripted and formulaic writing exercises to poetry that connects to the social issues important to children's lives. The authors argue that writing should provide a space for children to produce knowledge creatively rather than reproduce or parrot it. Critical literacy, for these authors, takes the form of student-centered inquiry and knowledge production rather than the examination of language and power. One question that remains for me is how this version of critical literacy differs from other forms of progressive pedagogy, including inquiry-oriented classrooms, although the case made for the importance of student-produced knowledge is strong.

By contrast, an examination of language and power among young children is at the center of the chapter by Exley, Woods, & Dooley, demonstrating that 4- and 5-year-olds can engage in critical literacy practices focused on language and text analysis. This work took place within a standard curriculum that prescribed scripted materials and worksheets. The authors point to the range of critical literacy approaches that the teacher drew upon, arguing that these approaches worked together to offer children robust experiences that included work with genre and critical language awareness.

Although it may come as a surprise that a volume on critical literacy would include five chapters that address issues of standardization, this is surely a sign of the current formidable limitations placed on critical educators. These chapters help to deconstruct the neoliberal agenda at the center of standardization and illustrate the ways that critical literacy is constrained and enabled by standardizing practices.

Reimagining the Possible: The Future of Critical Literacy

Like some of the authors in this volume, I have had to rethink what I mean by critical literacy at several junctures. Jean Ketter, Bettina Fabos, and I have identified three dimensions of critical literacy (2001): how texts position readers; how readers position texts; and how texts are positioned within socio-political contexts. The last dimension emerged out of a meeting with an African-American mother who preferred that her son have opportunities to read "melting pot" (Sims Bishop, 1992) books that had African-American characters living middle-class lives rather than books raising critical issues of discrimination or oppression. The mother's predominantly White rural community served as an important backdrop for this decision, a sociopolitical context that we, as educators, needed to consider as we thought about what critical literacy meant in that context and whose interests it would serve. At another juncture, after a year spent in a classroom that centered on the analysis and production of digital media texts that generated intensely emotional responses, I began to reimagine critical literacy as involving analysis, immersion, and emotion. Emotion, in that classroom, surfaced as a visible action that circulated through language and other forms of embodied communication in ways that were mobilized to produce identities and new forms of critical literacy (Lewis & Tierney, 2013).

Through these experiences and others, I have found, as Luke suggests in his chapter, that critical literacy is, indeed, "utterly contingent." Yet, this book makes it clear that, while new directions in critical literacy may embrace multimodality, embodiment, and spatiality in digital and global times of diversity and standardization, the underlying aims remain. Janks says it well in her chapter, suggesting that critique is "the ability to understand that discourses produce us, speak through us, and can nevertheless be challenged and changed." It is this potential for change—for reimagining possible worlds—that Morgan calls "the art of the possible" (1997), to which all of the authors in this collection aspire as they point the way to the future of critical literacy.

Note

1   In this chapter, I link embodiment/spatiality because together they signal a focus on how bodies are located in space and on how particular spaces affect people's lived realities. Digital technology/ globalization are linked because globalization is marked by increased "flows" (Appadurai, 2000) that depend on digital technologies to expand the connectivity between ideas, bodies, and identities.

References

Appadurai, A. (2000). Grassroots globalization and the research imagination. *Public Culture, 12* (1), 1–19.

Bakhtin, M. M. (1984). *Rabelais and his world.* Bloomington, IN: Indiana University Press.

Doerr-Stevens, C., Lewis, C., Ingram, D., & Asp, M. (in press). Making the body visible through dramatic/creative play: Critical literacy in neighborhood bridges. In M. Perry & C. Medina (Eds.) *Methodologies of embodiment: (in)scribing bodies in research in education and the performing arts.* New York, NY: Routledge.

Ellsworth, E. (1989). Why doesn't this feel empowering? Working through the repressive myths of critical pedagogy. *Harvard Educational Review, 59* (3), 297–324.

Ellsworth, E. (2004). *Places of learning: Media, architecture, and pedagogy.* New York, NY: Routledge.

Freire, P. (1970). *Pedagogy of the oppressed.* Trans. M.B. Ramos. New York, NY: Continuum.

Grande, S. (2004). *Red pedagogy: Native American social and political thought.* Lanham, MD: Rowman & Littlefield.

Halliday, M.A.K. (1978). *Language as social semiotic.* London, UK: Arnold.

Hull, G., Stornaiuolo, A., & Sahni, U. (2010). Cultural citizenship and cosmopolitan practice: Global youth communicate online. *English Education, 42* (4), 331–367.

Lensmire, T. J. (2011). *Bakhtinian pedagogy.* New York, NY: Peter Lang Publishing.

Lewis, C. & Tierney, J. D. (2013). Mobilizing emotion in an urban classroom: Producing identities and transforming signs in a race-related discussion. *Linguistics and Education, 23,* 289–304.

Lewis, C., Ketter, J., & Fabos, B. (2001). Reading race in a rural context. *International Journal of Qualitative Studies in Education, 14* (3), 317–350.

Morgan, W. (1997). *Critical literacy in the classroom: The art of the Possible.* London, UK: Routledge.

Pennycook, A. (2010). *Language as local practice.* New York, NY: Routledge.

Peters, M., & Lankshear, C. (1996). Critical literacy and digital texts. *Educational Theory, 46* (1), 51–70.

Santos, B. (2006). Globalizations. *Theory, Culture, and Society, 23,* 393–399.

Sims Bishop, R. (1992). Multicultural literature for children: Making informed choices. In V. Harris. (Ed.) *Teaching multicultural literature in grade K-8.* Norwood, MA: Christopher-Gordon.

Wohlwend, K. & Lewis, C. (2010). Critical literacy, critical engagement, digital technology: Convergence and embodiment in glocal spheres. In D. Lapp & D. Fisher (Eds.) *The handbook on teaching English and language arts,* 3rd edn (pp. 188–194). New York, NY: Taylor & Francis.

CONTRIBUTORS

JuliAnna Ávila is an Assistant Professor at The University of North Carolina at Charlotte where she teaches undergraduate and graduate courses in English Education. She received her Ph.D. from The University of California at Berkeley and has published in *Theory Into Practice*, *Pedagogies*, *Language Arts,*and *Teachers College Record*. With Jessica Zacher Pandya, she is the co-editor of *Critical Digital Literacies as Social Praxis: Intersections and Challenges* (Peter Lang, 2012).

Barbara Comber Research Professor, Faculty of Education at Queensland University of Technology, Australia Barbara Comber's interests include literacy education and social justice, teachers' work and identities, place and space, and practitioner inquiry. She has recently co-edited the *International Handbook of Research in Children's Literacy, Learning and Culture* (Hall, Cremin, Comber, & Moll, 2013) and *Literacies in Place: Teaching Environmental Communication* (Comber, Nixon, & Reid, 2007). She is currently conducting three Australian Research Council Linkage projects—Ethical leadership: How educators address learning, equity and accountability; Educational leadership and turnaround literacy pedagogies; and New literacy demands in the middle years: learning from design experiments.

Karen Dooley Faculty of Education at the Queensland University of Technology, Australia Karen Dooley lectures in English curriculum. She is interested in literacy education for students in linguistically and culturally diverse schools and high-poverty contexts. She has conducted studies looking at provision for refugee students and is currently looking at the use of iPads in kindergartens.

Beryl Exley Associate Professor and Researcher, Faculty of Education at the Queensland University of Technology, Australia. After enjoying a career in the classroom, Beryl Exley continues to be inspired by the many dedicated teachers she's met through her research work. She is passionate about teaching functional aspects of reading, writing, listening, and speaking in a multilingual, multicultural, multimodal world. Her particular passion is for pedagogies that liberate the student voice. Her most recent publications can be sourced from http://eprints.qut. edu.au/view/person/Exley,_Beryl.html.

Patrick J. Finn Associate Professor Emeritus State University of New York at Buffalo Patrick Finn is the author of SUNY Press' best seller *Literacy with an Attitude: Educating Working-Class Children in Their Own Self-Interest*, co-editor of *Teacher Education with an Attitude: Preparing Teachers to Educate Working-Class Children in Their Collective Self-Interest*. He is the creator and facilitator of Parent Empowering Workshops at School 4, Buffalo Public Schools. He developed and taught Organizing for Teachers at Antioch University, Los Angeles.

Seely Flint is an Associate Professor in the Middle Secondary Education Department at Georgia State University. Her research interests focus on teachers' professional development and identity around literacy; reading and writing pedagogy for young learners; and critical literacy in elementary classrooms. Amy teaches graduate-level courses in theories of reading process, critique of educational research, and early literacy development and policy. She conducts long-term professional development with elementary teachers in the metro-Atlanta area.

Jerome C. Harste Distinguished Professor Emeritus Department of Literacy, Culture & Language Education, Indiana University. He is an expert in early written language, language learning, and critical inquiry. In addition to authoring children's books (e.g., *It Didn't Frighten Me!; My Icky Picky Sister*), he has written *Language Stories & Literacy Lessons* with Woodward & Burke (1984), *Creating Classrooms for Authors & Inquirers* with Short & Burke (Heinemann, 1996), *Creating Critical Classrooms* with Lewison & Leland (Routledge, 2008), *Teaching Children's Literature: It's Critical* with Leland & Lewison (Routledge, 2013) and *Negotiating Critical Literacies with Teachers* with Vasquez and Tate (Routlege, 2013). He and his co-authors are currently working on a second edition of *Creating Critical Classrooms*.

Hilary Janks Professor, University of the Witwatersrand, South Africa. Hilary Janks' teaching and research are in the areas of language education in multilingual classrooms and literacy with a specific focus on critical literacy. Her work is committed to a search for equity and social justice in contexts of poverty. She has recently published *Literacy and Power* (Routledge, 2010), which develops an interdependent model that is concerned with the relationship between language/literacy and power, diversity, access and design/redesign and a new book, written with colleagues, entitled *Doing Critical Literacy: Texts and Activities for Students and Teachers* (Routledge, 2013).

Elisabeth Johnson is an Assistant Professor of Literacy and English Education. She began work in higher education after several years conducting research on small-school reform at the National Center for Restructuring Education, Schools, and Teaching. Prior to pursuing her doctorate, she spent six years teaching children and youth in the public schools of Compton, California; Buenos Aires, Argentina; and New Haven, Connecticut. Her work on embodiment and literacy has appeared in journals like *English Teaching Practice and Critique, Journal of Curriculum Theorizing*, and *English Education*.

Laura Ruth Johnson received her Ph.D. in Education at the University of California, Berkeley. She is an Associate Professor at Northern Illinois University, DeKalb, IL, where she teaches courses in qualitative and ethnographic research. Her current research focuses on civic engagement amongst urban Puerto Rican/Latino/a and African-American youth, with a focus on young mothers. She also conducts research on the design and implementation of community-centered research courses for graduate students.

Tasha Tropp Laman is an Associate Professor in the Department of Instruction and Teacher Education at the University of South Carolina where she teaches courses in literacy education. She studies multilingual students' writing practices, the impact of school/university partnerships on preservice teachers and classroom educators over time, and the role of critical literacy in children's literacy practices. Dr. Laman has published her research in journals such as *Language Arts, The Reading Teacher, Equity & Excellence in Teacher Education, Theory into Practice*, and *Voices in the Middle*. In addition, Dr. Laman is the author of *From Ideas to Words: Writing Strategies for English Language Learners,* published by Heinemann.

Cynthia Lewis is Professor of Critical Literacy and English Education at the University of Minnesota, where she holds the Emma M. Birkmaier Professorship in Educational Leadership. Her current research examines the role of emotion in urban classrooms, focused on critical media analysis and production. She has published widely on the intersection of social identities and literacy practices in and out of school.

Allan Luke is Professor of Education at Queensland University of Technology, Emeritus, Australia and Adjunct Professor of Education at the University of Calgary, Canada. Allan Luke teaches literacy education, educational sociology, and policy analysis. He has just co-authored the most extensive empirical study of Aboriginal and Torres Strait Islander school reform to date for the Australian federal government.

Michael T. Moore is a professor of literacy education at Georgia Southern University. He is a past editor of *English Education* and is interested in standards-based reform in the English/language arts.

Helen Nixon Adjunct Professor, Children and Youth Research Centre and Faculty of Education at Queensland University of Technology, Australia. Helen Nixon's research interests include young people's relationships with place, their meaning making using new media, and the implications of the changing landscape of communication for literacy curriculum and pedagogy. A recent book co-authored with Sue Nichols, Jennifer Rowsell, and Sophia Rainbird is *Resourcing Early Learners: New Networks, New Actors* (Routledge, 2012).

Jessica Zacher Pandya is an Associate Professor at California State University, Long Beach in Teacher Education & Liberal Studies, where she researches and teaches about urban children's literacy practices. In addition to having published many journal articles, she is the author of *Overtested: How High-Stakes Accountability Fails English Language Learners* (Teachers College Press, 2011), and the co-editor, with JuliAnna Ávila, of *Critical Digital Literacies as Social Praxis: Intersections and Challenges* (Peter Lang, 2012).

Enid M. Rosario-Ramos is an Assistant Professor of Educational Studies and Faculty Associate of Latina/o Studies at the University of Michigan, Ann Arbor. Her research focuses on studying the intersections between adolescents' civic engagement and their development of critical literacy skills. Recent work looked at the ways in which schools' institutional structures, teachers' discursive practices, and classroom instruction support and encourage adolescents to critically examine their worlds and their textual representations. Additional research interests include social justice education, culturally sustaining pedagogy, and teacher preparation.

Shinya Takekawa is a lecturer at Aichi University of Education in Aichi, Japan. His focus of research and teaching is in equity and quality issues of literacy, pedagogy, and curriculum. His current research includes a theoretical and practical investigation on literacy development and poverty in early childhood in the Japanese context, and a study of teacher training to develop critical awareness.

Vivian Vasquez is a Professor of Education at American University (AU), where she pursues her research interests in critical literacy, early literacy, and information communication technology. Her publications include eight books and numerous book chapters and articles in refereed journals, which are available at www.vivianvasquez.com. Prior to coming to AU, Vivian taught preschool and public school for 14 years. Since then she has held appointive and elective offices in scholarly organizations, including The National Council of Teachers of

English, The American Educational Research Association, The International Reading Association, and The Whole Language Umbrella. Vivian is host of the CLIP (critical literacy in practice) podcast, located at www.clippodcast.com.

Lalitha M. Vasudevan is Associate Professor of Technology and Education at Teachers College, Columbia University in the Communication, Computing, and Technology in Education Program. She engages participatory, ethnographic, and multimodal methodologies to study how youth craft stories, represent themselves, and enact ways of knowing through their engagement with literacies, technologies, and media. Lalitha has written several articles related to these areas of interest, and co-edited two volumes: *Arts, Media, and Justice: Multimodal Explorations with Youth* (2013) and *Media, Learning, and Sites of Possibility* (2008).

Annette Woods is an Associate Professor in the School of Early Childhood, Faculty of Education, QUT. She researches and teaches in the areas of literacies, school reform, and curriculum and pedagogy. Her current research projects include a large-scale survey of teachers' enactment of official syllabus documents, a school reform project in low-socioeconomic status communities that investigates the links between print and digital literacies, and a large-scale evaluation of a school leadership reform program that aims to improve the school outcomes of Indigenous students in Australia.

Don Zancanella is a professor in the Department of Language, Literacy, and Sociocultural Studies. His areas of interest include history and policy of English language arts; the teaching and learning of literature; and writing in literary forms. He is a former chair of the Conference on English Education.

INDEX

Printed in the USA/Agawam, MA
January 27, 2014

584659.063